The Resume Writing Guide

Also available by Lisa McGrimmon

Job Search Mistakes Exposed: Can't Find a Job? Find Out Why, and Get Back to Work!

The Resume Writing Guide
A Step-by-Step Workbook for Writing a Winning Resume

LISA MCGRIMMON

ISBN: 1502429322

ISBN-13: 978-1502429322

10|2018

DEDICATION

To my husband, Tim, who has always supported and trusted me no matter how crazy my plans may have seemed.

ACKNOWLEDGMENTS

I have had the privilege of working with some wise people over the years. Their input has made this book possible.

Charmaine Rodrick, who has supported me through my own career transition and generously provided valuable recommendations for the content of this book.
Cheryl Lepard, who is largely responsible for inspiring me to become a career coach.
Donna Whiteman, who taught me by example most of what I know about being a compassionate career coach.
Cathy Keates, who taught me how to write resumes. I couldn't have asked for a more thoughtful and generous mentor.
My clients, who have trusted me to help them achieve their career goals and have taught me a lot along the way.

Table of Contents

CHAPTER NINE
WORK HISTORY

CHAPTER FOURTEEN
BE READY FOR ANY TYPE OF JOB
CREATE YOUR FOUNDATION RESUME 223

CHAPTER FIFTEEN
SAMPLE RESUMES 238

CHAPTER SIXTEEN
RESOURCES 263

CHAPTER ONE
HOW TO GET THE MOST OUT OF THIS BOOK

WHAT YOU WILL FIND IN THIS CHAPTER

1. Get Yourself in a Mindset for Success

2. Learn From the Experience of 2000 Clients

3. Partners in Resume Writing

4. Getting the Most Out of This Book

> *"Your attitude, not your aptitude will determine your altitude." Zig Ziglar*

Get Yourself in a Mindset for Success

You can absolutely find a job in any economy, even if you have challenges that other job seekers might not have. You can free yourself from the whims of economic change or employer biases about age, education, work history or family situation if you know how to present yourself well and manage your career.

The biggest secret to conducting a successful job search is that you need to be willing to adopt a can-do attitude, and then do everything it takes to find the job you want.

The information is out there. It is easy to learn how to stand out from the crowd when looking for work, but you would probably be shocked by the number of job seekers who fail to take the few simple steps needed to distinguish themselves from other people competing for the same jobs.

That is unfortunate for other job seekers, and it is frustrating for career coaches, but it is great news for you!

If you have been unsuccessfully looking for work for a while, or if you are just starting a job search, you need to know that the things you have to do to find a job are not all that difficult, and almost anyone can do them.

You have more power in this process than you probably realize. You just have to do things slightly better than other job seekers.

That is all it really takes to stand out. Just be a tiny bit better than your competition. The extra steps are not difficult if you just commit to doing them consistently.

Push yourself a bit beyond your comfort zone, require just a little bit more of yourself, and you will be able to stand out.

Learn From the Experience of 2000 Clients

I know from experience that this is all true. It is not some pie-in-the-sky, fluffy, feel-good silliness that gets you pumped up for the moment but fails to provide you with tested, practical solutions to really achieve your goals.

Unfortunately, you will find a lot of resume writing advice out there that is just empty silliness. A lot of people who write resume books or online articles have no experience writing actual resumes with real clients.

You might be surprised by the number of people who write one resume for themselves and then decide they know enough about the process to write a book or a website about creating resumes. Unfortunately, those people don't know what they don't know, and they end up selling people a lot of bad advice.

Then there is resume writing advice written by employers who review a lot of resumes. They generally do know what works and what does not work on a resume, but what is missing from their information is the process.

They have not been involved in actually creating the resumes they review, so they know what a great resume looks like, but they typically do not know how to instruct someone step-by-step through the process of creating that great resume.

That is why I decided to write this book.

There are already resume writing books that do a good job of describing the general characteristics of good resumes, and there are resume books out there that provide excellent sample resumes. However, what is missing from every resume book I have ever read, is a clear description of a step by step process that takes you from the point where you are staring at a blank screen to the point where you are completely satisfied that you have written an excellent resume that shows your own unique skills and experiences in the best possible light.

"You have more power in this process than you probably realize. You just have to do things slightly better than other job seekers."

That is what this book will do for you. You will start from a blank page on your word processing software, and I will show you, one step at a time, how to work through the process of writing a winning resume, exactly the way I would work through the process with a client.

I have worked with about 2000 clients. I have personally written about 1000 resumes and supervised the writing of another 1000 resumes. I have helped all kinds of people from all walks of life find jobs, and because I have helped a lot of people from a lot of different backgrounds, I know the questions and worries people have.

There aren't many resume writing questions and concerns I haven't heard, answered and resolved for my clients.

As a job search workshop facilitator, I was required to maintain an 80% success rate over three months. That means, 80% of my clients had to be working within 3 months of attending my workshop. I consistently achieved those targets every year even in tough economic times, and even though my clients faced a lot of career-related challenges.

And what about the other 20 percent? A small number each year were impossible to contact when I did my follow-ups. Most found work; it just took them longer than three months, and some decided to return to school or start a business.

All of the participants in my workshop left at the end of the week with a resume that we wrote together with the help of my wonderful assistant. That is how I know for sure that the resume writing information in this book works.

It has worked for 2000 clients. It can work for you, too!

I cannot promise that you will find the perfect job within a specific time frame. That would be irresponsible because there are a lot of variables for each person, and resume writing is only one part of the job search process. I can promise that my resume writing recommendations have been tested by 2000 clients, and those clients have had excellent success in finding work.

The things I will ask you to do to write an effective resume are not extremely difficult, but you will need to commit some time and mental energy to brainstorm, write and revise your work. I will show you exactly how to do that little bit extra you need to do to stand out from the crowd.

You just need to commit to doing it.

Partners in Resume Writing

I always tell clients that we will be partners in resume writing. I never write the resume for them. We write the resume together, as a team.

In fact, you need to be wary of career experts who say they will write a resume *for you* with minimal input from you. Truly professional resume writers will write your resume *with you* using an enormous amount of input from you, so the content of the resume is a true reflection of the unique attributes, individuality and skills you have to offer employers.

So, throughout this book, you and I will be a team. I will be the expert on how to write a resume. You need to be the expert on your own career. We both bring to the table important information that is necessary to write an outstanding resume.

This book is not about me providing endless lists of stock phrases to include on your resume. It is about you learning how to take your own knowledge about your skills and experience and turn that into a great resume that shows employers who you are and why they should bring you in for a job interview.

If you simply copy run-of-the-mill, stock phrases from a book, you will only write a plain, vanilla resume that does not stand out from the competition. If you want to create a resume that demonstrates why you are great at the work you do, you need to use your own words and your own knowledge about your industry, your skills, and the unique attributes you bring to the job and use those ideas to write your own points on your resume.

Yes, that approach is initially more work than copying someone else's stock phrases, but it will pay off because your resume will be far more effective.

You will not be on your own in this process. I will show you what needs to be included and omitted on your resume, how to structure your resume to show yourself in the best possible light, and how to write a resume that minimizes concerns you may have (gaps in your work history, limited work experience, or incomplete degrees or diplomas are a few of the common concerns we will deal with). I will also show you how to brainstorm information about your job duties, skills and accomplishments, how to write about your skills and experience in a way that makes an impact, and where to find detailed job descriptions if you need some help remembering all of the important skills you use at work.

Your job is to take all of that information and apply it to what you know about your own career.

Together, we can create an effective resume.

Getting the Most Out of This Book

This book is a resume writing workbook, which means you will get the most benefit from the book if you complete the specific task or tasks set out in one chapter before you move on to the next chapter.

I will take you through the resume writing process step by step by asking you the first question I ask every time I write a resume with any client (What type of job are you looking for?), followed by the next question, and the next.

I will show you how to make crucial decisions about your resume along the way based on your answers to each question.

1. Are you making a career change?
2. Are you worried about age discrimination?
3. Do you have a gap in your work history?
4. Are you a recent graduate?

Your answers to these types of questions will provide the information you need to make important decisions about what to include on your resume and how to structure it in a way that shows you in your best light and minimizes any concerns about your work history.

I have designed this workbook to guide you the way a career coach would guide you through each step of the resume writing process. Please take your time to complete each task in each chapter to the best of your ability before you move on to the next chapter.

CHAPTER ORGANIZTION

You will notice there is a consistent organization in this book. Most chapters are organized as follows:

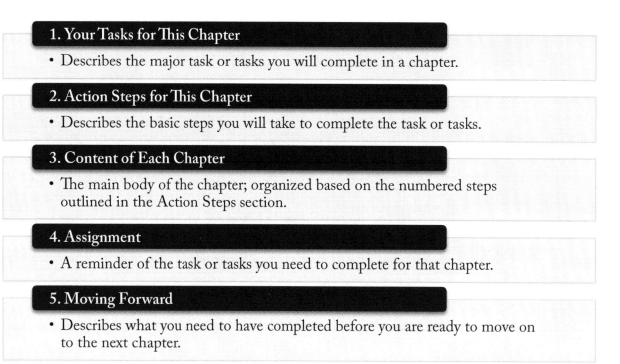

1. Your Tasks for This Chapter

- Describes the major task or tasks you will complete in a chapter.

2. Action Steps for This Chapter

- Describes the basic steps you will take to complete the task or tasks.

3. Content of Each Chapter

- The main body of the chapter; organized based on the numbered steps outlined in the Action Steps section.

4. Assignment

- A reminder of the task or tasks you need to complete for that chapter.

5. Moving Forward

- Describes what you need to have completed before you are ready to move on to the next chapter.

Each of these sections has a specific function and is designed to keep you moving forward in small steps to write a resume that shows you at your best. There is a lot of information in this book. The chapters are organized to break that information down into small, understandable, manageable pieces that you can act upon.

If you need to refocus yourself, you can refer back to "Your Tasks for This Chapter" to remind yourself what you are working to accomplish in a particular chapter. You can also refer back to "Action Steps for This Chapter" to remind yourself what steps you will take to complete that task. The "Moving Forward" section will let you know if you are ready to move on to the next chapter.

There are no tasks to complete in chapters one, fifteen and sixteen, so they are not organized in the same way.

Some resources to simplify the writing process and clarify concepts:

SAMPLE RESUMES

Chapter 15 includes several sample resumes that illustrate different resume formats, the sections within a resume and the strategies recommended in this book for minimizing concerns about your work history and highlighting your most marketable skills. It can be distracting if you have to flip back and forth to different sections within a book, and, if you have the Kindle version of this book and are reading it on a device with a small screen, you might prefer to view the sample resumes on a larger computer screen, so I have also included all of those resume samples on my website at careerchoiceguide.com/resumeexamples.

You might want to have your computer handy while you read through this book, so you can refer to the sample resumes easily. Alternatively, feel free to print the sample resumes from my website, so you have paper copies to refer to if you will not have easy access to a computer while reading this book and don't want to flip back and forth to different chapters. The examples will give you a deeper understanding of the concepts described in the book. You will also be able to refer back to them easily on my site while you are writing up your own resume.

If you look closely, you may notice there are some small formatting differences in the resumes on my site compared to the resumes in chapter 16 in this book. I made a few different formatting choices on my website simply because of the way the resumes sat on the page online compared to the way the resumes fit on the page in this book. Those slight variations will provide you with alternative ideas for formatting your information.

RESUME WRITING FORM

I also offer a free resume writing form on my website. It contains space to write all of the information you would need to include on virtually any type of resume. It is a little more efficient to just type your information directly into a blank Word document (or other word processing software), but some people will benefit from the added structure a form provides.

You can download a copy of my resume writing form at careerchoiceguide.com/resumeform.

You can type your information directly into the form, or print the form and hand write the information into each section if you prefer. Use whatever method helps you think best.

CHAPTER TWO
WHAT TYPE OF JOB DO YOU WANT TO TARGET?

YOUR TASK FOR THIS CHAPTER

1. Decide what type of job you are targeting.

ACTION STEPS FOR THIS CHAPTER

Step One: Know why you need to decide what type of job you want to target before you write your resume.

Step Two: Understand why you need a new resume for each job.

Step Three: Decide what job you want to focus on when you write your resume.

"If you don't know where you are going, how can you expect to get there?" Basil S. Walsh

Step One:
Know Why You Need to Decide What Type of Job You Want to Target Before You Write Your Resume

Before you start to write your resume, it is crucial to decide what type of job you want to pursue so you can write a resume that is targeted to that job.

Why you must write a resume for a specific job:

- To be effective, *a resume must be focused and demonstrate to the employer that you are an excellent candidate for the specific type of job* he or she needs to fill. General, untargeted resumes are less effective because they do not take every opportunity to demonstrate that you would be great at the specific job the employer needs to fill.

- Every decision you make about what to include on your resume hinges on the type of job you are seeking.

- Many decisions you make about how to format your resume also hinge on the type of job you are seeking.

"It is very difficult to write a great resume without targeting a specific job."

EXAMPLE

Imagine you are currently working as an adult education teacher. You think you might like to make a career change, and you have recently completed some training in addictions counseling.

If you want to write a resume to apply for another job as an adult education teacher, you will need to highlight your related work experience. The work experience section will be near the top of your resume, and you will go into detail describing your past experience working as an adult education teacher.

If, on the other hand, you want to write a resume to apply for a job as an addictions counselor, your education will be the most important feature to highlight. The education section will be near the top of your resume, and you will go into more detail describing your education. You will also need to write about your work experience in more general terms and highlight aspects of your job that demonstrate skills that would be useful if you were working as a counselor.

At this stage, do not worry about issues like whether you need to highlight your work experience or your education on your resume. We will look at that in detail later in the book. Just know that you need to target a specific job to make these types of decisions and write the most effective resume possible.

Writing a targeted resume is much easier than writing an untargeted resume.

It is very difficult to write a great resume without targeting a specific job.

When you write a resume, there are endless decisions to make including:

- How to format each piece of information
- In what order to present the information
- What to include
- What to omit
- How to describe each aspect of your professional experience

If you have a specific type of job in mind as you write your resume, all of these decisions become much easier to make.

Once you know what job you are targeting, you have an important point of focus. Everything you include on your resume should prove in some way that you would be great at the job you are targeting.

If you have a specific job in mind, before you include anything on your resume, you can ask yourself, *"Does this information help prove that I would be great at the specific job I am targeting?"* Asking that question helps you decide what should and should not be included on your resume.

Also, when you have a specific job in mind, you can also ask yourself, *"Have I included on my resume evidence that I have all of the skills and experience an employer in this field would be looking for?"* Asking that question helps you decide if you have missed any important information that should be on your resume.

- If the information does help demonstrate that you would be great at that job, it should be included on your resume.

- If the information does not help demonstrate that you would be great at that job, you either need to rewrite the information so it does prove you would be great at the job, or, if the information is completely irrelevant, you will omit it from your resume.

- If the information demonstrates an absolutely crucial requirement of the job, it must clearly stand out on your resume.

- If you have a specific type of job in mind while writing your resume, you will be able to make good decisions about how to describe your qualifications and how to organize your information in a way that presents you in the best possible light. It will be much easier to decide what to include, what to omit, what to highlight and what to minimize.

An unfocused resume is nothing more than a generic history of your work experience and education. A targeted resume is a powerful marketing tool that will demonstrate to an employer that you are a great candidate for a specific job.

Step Two
Understand Why You Need a New Resume for Each Job

If you are applying to more than one type job, you need more than one resume. Savvy and successful job hunters will even fine-tune and send slightly different resumes for the same type of job at different companies.

In fact, as more companies use specialized computer software called applicant tracking systems (or ATS for short) to screen the resumes they receive and decide which ones will be looked at by a human, it becomes even more necessary for job hunters to write a targeted resume for every single job they pursue. These applicant tracking systems, among other things, measure how closely a resume matches the requirements outlined in a job ad, so the more targeted your resume is to the job and the company, the better chance you have of making it through the ATS screening process.

We'll get into applicant tracking systems later in this book. At this point, just keep in mind that there is a possibility your resume will be screened by an AST, and you need to write a highly targeted resume to successfully make it through ATS screening. Generic resumes do not work well when an employer uses an applicant tracking system to screen resumes.

A resume must be targeted to address an employer's specific needs, and those needs will be different for each employer.

You might get away with using a single resume in a good economy or when there is a shortage of skilled workers in your field, but this approach is far from optimal because it will limit your job options.

Using a single resume is definitely not recommended in a competitive labor market.

A highly targeted resume will address each employer's needs and get you in the door to more interviews, even in a tough economy. In a less competitive environment, this strategy will still help you get invited to more interviews, open up more job options and allow you to find the job you want faster.

Don't worry about writing more than one resume at this stage of the process.

The idea of writing several resumes can be overwhelming, particularly if you have not even begun to write your first resume.

Focus on one specific job that you want to target, and concentrate on writing that resume for the time being.

Know that the most competitive job seekers fine-tune their resumes regularly, and once you have written your first resume, you will find instructions in chapter 14 that will make it very easy to write additional resumes as needed.

Step Three
Decide What Type of Job You Want to Target

This step may be very easy to complete, or very difficult. It all depends on where you are in your career development.

Because this book is a resume writing book, and not a book about choosing a career, I will not go into any detail about how to choose a career. If you have absolutely no idea what type of job you would like to pursue, and you want to explore that question, the resources section in the back of this book will direct you to that type of information.

If you know exactly what type of job you would like to target, your task for this chapter is easy.

If you are not certain what type of job you would like to pursue, or if you know that you want to write several resumes for several types of jobs that are quite different, I would suggest you start by writing a resume for a job that is similar to your most recent job.

The easiest resume to write is one that is targeted to a job that is similar to or the same as your most recent job.

If you are a recent graduate with limited work experience, the type of work you have trained for at school will be the easiest resume to write.

Writing a career change resume is a little bit harder than writing a resume for a job that you have done recently (career change resumes will be covered later in this book). Unless you know for sure that there is no way you would ever apply to jobs that are similar to your most recent job, I would suggest starting by writing a resume that is targeted to a job that is similar to your most recent job. Once you have written that resume, you can fine-tune it to target other types of jobs.

When you want to write a career change resume, starting with a completely blank page is a bit of a challenge. It will be easier to go back and adjust your first resume to create other versions of your resume that are targeted to other types of jobs once you have completed this base resume.

> *Remember: Don't let all of this talk about writing multiple resumes make you feel overwhelmed.*

You are concentrating on writing one resume for one single type of job right now. I will explain exactly how to fine-tune your resume for other jobs in chapter 14. Fine-tuning resumes to a variety of specific jobs is easier than you might think.

"*The easiest resume to write is one that is targeted to a job that is similar to or the same as your most recent job.*"

Assignment

Determine one specific type of job that will be the focus of the resume you are going to write.

Moving Forward

You are ready to move on to the next chapter if you...

1. Accept that you must target a specific job on your resume.

2. Understand that you will need more than one resume if you are applying to more than one job, but realize that your only task for the first several chapters will be to focus on writing one single resume.

3. *Have selected one specific type of job that will be the focus of the resume you will write.* Do not skip this step. It is absolutely crucial to writing an effective resume. Every other decision you make about writing and formatting your resume hinges on this decision.

CHAPTER THREE
APPLICANT TRACKING SYSTEM BASICS

YOUR TASK FOR THIS CHAPTER

1. Develop a basic understanding of what applicant tracking systems are and how they may affect your job search.

ACTION STEPS FOR THIS CHAPTER

Step One: Understand what an applicant tracking system (ATS) is.

Step Two: Know which employers might use an ATS.

Step Three: Understand how an ATS could affect your job search.

Step Four: Avoid confusion between ATS and human-reviewed resumes.

"Technology is nothing. What's important is that you have a faith in people, that they're basically good and smart, and if you give them tools, they'll do wonderful things with them. It's not the tools that you have faith in - tools are just tools. They work, or they don't work. It's people you have faith in or not." Steve Jobs

Step One
Understand What an Applicant Tracking System (ATS) Is

I will refer to applicant tracking systems (ATS for short) throughout the book, so I have included this chapter near the beginning of the book to provide a brief overview of applicant tracking systems for readers who are not familiar with this type of software. You will not need to worry about formatting your resume for an ATS until much later in the book. That information will be covered in chapter 13. For now, you just need a basic understanding of what an ATS is, so you know what I mean when I refer to them throughout the book.

An applicant tracking system is a software program that allows employers to manage the entire hiring process from posting the job, to receiving resumes, and tracking applicants all the way through the process. Sometimes they are called electronic resume management systems, (ERM) but ATS is the more common term, so that is the term I will use throughout this book.

There are several different applicant tracking systems in use, which each have their own capabilities and requirements. That fact can complicate issues a bit for job seekers who are trying to tailor a resume to an ATS, but there are a lot of common guidelines you can follow to create a resume designed to for optimal ATS screening.

In general, resumes are entered into the applicant tracking system, and the software reviews the content of each resume to determine how well it matches with the employer's criteria for the job. Resumes that best match the criteria and are formatted correctly for the software to read will score high enough to make it through the ATS screening process. Resumes that pass the ATS screening process will be viewed by a human. Typically, a human will not view the resumes that do not score well.

Although applicant tracking systems can be used by employers to help manage all aspects of the hiring process, as a job seeker, you just need to be aware of how this type of software is used at the resume screening stage. That is the stage in which an ATS can have a huge impact on whether you are considered for a job or not.

How does an ATS evaluate your resume?

ATS software can score resumes based on a variety of different criteria. Some of the things they may evaluate include:

Keywords and Phrases

- The ATS will search for keywords and phrases that match those in the job ad and/or synonyms for those keywords and phrases.

Job Titles

- The ATS will look for relevant job titles on your resume. Specifically, it may look for a job title that is an *exact match* for the job vacancy, and it may look for related job titles.

Date the Job Was Held

- An ATS may search for applicants who have the most current experience, so it will give a higher score to applicants who currently do, or recently have done the particular job.

Percent the Resume Matches the Job Posting

- Generally, the more the resume matches the job ad, the higher your resume will score in the ATS screening process.

Rarity of Keywords

- Some applicant tracking systems can rate a resume higher if they find qualifications that are relevant and rare. That is, if you have a relevant skill that most of the other applicants do not have, the ATS may give a lot of weight to that skill and rate your resume higher.

Step Two
Know Which Employers Might Use an ATS

Online job boards have made it easier than ever for job seekers to submit applications for jobs, which means companies receive more applications than ever before each time they advertise a job opening. Hiring managers need some way to wade through those piles of resumes and some are turning to applicant tracking system software to help with this task.

Unfortunately, it is not easy to pinpoint exactly what percentage of employers are using applicant tracking systems to screen resumes. You can find articles online that confidently state "most" or even "almost all" employers use applicant tracking systems. The problem with these assertions is that they are not backed up with any current, reliable data on what percentage of job openings are filled with the help of ATS software.

In addition, many online experts seem to be focused only on the hiring practices of very large companies. They constantly refer to their assumptions about the hiring practices of organizations like Google Inc. or Microsoft Corporation. They do not seem to be thinking about the experiences of job seekers who are applying to small and medium companies.

Based on my own experience working with plenty of job seekers, I know many, many people who are looking for work are *not* looking to apply to Fortune 500 companies. Many people are looking for work at small and medium-sized companies, and these are the companies that are much less likely to be using an applicant tracking system.

Applicant tracking systems are fairly expensive, so they are really only practical for employers who hire often. Therefore, if you are applying to a job with a large company, there is a greater likelihood the employer will use an ATS.

Also, if you are submitting resumes online frequently, you may begin to recognize the look of popular ATS software. You may notice the applicant tracking system's logo on the page, or you may recognize the ATS software's name in the address bar of your browser when you apply to a job online. All of these clues tell you the employer is using ATS software to screen resumes.

If you do not know whether an employer is using ATS software, consider calling the human resources department and asking. Of course, no human resources manager wants to field hundreds of inquiries about their resume screening process. Luckily for you, the vast majority of job seekers will not take this extra step, so HR staff will not be receiving an inordinate number of calls.

If it is not possible to contact someone in human resources, and you are not sure whether the employer uses ATS software, and you are emailing your resume, consider submitting two versions of your resume, one designed for a human reader, and one designed for an ATS. Be sure to name each file clearly so the purpose of each is obvious to the person who receives your email.

I do suspect the claims that "almost all" employers use an applicant tracking system are overblown. The likelihood that you will encounter ATS software when job searching depends largely on:

The type of employers you are targeting - Larger employers are more likely to use an ATS.

and

The way you find your job leads - Normally, the more you target unadvertised jobs in the hidden job market, the more opportunities you will have to avoid ATS screening.

However, applicant tracking systems do exist, their use by employers does appear to be growing, and you should know how to navigate the world of ATS resume screening in case you encounter it in your job search.

Step Three
Understand How an ATS Could Affect Your Job Search

If the employers you are targeting are using applicant tracking systems, your resume must be designed to pass the ATS screening, or it will never be seen by a human no matter how qualified you are.

Applicant tracking systems, at this point, have a lot of limitations, and well-qualified candidates can be screened out simply because they did not format their resumes correctly. In fact, there are several resume formatting strategies that are very effective for human screening, which are not advisable when a resume will be screened with an ATS.

The positive side of this situation is that, by the time you finish this book, you will know a lot more about how to write and format your resume for applicant tracking systems. If the companies that interest you are using an ATS, that knowledge will give you a big advantage over a lot of your competition.

If you think an employer will be using an applicant tracking system to screen resumes, you need to write your resume to please both the computer software and human readers. If you want your resume to reach the eyes of the human reader, you must first write effectively for the computer software.

Step Four
Avoid Confusion Between ATS and Human-Reviewed Resumes

Chapter 13 is all about optimizing your resume for ATS screening. That chapter will allow you to quickly and easily find all of the information about writing for applicant tracking systems in one place. You can refer back to it any time you need to write a resume that will be screened by an ATS.

Chapter 12 is all about formatting resumes for a human reader. As I mentioned earlier, some of the recommendations for writing for a human reader are different than the recommendations for writing a resume for an ATS. It can get a bit confusing! You really do not need to think about formatting of any type until much later in the resume writing process. Once you get to the formatting stage, though, if you become confused about whether a recommendation applies to a human-reviewed resume or an ATS-reviewed resume, refer to chapter 12 for human-reviewed resume guidelines and chapter 13 for ATS optimized resume guidelines.

Throughout the book, you will see I have included some general comments about optimizing your resume for applicant tracking systems. Those comments are just designed to help you see the differences between a resume that is ideal for human readers and a resume that is ideal for computer software.

Do not let yourself get too bogged down in thinking about applicant tracking systems while you are working on writing the first draft of your resume. As you work through this book, simply focus on getting all of your information down. Write a resume that shows you at your best before you think about writing for an applicant tracking system.

Once you have completed every section of your resume to the best of your ability, then you can go back and revise that resume each time you apply to a company that is using an ATS.

> *"If you want your resume to reach the eyes of the human reader, you must first write effectively for the computer software."*

ONE STEP AT A TIME!

I know the idea of writing a resume to pass a computer software screening, and revising your resume for every single job lead you pursue can sound a bit overwhelming. The reality is, it is absolutely necessary to submit highly targeted and well-formatted resumes if the employers you are interested in will use an ATS to screen resumes. In chapter 14, I will explain how to write a foundation resume that includes all of your skills and experiences. This foundation resume will make it much easier for you to write as many targeted resumes as you need.

Each chapter in this book contains just a few tasks to complete. Take one step at a time. You do not have to try to do everything all at once!

Moving Forward

You are ready to move on to the next chapter if you...

1. Have a basic understanding of what an applicant tracking system is, why employers use them, and how they might affect your job search. There is no need to understand applicant tracking systems in detail at this point. We will cover that topic in a later chapter.

2. Accept that if employers you are targeting are using applicant tracking systems to screen resumes, you will need to write highly targeted resumes that are written and formatted to make it through the software's screening process.

3. Understand that writing your resume will be easier if you simply write a traditional resume for human readers first, and then go back and revise that resume for applicant tracking system screening as necessary.

CHAPTER FOUR
WHAT TYPE OF RESUME SHOULD YOU WRITE?

YOUR TASK FOR THIS CHAPTER

1.   Determine what type of resume will show your skills and experience in the best possible light.

ACTION STEPS FOR THIS CHAPTER

Step One: Know features of the three main types of resumes.

Step Two: Know what type of job seeker will benefit from each type of resume.

Step Three: Understand that you may need to use different resume formats if you are looking for different types of jobs.

Step Four: Determine what type of resume you will write.

"Your persistence is your measure of faith in yourself." Proverb

Step One
Know the Features of the Three Main Types of Resumes

While resumes can vary a lot to meet specific needs, there are only three main types of resumes.

THREE TYPES OF RESUMES

- Chronological
- Functional
- Combination

Please note, although applicant tracking system optimized resumes are another distinct type of resume format, we will not examine ATS optimized resumes in this chapter. They belong in a section on their own and are used only in very specific circumstances. We will look at the ATS optimized resume format in chapter 13. At this point, please focus on chronological, functional, and combination resumes.

WHAT OTHER CAREER PROFESSIONALS MAY SAY

A few people who bill themselves as career experts will recommend writing your resume in a style that fits outside of these three main categories. Typically their rationale is that if you write a unique resume, it will stand out from the crowd and be noticed by employers.

However, anyone who has a significant amount of real world experience writing resumes for clients and helping people find work will tell you that resumes should be either chronological, combination and possibly functional in style.

Employers are used to reviewing these three types of resumes. They know where the information will be found on each type of resume, and, therefore, they can scan them quickly to find the information they want.

Similarly, traditional resume formatting is necessary if an applicant tracking system will be used to screen your resume. This type of software is designed to understand standard resume formatting. ATS software has a lot of limitations, and unusual resume formats can cause an ATS to have problems reading your resume.

OVERVIEW OF EACH RESUME FORMAT

To help you organize your thinking on the topic, on the next page you'll find an overview chart outlining the major features of each resume format. You can refer back to this chart any time you need some quick clarification.

Three Types of Resumes

Chronological Resume	Functional Resume	Combination Resume
• **Highlights:** Your work experience	• **Highlights:** Only your skills	• **Highlights:** Your skills and work experience
• **Standard sections are:** Contact information, profile, work experience, education, and possibly volunteer work.	• **Standard sections are:** Contact information, followed by an extremely detailed list of your marketable skills.	• **Standard sections are:** Contact information, profile, a list of your most marketable skills or accomplishments, work experience, education, and possibly volunteer work.
• **Information omitted:** Chronological resumes do not contain a summary of your skills and achievements. That information must be communicated in the other sections of your resume.	• **Information omitted:** A functional resume does not include details about your paid work experience, volunteer experience or education. It is simply a detailed list of your marketable skills.	• **Information omitted:** No relevant information is omitted from a combination resume. It is a combination of a chronological and a functional resume.
• **A good choice for:** People who have a solid work history showing progressive responsibility and no major employment gaps.	• **A good choice for:** NO ONE! I never recommend using functional resumes. Employers do not trust this resume format, and it is missing crucial information.	• **A good choice for:** Almost everyone. A combination resume will work for most people most of the time.

What other career professionals may say

Occasionally it makes sense to write a resume that has an extremely detailed list of your marketable skills followed by a short section that very briefly outlines your past work history without describing the jobs in detail.

Some career professionals call this type of resume a functional resume. In my opinion, this type of resume is still a combination resume because it includes both a skills summary and an outline of work experience.

In this book, when I refer to a combination resume, I am talking about any resume that includes both a skills summary (no matter how long or short) and a work history section (no matter how long or short). When I refer to a functional resume, I am talking about any resume that contains a detailed list of marketable skills and no work experience section.

Other career professionals are not wrong; this distinction is just a matter of opinion.

Step Two
Know What Type of Job Seeker Will Benefit From Each Type of Resume

Back in chapter 2 you decided what type of job you were going to pursue. Keep this job in mind as you decide which type of resume is best for you.

Who should use a chronological resume?

A well-written chronological resume will highlight your work experience. This resume style, when formatted correctly, can be read by both human readers and applicant tracking systems. *Job seekers who have a strong employment history should consider using a chronological resume.*

Do you have a strong employment history? Characteristics of a strong employment history include:

- You have worked for several years doing a job that is the same or similar to the type of job you are currently seeking.

- You are not making a career change.

- You have not been out of the workforce for an extended period of time. It has been less than six months since your last paid employment.

- You do not have gaps in the last few years of your work history.

- You have not held several jobs in a short period of time.

- Your work history shows professional growth and advancement over time through promotions and/or increased responsibilities.

LIMITATIONS OF CHRONOLOGICAL RESUMES

While a chronological resume can be a good choice when you want to highlight your work history, there are a few issues to be aware of if you choose to use this resume style including:

Your work history is completely front and center on this type of resume, so if there are any weaknesses at all in your work history, they will be harder to minimize if you use a chronological resume.

Employers often review resumes to see if job seekers have the basic skills that they require. There is no single place to highlight your relevant skills on a chronological resume, so your skills can easily get hidden if you use this format.

Because there is no place to highlight your skills, a chronological resume gives you fewer opportunities to include plenty of relevant keywords, which is particularly important if your resume will be read by an applicant tracking system.

"Job seekers who have a strong employment history should consider using a chronological resume."

A chronological resume can highlight your age if you are not careful. This issue can sometimes be a concern for more experienced workers (typically those 45 and older) as well as younger job seekers.

A chronological resume can get repetitive. If you have held the same type of job at two or more different companies, describing each job in detail, as you would in a chronological resume, can quickly become repetitive.

Who should use a functional resume?

A functional resume is designed to highlight skills that you can offer an employer, while hiding any issues that may exist with your work history.

Because a functional resume does not include a work history section, people will sometimes use this resume style to try to:

- Hide the fact that they do not have work experience that is related to the job they are seeking

- Hide the fact that they have held several different jobs in a short period of time

- Hide gaps in their work history

- Hide a recent, unpleasant work experience that they would rather not have to discuss

- Avoid age discrimination by hiding a short or lengthy work history

LIMITATIONS OF FUNCTIONAL RESUMES

Using a functional resume, in my opinion, is almost never a good choice.

In theory, a functional resume is supposed to hide all kinds of work history related issues. However, in reality, functional resumes hide nothing, and they raise all kinds of concerns in the minds of employers.

Most employers do not trust functional resumes because they know this resume style is designed to hide work history related issues. When most employers see a functional resume, they immediately assume the job seeker is trying to hide something.

Also, while a functional resume allows you to outline your skills in great detail, it does not show the context in which you used a particular skill. If your resume says that you are able to multi-task and manage conflicting demands, that information is usually not enough for the employer. He or she typically will want to know in what context you have demonstrated those skills.

A functional resume will not score well if an employer uses an applicant tracking system to screen resumes. The ATS will almost certainly look for specific work experience, and because a functional resume is just a long list of skills, the ATS will not find any work experience if you use this resume format.

WHEN SHOULD YOU USE A FUNCTIONAL RESUME?

The short answer to that question is *never!*

A functional resume is rarely the best format to use. I cannot imagine a situation in which I would recommend using a functional resume. In fact, I have written over one thousand resumes, and I cannot think of a single time when I wrote a purely functional resume for any client.

If you are thinking about using a functional resume to address some of the issues listed above (gaps in your work history, making a career change, concerns about age discrimination, etc.), please keep in mind that there are other, far more effective ways to address these issues. I will address these concerns throughout the book and show you how to minimize these issues by using a combination resume and a few subtle and effective techniques that do not raise huge concerns in the minds of most employers.

> *"Using a functional resume is almost never a good idea."*

Some people who believe they have absolutely no experience, such as students seeking their first job, consider using a functional resume. Keep in mind, it is extremely rare for people to have absolutely no experience to include on a resume.

In the very rare case that you truly have no experience to put on your resume, I would strongly recommend that you find ways (such as volunteer work or a school placement) to gain some experience. As soon as you start your volunteer work, you can put it on your resume, so it immediately improves your resume and your job prospects.

> *Functional resumes carry no credibility with employers. This problem is a profound weakness of this resume style, and in my opinion, functional resumes should never be used.*

Although I am no fan of the functional resume, it is a style that some people use. Since it exists, I do want to describe it, so you will understand all of the pros and cons of using this style of resume. You will be able to make an informed choice about using a functional resume, and if you choose this format, you will be able to write the best functional resume possible.

Who should use a combination resume?

A well-written combination resume is very effective for highlighting both your skills and your work experience. An applicant tracking system will be able to read a combination resume that is formatted correctly, and human reviewers can easily see relevant information on a combination resume. Job seekers who want to highlight their most marketable skills and provide clear information about their work history should consider using a combination resume.

A combination resume is an excellent choice for:

Career changers - A combination resume will allow you to demonstrate how your skills from your previous job are relevant to the new job you are seeking.

Recent graduates - A combination resume will allow you to highlight your skills and your education, which are probably bigger selling features than your work experience at this stage in your career.

People reentering the workforce after an extended period of time without paid employment - A combination resume will put the focus on your skills while still providing the employer with the work history information they expect to see.

People who have gaps in their work history - A combination resume will allow you to minimize the appearance of gaps by putting the focus on your skills.

People who have held several jobs in a short period of time - A combination resume will allow you to minimize any perception of job jumping and highlight your skills before your work history.

People who want employers to see their most important skills at a glance - Employers often scan resumes very quickly looking for evidence that job seekers have specific skills. A combination resume provides you with a place to highlight all of the most important skills that employers are seeking.

People in high tech jobs - People in high tech jobs need to list their technical skills in a way that is easy to see at a glance. You cannot rely on describing your technical skills within your job description, and you cannot assume employers know you have certain technical skills simply based on the types of jobs you have held. Without a summary of skills section, crucial skills will be buried in your job descriptions, and you may lose job opportunities simply because employers could not find your technical skills at a glance on your resume.

People who have done the same type of job at several different companies - A chronological resume can get repetitive if you describe the same type of job several times. A combination resume allows you to bring your skills into one section and avoid repetition.

Please note, while the issue of repetition can be a problem on human-reviewed resumes; repetition is not something to be worried about on ATS optimized resumes (for more on ATS optimized resumes, see chapter 13).

People who are concerned about age discrimination - Highlighting your skills takes a bit of the focus off of your work history, which allows you to minimize the appearance of a lengthy work history.

"Combination resumes work for most people most of the time."

LIMITATIONS OF COMBINATION RESUMES

Combination resumes have very few real limitations. They provide an enormous amount of flexibility to allow you to show your skills and experience in their best light.

A combination resume combines all of the strengths of the functional and chronological resumes. *This resume style works very well for most people most of the time.*

Step Three
Understand That You May Need to Use Different Resume Formats if You Are Looking for Different Types of Jobs

If you are looking for more than one type of job, you might need to write more than one type of resume.

For example, if you have a solid work history, and you are looking for work that is similar to the type of work you have done in the past, but you are also open to making a career change, you may decide to write a chronological resume targeting the type of work you have done in the past and a combination resume targeting the career change job.

If you find yourself in this type of situation, and you want to avoid writing two resumes in completely different styles, then writing a combination resume is your best option. A combination resume works for most people in most situations, and it offers the flexibility necessary to change sections and content around to highlight different aspects of your skills and experience.

You will still need to write more than one resume if you are looking for more than one type of job, but if you use a combination resume, you will not have to write a completely different resume in a completely different style. You will be able to make simple changes to your existing resume to target different jobs.

While you may decide that you want to write more than one type of resume, do not get bogged down by this idea at this point in the resume writing process. Stay focused on writing the best resume possible for the type of job you are seeking (the one you chose in chapter 2), and choose the resume style that will serve that purpose.

Step Four
Determine What Type of Resume You Will Write

If you are still unsure about what type of resume to write, I would suggest writing a combination resume. Most employers trust combination resumes, and they provide a lot of flexibility, which allows you to really control what information stands out.

Most of the resumes I have written for clients have been combination resumes. When I start to work with a client, I always consider using other formats; however, a combination style is usually the best option.

Combination resumes really do work for most people most of the time.

Assignment

Determine which type of resume will be most effective for highlighting your skills and experiences based on the type of job you are seeking.

Moving Forward

You are ready to move on to the next chapter if you...

1. Understand the features of combination, chronological and functional resumes.

2. Have thought through which of these resumes works best for someone with your specific background.

3. Understand that you may benefit from having two different styles of resumes if you are looking for two very different types of jobs, but realize that your main task for this chapter is to focus on choosing one single resume style that will work best for the job you chose in chapter 2.

4. Have selected the type of resume that will best highlight your skills and experiences based on the type of job you chose in chapter 2.

Remember: When in doubt, use a combination resume.

CHAPTER FIVE
BEFORE YOU START TYPING...

YOUR TASK FOR THIS CHAPTER

     1.   Understand how to write your resume efficiently.

ACTION STEPS FOR THIS CHAPTER

Step One: Understand why you should not format your resume while you write the content of your resume.

Step Two: Discover a more efficient way to write your resume.

> *"Efficiency is doing things right. Effectiveness is doing the right things." Peter F. Drucker*

Step One
Understand Why You Should Not Format Your Resume as You Write the Content of Your Resume

When most people write a resume, they are inclined to format as they write. They type out their contact information then set that information up in an attractive layout, perhaps putting their name in bold type, and spacing out their contact information nicely across the page. Then they proceed to format the rest of the resume while writing the content for each section.

THIS APPROACH IS EXTREMELY INEFFICIENT

There are several ways to format each section of your resume, and until you have determined all of the information you need to include on your resume, you will not know the best way to set it up. Therefore, it is best to get all of your information down on paper in a clear, organized (but not formatted) manner, and format your resume after you know what all of the content will be.

Formatting your resume is like organizing your closet.

If you decide to organize your closet and run out and buy several containers before you assess what is actually in your closet, chances are, all of your stuff will not fit well in your new containers.

If, on the other hand, you first assess what is in your closet, determine what items go together, what things are most important and need to be easily accessed, what things do not belong in your closet, and where everything will fit, and then you go out and buy containers based on your needs, you will know what sizes and shapes of containers to buy, and everything will fit and function perfectly.

Formatting a resume is the same.

If you try to contain all of your information into pre-formatted sections before you have written that information, your setup will not be the best possible fit, or you will waste a lot of time because you will have to rearrange things once you have finished writing all of your content.

If you wait until you know all of the content that you want to fit on your resume, and what information you want to highlight, and then you format sections to function based on the content you have written, you will create a great fit without wasting time.

AN EXAMPLE OF HOW FORMATTING CAN CHANGE BASED ON THE CONTENT OF YOUR RESUME:

If you have included all of the relevant information on your resume but still have a few lines of blank space left on the page, you will need to format your contact information to take up that extra space so your information sits well on the page. The contact information below is easy to read and is formatted to take up a bit of extra space, which may be exactly what you need to fill out the page.

Jane Somebody
123 Any Street
City, State
Zip Code
Phone: (000) 000-0000
janesomebody@emailprovider.com

On the other hand, if your resume is packed full of information, and you are short on space, you will need to format your contact information in a way that takes up less space. The contact information below is formatted in a way that is still attractive and easy to read, but it would take up a lot less space on your resume, leaving more room for other information.

Jane Somebody   (000) 000-0000

123 Any Street, City, State, Zip Code   janesomebody@emailprovider.com

You will not know all of the information you will need to work with, and how it fits on the page until you have finished writing the content of your resume. There is really no point in trying to format your resume until you know the full scope of what you are working with.

The formatting choices you make will have a huge impact on the impression your resume makes at first glance as well as its overall readability, so it is important to get the formatting right.

Also, you will format your resume differently depending upon whether you are writing for a human reader or an applicant tracking system. It is helpful to have an unformatted copy of your resume that you can go to and revise based on the specific submission requirements of the job you are pursuing.

At this point, we will not examine all of the different ways to format your resume. We will cover formatting resumes for human review in chapter 12 and formatting resumes for applicant tracking systems in chapter 13.

Step Two
Discover a More Efficient Way to Write Your Resume

Instead of formatting your resume as you go, simply type out the information in a clear manner. When you are finished writing the content of your resume, you can go back and format it in a way that works well with the information you have.

EXAMPLE

Once you have finished writing the content of your resume, you will have a document that looks something like the example below.

Please note, the example shows an outline for a combination resume. If you are writing a chronological or functional resume, the concept is the same, but your resume will have a few differences in terms of the sections that are included.

Jane Somebody
123 Any Street, Faketown, State, Zip Code
janesomebody@emailprovider.com
(000) 000-0000

Profile
Type your professional profile here.

Summary
List your most marketable skills here
Be sure to explain your skills in a clear manner
Do not worry about adding bullets or bolding any text at this point

Work Experience
Job Title, Company Name, City, Employment Dates
Describe your responsibilities and accomplishments at the job
Again, do not bother with bullets, bolded text or tabbing at this stage

Job Title, Company Name, City, Employment Dates
Describe your responsibilities and accomplishments at this job
Job Title, Company Name, City, Employment Dates
Describe your responsibilities and accomplishments at this job

Education
Name of Degree, Diploma, Certificate or Course, Name of School, City Dates

Provide details about your education here if it is appropriate to do so

Do not worry if you are not sure what content to include in each section. That information will be covered in upcoming chapters.

All you need to know right now is that *it is not efficient to format your resume as you write the content. It is smarter to type out your content in a plain, unformatted, but organized manner when you are writing the content of your resume.*

Moving Forward

You are ready to move on to the next chapter if you...

1. Understand that you should not format your resume until after you have written the content.

2. Understand how to type the content of your resume in an unformatted but organized manner.

CHAPTER SIX
YOUR CONTACT INFORMATION

YOUR TASK FOR THIS CHAPTER

1. Write the contact information section of your resume.

ACTION STEPS FOR THIS CHAPTER

Step One: Know what contact information to include.

Step Two: Know the most common mistakes people make with contact information on a resume.

Step Three: Understand why you might omit your mailing address from your resume

Step Four: Consider any additional, relevant information you might include

Step Five: Write your contact information.

"When you play it too safe, you're taking the biggest risk of your life. Time is the only wealth we're given." Barbara Sher

Step One
Know What Contact Information to Include

Writing out the contact information on your resume is fairly simple and straightforward, but there are a few common pitfalls you should be aware of and a few simple strategies that will make your job search a bit easier.

Your contact information consists of the following:

- Your name
- Your home address, although there are times when you may decide to omit this information
- Your email address
- Your home phone number and / or your cell phone number
- You may also consider including extra information such as your LinkedIn web address

Step Two
Know the Most Common Mistakes People Make With Contact Information on a Resume

1. Typos

Your resume must be completely free of errors. It is heartbreaking to discover an error in your contact information, particularly a mistyped telephone number, when you have already sent out several resumes.

Proofread your contact information meticulously, and be absolutely certain that it is free of errors.

2. Unprofessional email address

If you have a cute or funny email address that you use for personal emails, avoid using that address for anything related to your job search.

The email address you use for your job search should be professional and straightforward. An address that consists of your first name or your first initial followed by your last name is always a safe option.

Be very careful about adding periods, underscores or special characters to any email address that you intend to use for your job search. Under certain conditions, periods and underscores can be easily missed, and if an employer is entering your email address manually, he or she may miss a period or underscore, and you will not receive the message.

Also, be careful about adding numbers to the end of your name in your email address (as in joejobseeker65@emailprovider.com). Often, when people add a number to their email address, they use their birth year. Employers are aware of this practice. In the example above, many employers would assume that Joe Jobseeker was born in 1965, and that seemingly innocent number on his email address might open Joe up to age discrimination during his job search.

If some combination of your first and last names are not available through your email provider, try adding your middle name or middle initial or reverse your name (last name first, first name last) before you consider adding a period, underscore, special character or a number to your job search email address.

Internet service providers will normally allow customers to set up multiple email accounts at no additional charge. If your current email address is not suitable for job searching, simply create a new email account with a professional sounding address that you can use during your job search. Ask a technically inclined friend for help, or contact your Internet service provider's customer service department if you are not sure how to set up a new email account.

Alternatively, you may choose to use a free web-based email service to set up your job search email account. A service like Google's Gmail is perfectly respectable and acceptable to use for contacting potential employers. Do be aware that some web-based email is viewed more favorably than others. It may sound odd, but some people make a judgment about your technical savvy based on the email provider you use. Currently, Gmail is considered more favorably than some other free email providers. It is a safe option to choose for your job search email address.

HERE'S A TIP TO KEEP YOUR EMAIL ORGANIZED DURING YOUR JOB SEARCH:

Consider setting up a new email account that is only for job search related activities, even if your current email address is professional and appropriate.

A DEDICATED JOB SEARCH EMAIL ADDRESS WILL HELP TO KEEP YOUR REGULAR EMAIL ADDRESS SPAM-FREE.

During the course of your job search, you will probably end up posting your resume to a few resume posting sites.

If you are concerned about cluttering up your regular email address with emails and possibly spam, simply provide those sites with your job search email address. Any emails from resume posting sites will come to your job search email address, and when your job search is complete, you will not have to deal with an inbox full of emails from job search sites at your regular email address.

Do be aware, though, if you stop checking your job search email address after you find a job, you may miss an email with a fabulous opportunity. You might want to continue to check that account for a while.

A DEDICATED JOB SEARCH EMAIL ADDRESS WILL HELP KEEP YOUR JOB SEARCH ORGANIZED.

Creating a dedicated email address for all of your job search related emails will also help you stay organized. You will know that any mail coming to that address is related to your job search, and you will not risk missing messages because they will not be mixed in with your personal email.

A DEDICATED JOB SEARCH EMAIL ADDRESS WILL HELP YOU AVOID MISSING EMAILS.

Be sure to check your spam folder while you are job searching. Occasionally an important email will end up in your spam folder instead of your inbox. For example, if you have signed up for a service that sends relevant job ads directly to you through email, those messages may end up in your spam folder, and you may miss out on some good job leads.

Also, if you do set up a new dedicated job search email address, be sure to check it regularly. If you normally check email on your phone, be sure to add your job search email address to your phone's email application.

Do be extra vigilant about carefully checking for important emails when job searching.

3. Taking too long to return calls from employers

Not long ago, I told job seekers that including a cell phone number on a resume was optional, and they could omit that number if they were not heavy cell phone users and were not comfortable taking important business calls on a cell phone.

Today, cell phone use has become the norm, particularly in business, and, more and more, employers expect to be able to contact people immediately. For that reason, it really is wise to include a cell phone number on your resume whenever possible.

IF YOU ARE NOT A FREQUENT CELL PHONE USER...

Practice taking a few mock business calls on your cell phone so you can become more comfortable using it.

Be sure your family and other people you frequently spend time with know that you may receive important calls from potential employers on your cell phone. Ensure they know you might need immediate silence if your cell phone rings. A hand signal can be helpful to silently let family members know you are on an important call.

If you are not in the habit of leaving your cell phone turned on or keeping it with you during regular business hours, ensure it is always turned on and with you while you are job searching.

If you include your cell phone number on your resume, you must have voicemail for your cell phone. I do understand that adding voicemail to your cell phone account can be an extra expense at a time when you have limited income, but it really is crucial for employers to be able to contact you quickly and easily. You can cancel the voicemail service as soon as you have found work if it is not something you normally use.

IF IT IS NOT POSSIBLE TO INCLUDE A CELL PHONE NUMBER ON YOUR RESUME...

If you do not have a cell phone with voicemail, and it is not possible to get one for the duration of your job search, be sure to learn how to remotely check the voicemail on your home phone.

Most voicemail systems will allow you to check your messages from another telephone. Learn how to remotely check your voicemail messages, and any time you are away from home for more than a couple of hours during the day, check your messages remotely. That way, if a potential employer has left a message for you, you will know fairly quickly and be able to respond quickly.

4. No voicemail

While most people do have some type of answering machine or voicemail system, there are still some individuals who get by without one.

If you are job searching, *you absolutely must have an answering machine or other voicemail system connected to every phone number you have provided on your resume.*

Employers are not going to invest very much time trying to contact you if they are unable to leave a message the first time they call. If you do not have an answering machine or voicemail service, you will likely miss out on opportunities simply because employers will not be able to leave a message when you are unavailable to take their calls, and they will not call back. They will simply move on to the next candidate for the job if they cannot easily contact you.

Of course, if you are job searching, that often means you are trying to get by on less money than you normally have coming into your household, and it can be tempting to cancel your voicemail service to save a little cash. Having voicemail or an answering machine is not optional if you are job searching.

If you need to save money, perhaps, instead of renewing your voicemail service, you could look for a free or inexpensive answering machine by asking friends if anyone has a gently used answering machine you could buy or borrow.

TOP 5 CONTACT INFORMATION MISTAKES:

1. **Typos**
2. **Unprofessional email address**
3. **Slow to return employers' calls**
4. **No voicemail**
5. **Unprofessional voicemail greeting**

5. Unprofessional voicemail greeting

Many people have fun and cute greetings on their voicemail. Those messages are fine when you are not job searching, but if you are job searching, *your voicemail greeting must be brief and professional.*

Avoid allowing your kids to talk on your voicemail greeting, and avoid anything that you would not put on a workplace voicemail greeting. Stick to something simple like, "You have reached 000-0000. I'm sorry; I'm not able to take your call at this time. Please leave your name and number, and I will return your call."

ARE YOU CERTAIN YOUR VOICEMAIL GREETING IS PROFESSIONAL?

We record those greetings, and we often do not hear them again for months or even years at a time. If you are job searching, call any phone number that is listed on your resume, listen to the greeting, and ensure it is professional.

Step Three
Understand Why You Might Omit Your Mailing Address From Your Resume

Until quite recently, it was standard to always include your mailing address on your resume. Now some job seekers are choosing to omit their mailing address for a variety of reasons, and some are having good success with that strategy.

When you submit a resume, employers will either contact you by telephone or email, so they really do not need your full mailing address to contact you. However, employers might look at your mailing address for other reasons. Your address can give away more information about you than you might realize. There may be times when it is to your advantage to remove that information from your resume.

Reasons to omit your mailing address from your resume:

YOU HAVE SAFETY CONCERNS

It is easier than ever for people to post job ads, which means you do not necessarily know who is behind those ads. In addition, concerns about identity theft are on the rise, and your resume includes a lot of personal, identifying information.

If you have reasons to be concerned about safety or the security of your personal information, you may consider omitting your mailing address from your resume. In this case, you could omit the address entirely, or you could include your city, state and possibly your zip code if you wanted to indicate the general area where you live.

YOU LIVE FAR FROM THE JOB

In some locations, employers increasingly appear to be filtering out job applicants based on the distance they live from the job.

Applicant tracking systems make it easy for employers to filter out applicants who live far from the job location. If an employer uses an applicant tracking system to screen resumes, the employer can set the software to filter out resumes from anyone who lives more than a specified distance from the job location.

Even if resumes are being sorted by a human, it is not hard to filter by location and omit any applicants who would have to commute to work.

In fact, colleagues of mine have reported that clients who were seeking jobs several miles from their home often got no response (or limited response) to their resumes when they included their mailing address. As soon as they removed the mailing address their resumes, they began to get invited to interviews.

If you are looking for a job that is far from your home address, you may want to consider omitting your mailing address from your resume. In this case, you would omit your entire address.

YOU MAY BE JUDGED NEGATIVELY BASED ON YOUR ADDRESS

If you live in a neighborhood that is considered a "rough" part of town, unfortunately, people might judge you based on your neighborhood. I truly wish that was not the case, but it is a fact that can impact your job search success.

If you know that some people make unfair, negative assumptions about people who live in your neighborhood, you might want to consider omitting your address from your resume. In this case, you can omit the mailing address completely, or you could include the city and state if you want to provide general information about your location.

Reasons to include your mailing address on your resume:

YOU LIVE CLOSE TO THE JOB

Just as employers may filter out job seekers who live far from the job location, they may also give preference to people who live close by. If you do not have any concerns about providing your mailing address, and you want to show the employer that you live very close, then it is wise to include your full mailing address on your resume.

YOU HAVE NO REASON TO OMIT YOUR MAILING ADDRESS

If none of the concerns listed above are relevant to you, and you have no reason to omit your address, you may decide to include your full address on your resume. Although employers do not need that information to contact you, the mailing address has been a standard part of the resume for a long time. In the future, it may become standard to omit your address, but the trend has not reached that point, and some employers may wonder why you have omitted your mailing address.

Should you omit your mailing address from your resume?

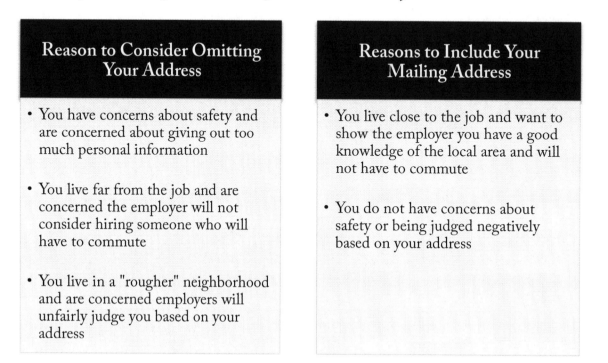

Reason to Consider Omitting Your Address	Reasons to Include Your Mailing Address
• You have concerns about safety and are concerned about giving out too much personal information	• You live close to the job and want to show the employer you have a good knowledge of the local area and will not have to commute
• You live far from the job and are concerned the employer will not consider hiring someone who will have to commute	• You do not have concerns about safety or being judged negatively based on your address
• You live in a "rougher" neighborhood and are concerned employers will unfairly judge you based on your address	

The decision to omit your mailing address from a resume is a judgment call. It is a newer trend, which means it will not be accepted by all employers. However, I have seen evidence that this strategy can help people find jobs when their home address could be a negative factor to a potential employer.

If you have a reason to be concerned about including your mailing address on your resume, consider omitting it. Do watch the response rate to your resumes, though if you make this change. Look for any indication that it is working for you or against you. Your biggest clue about how well this strategy works will be the number of invitations to interviews you receive. If the strategy seems to be working for you after submitting several resumes, continue to omit your address. If it seems to be working against you, consider adding your address back on to your resume.

Keep in mind, you might decide to include your mailing address on some resumes and omit it on others. For example, if you are applying to jobs that are close to your home, you may decide to include your mailing address on those resumes, but if you are also applying to jobs that are farther away, you may decide to omit your mailing address on those resumes.

Step Four
Consider Any Additional, Relevant Information You Might Include

If you have a LinkedIn account that would make a great impression on employers, you may include your LinkedIn profile web address (also known as a URL) on your resume. Ideally you should create a custom address on LinkedIn because it is more professional looking and user friendly. Avoid using the address with random characters that LinkedIn provides when you first sign up.

Including this information is optional, and it is only advisable if your LinkedIn account would help an employer to decide that you are a strong candidate for the job. If your account information is complete with information that enhances your resume, and if you have plenty of connections and endorsements that show you are well known and respected by people in your industry, that information can validate your claims on your resume and help you make a good impression.

Step Five
Write Your Contact Information

Finally, it is time to put something on paper! Open up your favorite word processing program, and type your contact information in a plain, unformatted style. When you are finished, you will have something that looks like this:

Jane Somebody
123 Any Street, Faketown, State, Zip Code
janesomebody@emailprovider.com
(000) 000-0000

Or, if you have decided to omit your mailing address and include your LinkedIn profile URL, it will look like this:

Jane Somebody
janesomebody@emailprovider.com
(000) 000-0000
www.linkedin.com/in/janesomebody
Proofread your contact information carefully.

Save your document.

Assignment

Type your contact information for your resume.

Moving Forward

You are ready to move on to the next chapter if you...

1. Understand the common mistakes people make when including contact information on a resume so you can avoid making those mistakes.

2. Have considered whether your email address is professional enough to use during your job search and created a new email account with a professional sounding address to use during your job search if necessary or desired.

3. Have ensured that you have an answering machine or voicemail system connected to any phone number you include on your resume and have checked to confirm the greeting is professional.

4. Understand reasons why you might choose to omit your mailing address from your resume and have made a decision about whether you will include that information on your resume.

5. Have determined whether you will include your LinkedIn address on your resume if you are active on that site.

6. Have typed your contact information and proofread it carefully.

CHAPTER SEVEN
PROFILE

YOUR TASKS FOR THIS CHAPTER

1. Understand why profiles are more effective than job objectives.
2. Write the profile section of your resume.

ACTION STEPS FOR THIS CHAPTER

Step One: Understand the features of job objectives and profiles.

Step Two: Understand how a profile makes your resume more appealing to employers.

Step Three: Understand why you cannot write an effective resume if you do not have a specific profile.

Step Four: Determine whether you will write a job objective or a profile.

Step Five: Know how to write an effective job objective and an effective profile.

Step Six: Write your job objective or profile.

"Concentrate all your thoughts upon the work at hand. The sun's rays do not burn until brought to a focus." Alexander Graham Bell

Step One
Understand the Features of Job Objectives and Profiles

In my opinion, all good resumes have a profile section immediately following the contact information. Whether you are writing a combination resume, a chronological resume or a functional resume, you will need to include a profile.

In the recent past, it was acceptable to use a job objective on your resume instead of a profile. However, job objectives are falling out of favor. Using a job objective can make your resume appear out of date to some people, and profiles generally do a better job of communicating your value to potential employers.

I will cover both profiles and objectives in this chapter because you will almost certainly find information about using a job objective if you research other sources for resume writing tips. My bias is clearly towards using a profile instead of an objective. You can review the information in this chapter, and make a more informed decision for yourself about which option is best for you.

What is a job objective?

A job objective is a simple statement that indicates the type of work you are seeking.

SOME EXAMPLES OF JOB OBJECTIVES

Seeking a part-time position as an administrative assistant.

To obtain a position as a retail sales clerk.

To obtain an entry-level position as a customer service representative.

Seeking a shift supervisor position at XYZ Company, job reference number 1234567.

What is a profile?

Profiles are slightly more complex than job objectives. A profile usually consists of two or three sentences that describe the type of work you are seeking as well as some of the most important skills and experiences you can offer to an employer.

SOME EXAMPLES OF PROFILES

Customer service manager with seven years of progressive professional experience. Results oriented with a proven ability to improve customer retention and increase team productivity. Seeking a position with XYZ Company, job reference number 1234567.

Bilingual events coordinator with exceptional project management skills. Over ten years of experience working with volunteers, diverse teams and community leaders. Strong leadership skills with the ability to build the trust of others with integrity and consistently meet and exceed targeted results.

Step Two
Understand How a Profile Makes Your Resume More Appealing to Employers

Whether you use a profile or an objective, *the purpose of this section of your resume is to allow employers to understand, at a glance, the type of job you are seeking and are qualified to do.* This section helps employers to read your resume more quickly and intelligently.

An objective or profile will help to orient the employer's focus as he or she quickly reviews your resume. This section makes it clear to employers that all of the information on your resume, when added together, will demonstrate that you are very well suited to the type of job you have noted in your profile or objective. It eliminates reader confusion and pulls the employer deeper into the content of your resume.

When a resume does not have a clear profile, it is much more difficult to read quickly. Resumes without profiles are harder to decipher because it is not clear at a glance what type of work the individual is seeking and qualified for. When there is no profile, an employer reviewing your resume wastes the first few precious seconds trying to determine your career focus.

You may hear some people say that a profile or objective is unnecessary. I am certain that people who say that have never had to sort through piles of resumes to find the most likely candidates for a job. A profile or objective truly makes your resume more readable at a glance. Resumes that do not have a profile or objective are much harder to review quickly.

When there is a profile or objective, an employer can quickly jump into understanding and assessing your skills in the context of the job you are seeking without any confusion about your career background.

DO NOT UNDERESTIMATE THE IMPORTANCE OF ENSURING EMPLOYERS CAN READ YOUR RESUME QUICKLY AND INTELLIGENTLY.

When moving through the hiring process, employers are typically sorting through huge stacks of resumes searching for just a few suitable candidates to interview. If they do not get the information they need in a few quick seconds, your resume will be tossed in the 'no' pile, even if you are qualified for the job.

A PROFILE CAN HELP YOUR RESUME SCORE BETTER IF IT WILL BE SCREENED WITH AN APPLICANT TRACKING SYSTEM.

If your resume will be screened with an applicant tracking system, it is important to include relevant keywords, including the job title of the job you are pursuing exactly as it is written in the job ad. A profile allows you to include relevant keywords and an exact match for the job title fairly easily and near the top of your resume.

You will notice in two of the examples at the beginning of this chapter, the objective or profile includes the job title as well as the company name and job reference number. Including the company name on your resume, in some cases, might help increase the score your resume receives when screened with an applicant tracking system.

Step Three
Understand Why You Cannot Write an Effective Resume if You Do Not Have a Specific Profile

Some job seekers are hesitant to state a specific job on their resumes. Normally when people hesitate to state a specific job it is either because they do not know what type of job they are seeking, or they are concerned that if they state a specific job on their resume, they will not be considered for other jobs.

While these concerns should be addressed, they are not valid reasons for omitting a profile or objective from your resume.

If you have no idea what type of work you are seeking:

Consider writing a resume targeted to the type of work you have done in the past. Even if you think you do not want to do that same type of work again, this type of resume is the easiest to write and can be a good starting place. Writing a resume that is targeted to the type of work you have done in the past can provide a lot of content and clarity, which will help you write resumes targeted at other types of jobs that are of interest to you.

or

You may not be at the resume writing stage of the job search process. If you have absolutely no idea what type of job you want to target, and writing a resume for the type of work you have done in the past does not seem appropriate, you may need to take a step back and explore your career options before you start to write your resume. You will find a link to career exploration resources in chapter 16.

> *" If you try to appeal to every employer by being vague, you will end up appealing to no one."*

If you are concerned you will not be considered for other jobs:

Remember, if you are looking for more than one type of job, you will need more than one resume. You will simply need to write different resumes with different objectives or profiles and slightly different content throughout the resume if you want to be considered for other jobs.

If you are concerned that you will not be considered for different jobs within a single company, a profile is definitely a better choice than an objective. A profile provides a little more flexibility and allows you to put more focus on the skills you have to offer as opposed to focusing on a specific job title. A well-written profile can allow the employer to focus on your general area of expertise but still consider you for different jobs within an organization.

WHATEVER YOU DO, DO NOT WRITE A VAGUE, UNFOCUSED OBJECTIVE OR PROFILE.

When people are hesitant to state a specific job, they tend to make the mistake of writing a vague objective like:

To obtain a position that will utilize my skills and experience.

This type of general, vague job objective is just not effective. It does not provide the employer with any evidence that you are a great candidate for the job you are seeking.

A general job objective does not communicate to employers that you are open to considering a variety of jobs. Instead, it gives employers the impression that you are completely unfocused and not specifically interested in or qualified for any of the jobs they are trying to fill.

You make a much stronger and more positive impression on employers if you come across as a person who is focused, is searching for a specific type of job and has a specific set of skills to offer.

Also, if your resume will be screened with applicant tracking system software, your resume must be highly targeted to the specific job you are applying to. A general resume will not score well in ATS screening. The use of this type of software to screen resumes has drastically raised the importance of submitting a highly targeted resume every time you apply for a job.

If you try to appeal to every employer by keeping your objective or profile vague, you will end up appealing to no one.

Step Four
Determine Whether You Will Write a Job Objective or a Profile

WHY PROFILES ARE BETTER THAN JOB OBJECTIVES

The use of job objectives on resumes has become somewhat questionable. Objectives are starting to fall out of fashion, and, in my opinion, profiles have always been stronger than job objectives anyway.

An objective can make your resume appear outdated.

Because objectives are falling out of fashion, using one can subtly communicate to some employers that you might also be outdated professionally. This generalization, of course, is not fair, but keep in mind, employers make quick decisions based on immediate impressions when they are initially sorting through a pile of resumes.

Of course some employers do not care whether you use an objective or a profile, but some will. It is just as easy to write a profile as it is to write an objective, so you might as well use a profile and avoid the possibility that an objective could make you appear outdated in the mind of an employer.

Profiles are focused on what you can offer the employer.

Objectives focus on what you want. They tell an employer you want a job as an administrative assistant, or a retail sales associate, or whatever other type of job you are seeking.

Profiles focus on what you have to offer. They tell an employer you can offer years of experience in a field, or a high level or education, or a depth of knowledge in a specific area of expertise that is important to that employer.

When you write a resume, it is important to constantly focus on demonstrating how you can meet that employer's needs. Of course, you are writing a resume because you have your own need to land a job. However, to get invited to interviews, you have to convince employers you can meet their needs. When you write a resume, every point on it must demonstrate ways in which you can meet the needs of the employer, and a profile does a better job of addressing the needs of the employer.

Bottom line: Objectives come with some pitfalls; profiles do not, so you might as well use a profile and avoid those potential pitfalls.

WHEN TO USE A JOB OBJECTIVE

In the past, I would sometimes use a job objective on a resume for a client who was seeking an entry-level job. I have never recommended objectives for people seeking mid-level or senior positions or jobs that require specialized training.

At this point, though, I would not recommend the use of a job objective, even if you are pursuing an entry-level job.

WHEN TO USE A PROFILE

Profiles can be used in any circumstance. They are effective when:

- You have experience and an established career

- You are making a career change

- You are a recent graduate

- You are returning to the workforce after a period of time without paid employment

- You want to put the focus on your skills more than on a specific job title

- You have a few key skills or experiences that you want to highlight to employers

- You are seeking an entry-level job

If you are not sure whether to write a job objective or a profile, remember:

- Objectives may seem outdated to some employers

- Profiles are stronger than objectives

- Profiles are appropriate in all situations

When in doubt, write a profile instead of a job objective.

Step Five
Know How to Write an Effective Job Objective and an Effective Profile

How to write an effective job objective:

A job objective is one sentence that states the specific type of job you are seeking. Although job objectives are fairly simple, they can be used to state more than just a job title.

EXAMPLES OF JOB OBJECTIVES THAT EXPRESS EXTRA INFORMATION

> To obtain a position at ABC Company where I can support clients using my counseling and group facilitation skills and experience.

This type of job objective may work in a situation where you would like to target a specific company, you know they employ people with your background, but you do not know what specific jobs may be available at that company. This type of objective is not recommended if you are applying to a specific job. It is also not recommended if your resume will be screened with an applicant tracking system because the objective is too vague to be effective.

In the example, the company name has been specified, so the objective is not completely generic, and then a couple of key skills that would benefit the company are noted. In this case, the job seeker is indicating that he or she would fit well in a front line job working with clients in a few different types of roles, perhaps as a counselor, workshop facilitator or teacher.

Seeking a position as a sales manager trainee at XYZ Company.

This objective would be used if you were applying to a specific company. If you know the exact title of the position you are seeking and the company where you would like to work, it is perfectly reasonable to be that specific in your job objective. In fact, including the exact match job title and company name as shown in this example is effective when a resume will be screened with an applicant tracking system. Also, if there is a reference number associated with the job posting, you could include the reference number in your objective as well.

Just remember to change your objective if you apply for the same job at a different company. If your resume says you want to work at XYZ Company, and you send it off to ABC Company, you are not going to get called for an interview at ABC Company.

To obtain employment with an organization that will benefit from my exceptional customer service, problem solving, planning and organizational skills.

This job objective is really not ideal because it is more generic than it should be. However, I have included this example because clients often ask what type of objective statement they should write when they really do not know what type of job they are seeking. Although this example is generic, at least it notes some important skills that the job seeker can bring to the organization.

You really should include a type of job, industry and/or company name in your objective to avoid appearing vague and unfocused. Use the example above as a model as a last resort only, and always avoid extremely general statements like, "To obtain a position that will use my skills and experience."

> To obtain a part-time position as a sales associate.

If you are specifically looking for part-time work, say so in your objective statement. Employers who are hiring part-time staff often worry that the person they hire will leave as soon as they find full-time work, and all of the time they invested in hiring and training that person will be wasted. Therefore, if you really want part-time work, say so. You will communicate to the employer that you will not treat their part-time job as a temporary position.

> Seeking a full-time position as an administrative assistant in the publishing industry.

If you are seeking a type of job that can be found in many different industries, consider noting a specific industry in your job objective. This job objective example would work well for someone who has experience working as an administrative assistant in the publishing industry and is seeking the same type of job in the same industry.

When the work that you do fits into many different industries, noting the industry that is of interest to you communicates to the employer that you are not just any administrative assistant, you are an administrative assistant who already has an excellent understanding of that company's industry.

To write an effective job objective, keep it simple. State the type of job you are seeking, and, if you like, note any other important considerations such as a preference for part-time work, or interest in a specific industry.

How to write an effective profile:

A profile is normally at least two sentences and no longer than three sentences. It indicates the type of work in which you have expertise and provides a very brief summary of the most important skills you can offer an employer.

1. DETERMINE THE JOB TITLE YOU WILL USE

The first part of a profile normally states your job title. You do not have to use the exact job title you had at your last job if it is not the best fit for the work you are currently seeking. If you think your resume will be screened with an applicant tracking system, ideally, you should use the exact job title that is stated in the job ad, assuming that job title is an accurate reflection of your area of expertise.

Remember, the job title you use must be an honest reflection of your professional experience. You cannot just call yourself a bookkeeper if you have absolutely no experience or training in that profession. The job title you use must also be a good fit with the type of work you are currently seeking.

HERE ARE A FEW EXAMPLES TO HELP YOU TO DECIDE WHAT JOB TITLE TO USE FOR YOUR PROFILE:

If your most recent job involved working as an adult education teacher, but you have experience and training to teach music, and you are applying for a job as a music teacher, you would use the job title music teacher, not adult education teacher, in your profile.

If your most recent job involved working as a health and safety manager, but your actual job title was very company-specific, and no one outside of your organization would know what your job title actually meant, you would use the job title health and safety manager, which would be understood by people outside of your current company.

If your current job is very specialized in your industry, and you are open to more generalized jobs in your field, use the more general title. For example, if you are currently working as a vocational rehabilitation case manager (a specialized niche in career counseling), but you are willing to consider all kinds of career counseling jobs, you would use the more general job title, career counselor, on your profile.

If your most recent job title is a perfect, or very close match for the new job you are seeking, then use your most recent job title on your profile. Use the exact title of the job you are pursuing if there is a chance the employer will use an applicant tracking system to screen resumes.

2. HIGHLIGHT YOUR MOST MARKETABLE SKILLS AND ACCOMPLISHMENTS

Marketable skills and accomplishments are the skills and accomplishments that employers in your line of work are looking for. They are the skills that demonstrate that you are an excellent candidate for the job you are seeking. Marketable skills and accomplishments set you apart from other, less qualified job seekers.

Your most marketable skills and accomplishments might not be your favorite skills. They might not be the accomplishments that you are most proud of, and, particularly if you are making a career change, they might not even be the skills you use most often at your current job.

As you work to determine the two or three most marketable skills and accomplishments that you want to highlight on your profile, ask yourself, "What does an employer in my field need to know about me in order to know that I am an excellent candidate for the job?"

If you are applying to an advertised job, review the job ad carefully to determine which skills are most important to the employer. Look for job requirements that are mentioned more than once in the ad. Also, look for a section labeled something like "requirements for success" in the ad. This section tells you the absolutely necessary skills and experience you must have to be considered for the job.

3. CONSIDER YOUR SOFT SKILLS AND YOUR HARD SKILLS (ALSO KNOWN AS TECHNICAL SKILLS)

Soft skills are interpersonal skills or personality traits that you possess which make you well suited to your job. Although it is possible to work to improve certain soft skills, they are generally skills that you develop through life and are not learned through specific coursework.

SOME EXAMPLES OF SOFT SKILLS ARE:

- Self-directed
- Reliable
- Courteous
- Dependable
- Team player
- Adaptable
- Cooperative

Hard skills, also known as technical skills, refer to the technical requirements of your job. They typically refer to skills that you had to actively learn.

SOME EXAMPLES OF HARD SKILLS ARE:

- Proficiency with computer software that is relevant to your work
- Ability to operate machinery and tools that are relevant to your work
- Ability to analyze information that is relevant to your work

Consider the type of skills required for the job you are seeking. If soft skills are crucial, those are the skills you should highlight in your profile. If hard skills are more important in the job you are seeking, hard skills should be featured in your profile.

Many jobs require a balance of soft and hard skills. If that is the case for the job you are seeking, highlight both soft and hard skills in your profile.

4. DO NOT TRY TO INCLUDE TOO MUCH INFORMATION IN YOUR PROFILE

Keep in mind, you should not try to say everything in your profile. There is no need to describe all of your marketable skills here. Instead, your goal should be to highlight a couple of important skills that will pique the employer's interest and cause him or her to want to read more.

Once you have determined two or three skills or accomplishments that you want to highlight, work them into a very concise, two or three sentence paragraph that will be your profile.

A FEW EXAMPLES OF PROFILES:

> Administrative professional with seven years of experience in the nonprofit sector. Able to prioritize and manage conflicting demands. Exceptional technical skills including proficiency with Word, Excel, PowerPoint and Prezi.

This profile is concise. It highlights the amount of experience this job seeker has and indicates specific experience working with nonprofit organizations. It expresses some soft skills that are important to the job, as well as crucial technical skills. The profile does not provide all of the information the employer needs, but it does provide enough information to encourage the employer to read further in the resume.

> Music teacher with five years of teaching experience. Proven ability to plan and implement lessons that meet both individual and group needs, and committed to developing positive relationships with students, parents and staff. Areas of expertise include teaching group and individual piano and flute lessons and early childhood music classes.

This profile is for the teacher mentioned earlier who currently teaches adult education but has experience teaching music and is applying to a music teaching job. This job seeker has combined all of his or her years of teaching experience. He or she may have taught music for four years and adult education for one year, but rather than breaking it up, the experience has been grouped and stated as "five years of teaching experience" in the profile.

Also, the adult education experience is not mentioned in the profile. This job is still relevant and will be described later in the resume, but it is not the most crucial piece of information that the employer needs, so it has not been highlighted in the profile.

> Career counselor with over five years of counseling experience. Self-motivated, with a proven ability to work independently. Areas of specialization include working with clients who are injured workers, long term unemployed and experienced workers.

This profile belongs to someone who currently works as a job search workshop facilitator and is applying to a job that is within the realm of career counseling, but does not involve facilitating workshops. Also, this resume is targeted at a job that would involve working from a home office.

The more general job title, career counselor, was used instead of the more specific title, job search workshop facilitator, because this individual is not seeking a job that involves leading group sessions. The sentence, "Self-motivated, with a proven ability to work independently." is important because the job this person is applying to involves working from home. In a job that did not involve working from home, this skill would be less crucial, and, therefore, would not be included on the profile.

AVOID CONFUSION

I have included in this chapter a lot of information about how to write job objectives, immediately after saying I do not recommend using a job objective. I realize that might, understandably, cause some confusion for some people.

To clarify, *I do not recommend the use of job objectives*. As I explained earlier, there are pitfalls associated with using job objectives, and you can avoid those pitfalls by using a profile instead.

However, if you seek out resume writing information from other books or websites, you will find information about job objectives. For that reason, I wanted to present you with information about both job objectives and profiles. That way, you can make your own informed decision about which to use on your resume, and if you do decide to use an objective, you will be able to write one that is as effective as possible.

Step Six
Write Your Job Objective or Profile

If you are writing a job objective...

Writing a job objective is fairly simple. Most job objectives start with a phrase like "To obtain a position as" or "Seeking a job as" and then state the specific job the job seeker wants to pursue.

You may want to add slightly more detail. Ask yourself if you want to highlight any of the following in your job objective:

- A preference for part-time work
- Interest or experience in working in a specific industry
- One or two of your most marketable skills

Work any additional, important information into your objective.

Open up the document where you saved your contact information from chapter 6, and write your job objective. When you are finished, you will have something that looks like this:

Jane Somebody
123 Any Street, Faketown, State, Zip Code
janesomebody@emailprovider.com
(000) 000-0000

Job Objective
Seeking a position as an administrative assistant in a local nonprofit organization.

If you are writing a profile...

Writing a profile is just slightly more complex than writing an objective.

- Determine the best job title to use. Be sure it is an honest reflection of your professional experience and a good match for the work you are currently seeking.
- Determine two or three marketable skills that you want to highlight in your profile.

If you are feeling a bit stuck, try this simple formula for writing your profile:

1. Note the most appropriate job title.

2. List the number of years of experience you have doing this type of work.

3. Mention a couple of soft skills that are important to the work you are seeking.

4. Mention a couple of technical skills that are important to the work you are seeking.

WRITE YOUR OBJECTIVE OR PROFILE

Open up the document where you saved your contact information from chapter 6, and write your job objective. When you are finished, you will have something that looks like this (notice the profile was written using the formula described above):

Jane Somebody
123 Any Street, Faketown, State, Zip Code
janesomebody@emailprovider.com
(000) 000-0000

Profile
Administrative professional with seven years of experience in the nonprofit sector. Able to prioritize and manage conflicting demands. Exceptional technical skills including proficiency with Word, Excel, PowerPoint and Prezi.

Assignment

Decide whether you will write an objective or a profile, and then write your objective or your profile.

Moving Forward

You are ready to move on to the next chapter if you...

- Understand the basic features of job objectives and profiles.

    1. Know why profiles are more effective than job objectives.

    2. Have made a choice, based on your specific background, between writing a job objective or a profile.

    3. Have written your job objective or profile.

CHAPTER EIGHT
SUMMARY OF SKILLS

YOUR TASKS FOR THIS CHAPTER:

1. Decide if you need to write a summary of skills.
2. Understand how to write to promote yourself effectively on your resume.
3. Write your summary of skills if required.

ACTION STEPS FOR THIS CHAPTER

Step One: Understand the features of a summary of skills.

Step Two: Understand the benefits of using a summary of skills.

Step Three: Understand how to determine what information should be included in a summary of skills.

Step Four: Know how to describe your skills and accomplishments in a way that makes a strong, positive impact.

Step Five: Know how to organize your summary of skills.

Step Six: Write your summary of skills

"Always define WHAT you want to do with your life and WHAT you have to offer to the world, in terms of your favorite talents/gifts/skills not in terms of a job title." Richard Nelson Bolles

If you are writing a combination resume or a functional resume, you will need to write a summary of skills. If you are writing a chronological resume, you will not include a summary of skills on your resume. However, even if you are not including a summary of skills on your resume, you should read this chapter because it contains information about how to effectively describe your work that can also be applied to writing the work history section of your resume.

For many people, writing a summary of skills is the most difficult part of the resume writing process. If you are not accustomed to writing or talking about yourself and your professional experience, then remembering all of your relevant skills and describing them in a way that is concise, meaningful and impressive to employers can take a lot of thought.

If you feel overwhelmed by the thought of writing your skills summary when you finish reading this chapter, feel free to skip this section and work through chapters 9 through 11 (work history, education and volunteer work) first. These sections are often easier to write than the skills summary, and writing those sections can help you gain the focus necessary to write your summary of skills. Come back to this chapter, and write your summary of skills once you have completed the other sections of your resume.

I almost always work on the summary of skills section last when I write resumes with clients. The summary of skills is extremely important, but it also tends to be difficult to write. It is often much easier to write a great summary of skills after you have warmed up by writing the other sections of your resume first.

Step One
Understand the Features of a Summary of Skills

A summary of skills is a list of about five to eight of your most important skills or accomplishments. You choose which skills and accomplishments are most important based on the type of job you are currently seeking. It is one of the first things an employer focuses on when reviewing your resume, so it is an extremely important section of your resume.

The skills and accomplishments listed in this section should include those that are crucial to the job you are seeking and impressive enough to draw the attention of an employer who reads your resume.

It is possible to list more than eight skills in this section, and, if you are writing a functional resume, you must list more than eight skills. If you have a long list of skills that you need to highlight, simply organize your skills into sub-headings and keep each list to eight points or less.

You will find more information about organizing a long list of skills and accomplishments later in this chapter.

For the sake of simplicity, I will refer to this section as the summary of skills. However, this section of your resume can be given many different headings depending upon how you choose to organize your skills and accomplishments, so keep in mind that you can choose the heading or headings that are most appropriate for you.

You will find more information about choosing the best heading or headings for this section of your resume later in this chapter.

Step Two
Understand the Benefits of Using a Summary of Skills

Benefits of using a summary of skills:

A summary of skills:

- Brings your most important skills to the top of your resume so they do not become hidden within your work history and are easy to find at a glance

- Provides a single place where employers can look to quickly see if you have the most crucial skills required for the job

- When written well, draws employers deeper into the body of your resume

- Provides an enormous amount of flexibility in terms of where you can place each point, so if you have important skills that were demonstrated at a job you held several years ago, you can get those skills up to the top of your resume where employers will notice them

- Allows you to show how skills from one type of job transfer into a different but related job more easily than you can in the work history section of your resume

- Helps you avoid repetition if you have held basically the same job at several different companies

- Allows a huge amount of flexibility to customize your resume and tailor it to each job

- Provides extra opportunities to include important keywords and phrases that can help your resume rank well if it is reviewed by an applicant tracking system

Potential problems when using a summary of skills:

A summary of skills takes up space on your resume. If you include a summary of skills on your resume, you will have less space for your work history, education, and any other information you choose to include. However, some of the information you include on a summary of skills would have been included in the work history section if you did not have a summary of skills, so you will be able to make your work history more concise than you could if you did not use a summary of skills.

It can be difficult to show exactly when you used a specific skill when it is listed in your summary of skills instead of your work history because there are no dates associated with the summary of skills section. This fact can be both positive and negative. It is a positive if you want to bring older skills up to the top of your resume, but it can be a negative to some employers because they may want to know exactly when you used certain skills or achieved a specific accomplishment.

The majority of employers will look to your work history to determine when you used those skills, so this issue is rarely a large cause for concern and should not prevent anyone from using a summary of skills.

If you do want to note when you used a specific skill, you may mention the job you were doing when you demonstrated that skill or you may specify the date.

EXAMPLE

Imagine you worked as a receptionist from 2008-2010, you worked as an administrative assistant from 2010-2012, and you worked as a legal administrative assistant from 2012-2014. You have an important skill or impressive accomplishment that is very recent, and you want to clarify on your skills summary that the skill or accomplishment is tied to your most recent job, and not one in the more distant past.

The point you write might look something like this:

> As a legal administrative assistant, developed new database system to efficiently compile and analyze large volume and variety of client data, which reduced time to complete monthly, quarterly and annual reports by 50%

or like this...

In 2014, developed new database system to efficiently compile and analyze large volume and variety of client data, which reduced time to complete monthly, quarterly and annual reports by 50%

By noting the job you held or the year when you completed an accomplishment or demonstrated a skill, you can pinpoint it to a specific time.

Please be aware that it is neither necessary nor desirable to link every skill you list with a specific date or job. Doing so would create a very awkward and difficult to read summary of skills. However, if you feel it is important to link one or two of the points in your summary of skills to a specific time or job, this strategy will work.

Also, please be aware that it is not advisable to include dates in the summary of skills section if an applicant tracking system will be used to review your resume. Dates in unexpected places on your resume may cause some applicant tracking systems to interpret your resume incorrectly.

Step Three
Understand How to Determine What Information Should Be Included in a Summary of Skills

A summary of skills should include the most crucial and impressive skills you have to offer an employer as well as accomplishments that are *related to the type of job you are currently seeking*.

The last part of the previous sentence is important. This section of your resume builds the employer's first impressions of you, and you want to create the impression that you are a great candidate *for the specific type of job that you are seeking*.

The types of skills and accomplishments that are important to the job you are currently seeking may or may not be the skills you use most frequently in your current or most recent job.

When you are deciding which skills to include, do not simply create a list of the job duties you perform on a regular basis at your current job. Instead, determine which skills and accomplishments would be important to someone who is doing the type of job you are currently seeking. Next, ask yourself whether you have those skills, and if you do, think about how you demonstrated those skills at work, or school or through volunteer work if you have limited relevant paid work experience. Those are the types of points that should be included in your summary of skills.

Some tips about the types of skills you should include:

You can and should change your skills summary to target each job you apply to. You will find more information about how to write many resumes targeted to specific jobs in chapter 14.

If the job you are applying to is an advertised job, review the job ad and note what skills the employer has asked for. The skills an employer asks for in a job ad represent the most crucial skills that a person must have to be considered for the job. If you have the skills noted in the job ad, be sure to include evidence that you have them in your skills summary. This step is particularly important if your resume will be screened with an applicant tracking system. You will find more details about how to write an effective skills summary for an ATS in chapter 13.

If you know the name of the company you are applying to, review the company's website and their social media accounts and note specific information about the company's business and culture. Try to answer questions like:

- What values are important within the company?

- What types of customers or clients do they work with?

- What type of work do they do?

- What makes the company stand out from other companies in the same industry?

As you answer these questions, think about how your skills and accomplishments match with the company's work and culture. Include those points on your summary of skills.

If you do not have a job ad or information about the company, think carefully about the type of job you are applying to and determine which skills are most important in that type of work. In chapter 16, you will find a list of websites that provide detailed job descriptions for thousands of jobs. Use these sites for inspiration if you need help thinking of all of the important skills related to the type of job you are seeking.

Think through the accomplishments you have achieved throughout your career and ask yourself if each accomplishment makes a strong case for the fact that you would be great at the job you are seeking. If an accomplishment helps to prove that you would be great at the type of job you are currently seeking, it should be included in your summary of skills.

Remember, unless you are writing a functional resume, a summary of skills will not contain all of your relevant skills, you will use other sections of your resume to demonstrate that you have other skills that are relevant to the job you are seeking. However, your summary of skills must include *the most important skills and accomplishments* an employer needs to know about to know you would be great at the job.

This section of your resume is prime real estate, do not waste it by including irrelevant or only moderately important information.

Step Four
Know How to Describe Your Skills and Accomplishments in a Way That Makes a Strong, Positive Impact

Avoid common mistakes.

Before you begin brainstorming points to include on your summary of skills, you should be aware of a few common mistakes people make when writing this section of a resume so you can avoid making the same mistakes yourself.

COMMON MISTAKES INCLUDE:

1. MINIMIZING THE VALUE OF YOUR SKILLS

Many job seekers neglect to mention certain skills when writing a resume because the skills come so naturally to them or are used so frequently, the job seeker does not even think of them as skills.

An administrative assistant may think, "Well, of course, I am well-organized, detail oriented and able to multi-task. Isn't everyone?" In fact, everyone is not well-organized, detail oriented and able to multi-task, but if those skills are second nature to you, you might make the mistake of thinking they are not important or not worth mentioning on your resume.

If a skill is crucial to the type of work you do, it should be included on your resume. Do not minimize the importance of your skills simply because they come easily to you.

2. PROVIDING LITTLE OR NO DETAIL

Some job seekers believe that they do not need to include a lot of detail on a resume because they think an employer should be able to infer what skills they have, based on the types of jobs they have held. Just because an employer may know, based on your work history, that you have worked as a quality assurance technician for five years, you cannot assume that the employer knows exactly what you did on the job or how well you did it.

Employers review resumes very quickly. They are typically looking for evidence that a job seeker has specific skills or experience, and you need to make that task as easy as possible for them. If your most crucial and impressive skills and experience are not spelled out clearly on your resume, you will most likely not be invited to a job interview.

Resume writing goes beyond listing a basic job description. The phrases you include on your resume should show employers that you have a deep level of understanding of your field of work and should be used to demonstrate how and why you are particularly good at your job compared to other job seekers.

3. TRYING TO PHRASE THINGS PERFECTLY ON THE FIRST DRAFT

Be aware that you will almost certainly need to write several drafts of your summary of skills before it is fully polished and describes your skills and accomplishments in their best possible light. With that thought in mind, be willing to approach the task of writing this section of your resume as a brainstorming session. Write down everything that comes to mind, and do not worry about phrasing things perfectly or organizing the information perfectly. Simply start by getting your thoughts written down.

Start brainstorming.

1. BRAINSTORM YOUR SKILLS

Begin by brainstorming the skills you have demonstrated throughout your career.

Make a list of *technical skills* you have that are relevant to the type of job you are currently seeking. Technical skills refer to skills and knowledge that are relevant to a specific type of job. These skills can usually be easily demonstrated and must be actively learned in some way. You are not born with your technical skills; you must develop them.

Examples of technical skills are: computer software skills, typing speed, ability to operate specific types of heavy equipment and knowledge that is relevant to a specific field such as accounting or engineering.

Now make a list of *soft skills* you have that are relevant to the type of job you are seeking. Soft skills refer to your personality traits, communication style, and personal habits that make you suited to the type of job you are currently seeking. While people are often born with soft skills, they can also be developed with practice.

Examples of soft skills are: communication skills, work ethic, adaptability and ability to work as a part of a team.

You may find that your list of soft skills and technical skills are not equal. That is fine. Different types of jobs require different types of skills; some jobs require the use of more technical skills, while other jobs require more soft skills.

To determine whether you should focus on technical skills or soft skills on your resume, think about the type of job you are targeting, and ask yourself whether the skills required to do that job well tend to be more soft skills or more technical skills.

Later in this chapter, you will find a list of soft skills that are valued by many employers. Use this list to help you think through your own soft skills. You will not find a corresponding list of technical skills simply because technical skills are specialized and, therefore, they are very job specific. Please refer to chapter 16 for a list of resources that provide detailed information about the skills required in specific jobs. Those resources can be used to brainstorm technical skills that are required for the type of job you are seeking.

2. BRAINSTORM YOUR EXPERIENCE

Think through and make note of all of the practical experience you have that is related to the type of work you are currently seeking. Make note of any impressive and relevant experience gained through paid employment, internships, school placements or volunteer work.

3. BRAINSTORM YOUR ACCOMPLISHMENTS

Now, think through, and make note of, your most impressive career-related accomplishments. At this stage of the resume writing process, instead of asking yourself what you did at your job, *ask yourself why you were good at your job*. What have you achieved throughout your career that demonstrates you would be great at the type of job you are targeting?

General tips for writing about your soft skills:

Soft skills are the personality traits, personal style and interpersonal skills that have a positive impact on the work that you do.

Job seekers often underestimate the importance of soft skills because they are not aware that many employers consider soft skills to be a crucial factor in their hiring decisions. The fact is, although people can decide to work on improving their soft skills, it is often much easier for an employer to train someone to develop a technical skill than it is to train someone to develop a soft skill.

For example, imagine an employer is comparing two candidates for a job. One candidate has all of the technical skills required for the job but does not appear to be particularly enthusiastic about the work. The other candidate has almost all of the technical skills; she is not familiar with PowerPoint (which is a requirement of the job), but she was able to demonstrate that she is extremely enthusiastic about the job. Many employers would choose to hire the candidate who demonstrated enthusiasm for the job in spite of the fact that she would have to be trained in PowerPoint.

Most employers feel that a soft skill like enthusiasm is crucial, and it is far easier to train someone to use PowerPoint effectively than it is to try to train someone to be enthusiastic about the job. Technical skills are still important, but they are not the only factor in most employers' decision making process.

Below you will find a list of soft skills that many employers value. There may be other soft skills that are important in the type of job you are seeking, so do not consider this list to be a complete list of soft skills. It is a starting point to help you begin to think through the types of skills you want to include on your resume.

For the most part, you should avoid simply writing lists of soft skills on your resume. It will start to look like a list of catch phrases that employers see over and over. It will not stand out from the crowd if you simply write a list of unproven soft skills.

Instead, consider the soft skills you want to express on your resume, and then think about how you demonstrated those skills on the job. By describing ways in which you demonstrated specific soft skills on the job, you will "prove your brags" to employers, that is, you will give evidence that you have the skills you claim to have, which will make your resume stand out from the competition.

EXAMPLE ONE

Instead of writing:

- Committed, quick learner with exceptional leadership skills

Use a specific example that demonstrates that you have those skills such as:

- Promoted from retail sales associate to assistant store manager within 8 months of being hired

EXAMPLE TWO

Instead of writing:

- Strong communication and public speaking skills

Use a specific example to demonstrate that you have those skills such as:

- Teach history and English to groups of up to thirty students in grades nine through twelve

EXAMPLE THREE

Instead of writing:

- Able to write effectively and persuasively and committed to company success

Use a specific example to demonstrate that you have those skills such as:

- Designed and wrote copy for program marketing materials, which increased workshop attendance by 30%

If you really think about the first points in each example, you will see that they do not say much about the job seeker. Anyone can say those positive things about themselves, but without a specific example, there is no evidence that the job seeker has the skills he or she claims to have.

The second points demonstrate the skills instead of simply mentioning the skills. These points make a stronger impression because they provide some evidence that the job seeker actually has the soft skills the employer values.

The list of soft skills below is provided to give you some inspiration, not to be simply copied to your resume. Use the list as follows:

- Review the list, and ask yourself whether each skill is important to the type of job you are seeking.

- If the skill is important to the type of job you are seeking, ask yourself whether you possess that skill.

- If you answered yes to points 1 and 2, think about specific situations at work when you demonstrated a skill, and use that situation as the basis for a bulleted point form statement that demonstrates you have a specific skill (or skills).

Soft skills and personal attributes that many employers value

COMMUNICATION SKILLS

Speak effectively
Facilitate groups
Attentive and active listening skills
Excellent verbal and written grammar
Able to write clearly and concisely
Express ideas, opinions and feelings effectively
Accurately perceive nonverbal communication
Able to negotiate
Able to be persuasive
Network effectively with coworkers and business partners

COMMITMENT

Dependable
Enthusiastic
Accept responsibility
Dedicated to improving performance
Set and achieve professional goals
Meet or exceed goals
Strong work ethic
Committed to contributing to success of business

Tenacious

INTEGRITY

Honest
Discreet
Demonstrate professionalism
Take responsibility for actions
Believe in self-worth
Exercise good judgment

ADAPTABILITY

Willing and able to learn new tasks
Willing and able to take on new responsibilities
Able to manage multiple priorities
Able to work in a constantly changing environment
Able to manage conflicting priorities
Able to deal with ambiguity

INTERPERSONAL SKILLS

Positive attitude
Work well as a part of a team

Able to work in a competitive team environment
Able to prevent or mitigate conflict
Able to inspire others to action
Able to work with diverse populations of people

DECISION MAKING AND PROBLEM SOLVING

Research skills
Gather, organize and interpret information or data
Analytical
Accept responsibility
Creative
Resourceful
Able to identify root cause of problems
Able to imagine alternatives and solutions
Able to predict outcomes
Able to define needs
Develop, implement and evaluate strategies

TIME MANAGEMENT

Able to organize and allocate use of time effectively

Able to set and meet goals
Able to prioritize
Able to manage conflicting demands
Work well in a fast paced environment
Work well with minimal supervision
Able to manage complex projects
Complete projects within time allotted
Able to maximize effectiveness and work efficiently
Manage and work well under stress

LEADERSHIP SKILLS

Persuasive
Self-motivated
Persistent
Demonstrate high personal standards
Initiate new ideas and promote change
Manage staff
Delegate responsibilities
Coordinate tasks and projects
Manage conflict
Effectively allocate resources

Determine which points to include and which points to omit.

After you complete a thorough brainstorming session, you will have a list of skills, experiences and accomplishments that may be included on your resume. Before you begin the work of rewriting your points into more polished phrases, determine which points should be included in your summary of skills and which ones should be left out.

As you are working through your brainstormed list of points, do not delete any points that you decide to omit from your summary of skills. Some points may make more sense in the work history section of your resume, and some points may not belong on the resume you are currently writing, but they may be important points to include on a different resume that you may write for a different job.

You will find more information about writing about your work history and writing additional, targeted resumes later in this book. For the time being, simply save a copy of all of the points you have brainstormed because you may want to use them in the future.

Remember that a summary of skills usually contains five to eight points, but if you want to include more points, you may simply group your points into sub-categories.

You will find more information about categorizing your points later in this chapter.

When determining whether a point should be included in your summary of skills consider the following:

IS THE POINT RELEVANT TO THE TYPE OF JOB I AM CURRENTLY SEEKING?

If the point does not add any information that helps to prove that you would be great at the type of job you are currently seeking, it does not belong in your summary of skills.

IF THE JOB IS AN ADVERTISED JOB, HAVE I INCLUDED ALL OF THE SKILLS, ACCOMPLISHMENTS AND EXPERIENCES I HAVE THAT WERE REFERENCED IN THE AD?

If an employer specifies certain skills in a job ad, he or she feels that these skills are crucial. If you have those skills, be sure to demonstrate them in your summary of skills.

IF THE NAME OF THE COMPANY IS KNOWN, HAVE I INCLUDED POINTS THAT INDICATE THAT I WOULD BE A GOOD FIT WITH THE COMPANY'S EXISTING BUSINESS AND VALUES BASED ON MY COMPANY RESEARCH?

Targeting a resume to this extent is an extra step that most job seekers do not take. Therefore, adding a point or two that demonstrates that your skills and experience fit with the company's needs and values based on company research you completed will go a long way to help your resume stand out from the rest of the competition.

DOES THE POINT DEMONSTRATE A SKILL OR ACCOMPLISHMENT THAT IS PARTICULARLY IMPRESSIVE OR SPECIAL THAT OTHER JOB SEEKERS MAY NOT HAVE?

Keep in mind, you are not simply trying to use your resume to demonstrate that you have the basic level of required skill or experience. You are also trying to demonstrate that you are more competent with those skills than other job seekers who have similar skills and experience.

Listing your most impressive accomplishments helps to demonstrate that you are highly competent. On the other hand, trying to over-play very basic skills or experiences makes you appear as though you do not have significant accomplishments, and you are attempting to pad your resume.

DOES THE POINT DESCRIBE A SKILL OR ACCOMPLISHMENT THAT WAS USED OR ACHIEVED FAIRLY RECENTLY?

Skills and accomplishments that were demonstrated or achieved fairly recently make a stronger case for your suitability for a job than skills or accomplishments from the distant past. If you are trying to choose between a couple of similar points, and one point refers to something more recent, while the other refers to something in the distant past, choose the point that is more recent.

Similarly, if you have mentioned an achievement from the distant past, and it demonstrates a skill that is crucial to the job you are seeking, ask yourself whether you have demonstrated that skill at work in another way more recently. While it is acceptable to note skills that were demonstrated in the past, those that have been used more recently make a stronger impression on employers.

DOES THE POINT DESCRIBE A SKILL THAT WAS DEMONSTRATED THROUGH PAID EMPLOYMENT, OR WAS IT DEMONSTRATED IN SOME OTHER WAY?

Employers generally give more weight to skills and experience gained through paid employment. While it is perfectly acceptable to include skills developed through volunteer work, education, placements or internships, if you can link the same skill to related paid employment, your resume will make a stronger impression on most employers.

Rewrite your points so they are clear, concise, attention-grabbing statements.

BE SPECIFIC

General and over-used phrases do not make a strong impression on employers. Generic phrases do not paint a memorable, vivid picture of your accomplishments, and they do not help you stand out from the competition. The more specific you can be about your skills and accomplishments, the better impression you will make on employers.

EXAMPLE

Imagine you are a music teacher, and during your brainstorming session, you wrote that you "work well as a part of a team." That skill is valued in many work settings, but the phrase is generic and does not provide much information about how you worked as a part of a team.

To paint a more vivid picture of your skills and experience, you could rephrase the point to describe the type of teamwork you have experienced in your career.

Work well as a part of a team could become:

> Collaborate with students and parents to establish long and short term goals and plans including participation in recitals, competitions and examinations.

QUANTIFY

Quantifying - using numbers in your descriptions - is an excellent way to make your descriptions more specific and memorable. Any time you take the opportunity to quantify your accomplishments on your resume, you make a strong, positive impression on employers. General words that refer to amounts, such as increased, improved, a lot and many do not really provide the full picture of what you accomplished. You may have increased sales, but without a specific number, employers will not know if you increased sales by 1 percent or 50 percent.

EXAMPLE

Imagine you are a retail sales manager, and during your brainstorming session, you wrote down that you have a "track record of success." That is a great idea to express in your summary of skills, but you need to express it in a way that is more meaningful to potential employers.

To be more specific, you could quantify, and "track record of success" could become:

> Exceeded sales targets for five consecutive years, and increased sales by an average of ten percent each year in an environment of growing competition.

USE STRONG VERBS

You have a small amount of space to communicate a lot of crucial information, so it is important to choose each word with care. Some words are overused and do not communicate much information. Avoid repeatedly using words or phrases like "responsible for" or "duties included" which do not provide much information to employers. Occasionally one of those phrases may be the only thing that makes sense, but do avoid them whenever possible.

You will find a list of strong verbs to help with your resume writing in chapter 16.

USE DESCRIPTIVE WORDS

Instead of simply telling employers that you did a task, make a point of also describing how you did that task. When you add descriptive words to your points, you add important information about how you approach your work and you distinguish yourself from other job seekers.

EXAMPLE

Imagine that during your brainstorming session you noted that you "manage client data." Some descriptive words and phrases would make that phrase stronger:

> Accurately manage client data using Excel

If you combined those descriptive words with a specific number, you would have an even stronger point:

> Accurately manage client data for a caseload of up to 500 clients using Excel

You will find lists of adverbs and adjectives that you may use to include more descriptive words on your resume in chapter 16.

For more information...

There is more information about writing effectively in chapter 9, Work History. The tips on describing your work history effectively can also be applied to writing an effective summary of skills. Although the tips for writing well apply to each resume section, I have tried to avoid too much repetition within this book, so you will find different tips on writing well included in each chapter. A review of the tips on writing well that are included in chapter 9 will provide you with even more information and examples for writing effective points for your summary of skills.

Also, in chapter 13, you will find detailed information about writing to score well if your resume will be screened with an applicant tracking system. There are some very specific guidelines that are important to follow if your resume will be screened with an ATS. I have not included those ATS guidelines in this chapter because I wanted to avoid overwhelming you with too much information. You can always refer to chapter 13 whenever you need to revise your resume for an ATS.

Step Five
Know How to Organize Your Summary of Skills

Group your skills into logical sections.

IF YOU HAVE BETWEEN FIVE AND EIGHT SKILLS IN YOUR LIST...

As noted earlier in this chapter, your summary of skills should include five to eight points. If you are writing a combination resume, and you have a list of five to eight points that you would like to include in a summary of skills, you do not need to subdivide your list of skills into separate categories. You may move on to deciding the order in which your skills will appear on the list (look ahead a few paragraphs in this chapter for the heading Organize Each Point).

Please keep in mind that the rule about limiting your list to five to eight points is not a precise rule. Five to eight points per section are recommended because that is the number of points that can typically be read quickly and easily when grouped together. If the list gets much longer than eight points, it can become difficult to read.

Do use your best judgment. If you have nine points that you want to include in your summary of skills, and you do not want to subdivide your skills into sub-headings for the sake of one extra point, that decision is perfectly reasonable.

IF YOU HAVE MORE THAN EIGHT SKILLS IN YOUR LIST...

If you have a long list of points that you would like to include in a summary of skills, you will need to divide them into logical, meaningful groups. Each of those groups should include approximately five to eight points.

If you are writing a combination resume, you might decide to divide your skills into more than one group, and if you are writing a functional resume, you will definitely need to group your skills into more than one group because your list will need to be quite long to fill out the resume.

One way to divide your points into smaller groups is to separate your accomplishments and your skills into two separate headings. Any point that describes an accomplishment would be listed under the heading Accomplishments, and any point that describes a skill would be listed under the heading Summary of Skills.

Another option for dividing your skills is to simply think about the broad types of skills you use at work and then use these groupings as headings. For example, an instructor may use teaching skills, administrative skills and computer skills at work; any point related to teaching would be placed under the heading Teaching, any point related to administrative work would be placed under the heading Administration, and any point about computer skills would be placed under the heading Computer Skills.

Please be aware that dividing a long list of skills into sub-categories works well when a human reader will be screening your resume. It can cause problems if your resume will be screened by an applicant tracking system because multiple and uncommon section headings can cause the ATS to misinterpret your resume. You will find more information about how to structure your skills summary to pass an ATS screening in chapter 13.

Name your headings.

As you can see, if you choose to divide your skills based on the broader types of skills you use at your job, you could use almost any number of headings depending upon the types of skills that are important in the work that you do. However, there are several types of skills that are commonly used in many types of jobs, so I have provided the following list of possible headings to give you some ideas about how to divide your own list of skills into logical groups.

Use whichever headings make the most sense based on the types of skills you decide to include on your resume, and, if necessary, use your own headings that are specific to the type of work you are targeting.

POSSIBLE HEADINGS FOR YOUR LIST(S) OF SKILLS AND ACCOMPLISHMENTS

GENERAL HEADINGS

Summary of Skills
Skills Summary
Accomplishments
Professional Qualifications
Key Strengths
Highlights of Qualifications
Relevant Experience
Professional Experience

MORE SPECIFIC HEADINGS

Computer Skills
Technical Skills
Management
Communication
Administration
Organization
Languages

Put your skills in the best order.

ORGANIZE YOUR GROUPS OF SKILLS

Once you have grouped your skills into appropriate sections, you will need to put them in the best order.

First, if you have divided your skills into two or more groups, determine which group of skills is most crucial or most impressive to potential employers. That group of skills is the first thing you want employers to read.

EXAMPLE

Imagine you were writing a resume for a job as a teacher, and you divided your skills and accomplishments into four separate sections: Teaching Skills, Administrative Skills, Computer Skills and Professional Achievements. The professional achievements and the teaching skills are the most impressive and crucial points for an employer to read. The computer skills are necessary, but you know that most teachers applying for the same job would posses these skills, so they need to be on the resume, but they do not need to be a focal point.

In this situation, you would organize your sections as follows:

Professional Achievements
Teaching Skills
Administrative Skills
Computer Skills

ORGANIZE EACH POINT

Once you have determined the best order for your groups of skills, you will need to determine the order of each point included in your skills summary.

Keep in mind, when employers quickly read through resumes, they tend to read the first two or three points in a list, and they only read further in that list if the first couple of points grab their attention. Therefore, you should put the most important or impressive couple of points at the top of the list and other supporting points should follow. Repeat this step for each list of skills if you have grouped your skills into more than one heading.

Step Six
Write Your Summary of Skills

Open up the document where you have saved the draft of your resume, and write the summary of skills section. Your resume will have some differences compared with the example depending upon choices you have made along the way, but when you are finished writing up the summary of skills section of your resume, your document will look something like this:

Jane Somebody
123 Any Street, Faketown, State, Zip Code
janesomebody@emailprovider.com
(000) 000-0000

Profile
Administrative professional with seven years of experience in the nonprofit sector. Able to prioritize and manage conflicting demands. Exceptional technical skills including proficiency with Word, Excel, PowerPoint and Prezi; type 80 words per minute.

Summary of Skills*
Proven ability to meet strict deadlines, ensure accuracy of work and manage conflicting demands effectively**
Thorough knowledge of and ability to research community resources developed over 7 years working at local, non-profit community organizations
Able to resolve common computer hardware issues for staff and clients in resource center
Exhibit a professional and welcoming demeanor to clients and co-workers; earned reputation as a resourceful problem solver with high degree of integrity
Bilingual in English and Spanish

*Your resume will include this section if you are writing a combination resume. You will not include a summary of skills section if you are writing a chronological resume. If you are writing a functional resume, this section will be much longer because it must describe all of your skills and experience.

**Each point is not bulleted in the example because it is not necessary to format your resume until you have written all of the content of your resume. If you find it difficult to read without the bullets, feel free to add them at this stage.

Assignment

Write up the summary or skills section of your resume. Remember, many people find that writing this section is the most challenging part of resume writing. If you feel stuck, go ahead to chapters 9, 10 and 11 and write the work history, education and volunteer work sections of your resume and then come back to the summary of skills.

Moving Forward

You are ready to move on to the next chapter if you...

1. Know what information should and should not be included in your summary of skills.

2. Understand how to write about your skills and achievements in a way that is compelling.

3. Understand how to organize your skills and achievements within this section of your resume.

4. **Have written your summary of skills (not necessary if you are writing a chronological resume, but writing a skills summary can help you think of points to include in your work history).**

   or

5. **Have determined that you would prefer to move on and write the rest of your resume first and then return to this section once you have written about your work history, education and volunteer work.**

CHAPTER NINE
WORK HISTORY

YOUR TASKS FOR THIS CHAPTER

1. Understand the features of the work history section of a resume.
2. Discover how to write effective statements about your job duties and accomplishments.
3. Learn how to minimize any concerns you may have with your work history and highlight the most positive aspects of your work history
4. Write the work history section of your resume.

ACTION STEPS FOR THIS CHAPTER

Step One: Understand the features of the work history section.

Step Two: Know what employers are trying to discover when they read your work history.

Step Three: Understand what information should be included in your work history.

Step Four: Understand how to describe your work experience to make a great impression.

Step Five: Know how to address common concerns with the work history section of your resume.

Step Six:	Determine what heading to use for the work history section of your resume.
Step Seven:	Write your work history.

"Follow your heart, but take your brain with you."
Alfred Adler

Before we dive into understanding the work history section of your resume, you will need to decide whether you will be including a work history section on your resume or not.

If you have decided to write a combination resume or a chronological resume (see chapter 4), you will include a work history section on your resume. If you have decided to write a functional resume (see also chapter 4), you will not include a work history section on your resume.

Please be reminded that the vast majority of employers expect to see a work history section on each resume they review. Many employers do not trust functional resumes and will not invite someone to a job interview if his or her resume contains no work history.

Also, it is necessary to include a work history section on your resume if the employer uses an applicant tracking system to screen resumes. Applicant tracking systems are set up to look for work history information, and if that information is not included on your resume, it will very likely not score well in the ATS screening stage.

While some job seekers choose to use a functional resume to hide issues with their work history, such as gaps in employment or limited related experience, this strategy usually backfires.

Employers know you are trying to hide something when you use a functional resume, so they immediately lose trust when they see this resume style. There are far more effective ways to minimize issues with your work history, as you will see in this chapter, and I would strongly urge all job seekers to use a combination or chronological resume format, which includes a work history section.

I realize that I am repeating myself on the idea that you should avoid using a functional resume, but it is important for you to fully accept that using a functional resume can do serious damage to your job search efforts.

Step One
Understand the Features of the Work History Section

The work history section of your resume provides employers with information about where you worked, for how long and what practical experience you can offer a company.

In this section, you will simply list your work experience, usually in reverse chronological order (most recent job first, older jobs last) followed by a point form description of your responsibilities and achievements.

Although there are exceptions, which we will explore throughout this chapter, each entry in the work history section normally includes the name of the company where you worked, the city where you worked, your job title, the dates you held the position, and a point form description of the job you performed.

Step Two
Know What Employers Are Trying to Discover When They Read Your Work History

While this section of your resume may, on the surface, seem like a simple, straightforward list of dates, previous employers, job titles and job duties, you may be surprised by the conclusions employers will make about your suitability for a job based on the way you describe your work history on your resume.

Here are some things that your work history may say about you in the minds of employers:

Negative perceptions that can be created by your work history:

THIS PERSON'S SKILLS MAY BE OUT OF DATE.

If you have gaps in your work history, employers may worry that your skills or knowledge of your industry is not up to date. Gaps are typically defined as more than six months without paid employment, and gaps in the present are a bigger concern than gaps in the past.

THIS PERSON MAY NOT BE EFFECTIVE AT HIS OR HER JOB.

If you have held a lot of jobs in a short period of time, employers may worry that this is evidence that you were not effective at those jobs and, therefore, were fired. Similarly, if you have a large gap in your work history, employers may be concerned that you have had difficulty finding a new job because of a spotty track record at previous jobs.

THIS PERSON IS NOT COMMITTED TO HIS OR HER CAREER.

If you have gaps in your employment history or have held several jobs in a short period of time, employers may be concerned that you are not committed to your career, and, therefore, will not be committed to a job at his or her company.

THIS PERSON WILL LEAVE THE COMPANY IN A SHORT TIME, AND I WILL HAVE TO SPEND TIME HIRING AND TRAINING ANOTHER PERSON.

The process of hiring and training new staff is time consuming and often expensive, so employers want to hire people who will stay at the job for a reasonable length of time. What is considered reasonable depends upon the industry you are in and the type of job you are seeking. If you have held a lot of jobs in a short time, employers may be concerned that you will not stay at the new job for very long.

The concern that a new employee will leave the company after a short time is also a primary issue behind employers saying a job candidate is over-qualified. If you have a well-established career, but you are currently looking for a less responsible position, an employer may assume that you will become bored or that you see the job as a short term solution to unemployment and you will leave as soon as you find a higher level job at another company.

THIS PERSON HAS VERY LITTLE RELEVANT EXPERIENCE.

If your work experience is limited or if you are making a career change, employers may be concerned that you do not have the experience required to do the job or that they will have to invest a significant amount of time in the training process.

Alternately, you may have plenty of related work experience, but if you do not describe your experience and responsibilities in clear, descriptive terms on your resume, employers will not know you have the experience they need.

DON'T PANIC!

Few people have a completely perfect work history. The fact that you have a gap in your work history or are making a career change does not mean you are not an effective employee. Plenty of people who are brilliant in their jobs have experienced career changes and challenges.

That being said, it is important to remember that employers normally have to review a lot of resumes to narrow the competition down to a few people who will be invited to a job interview. They need to manage their time well, and they need to ensure the person they bring into the company is effective and positive. Therefore, as employers scan a resume, they are looking for any reason to exclude that candidate from being invited to an interview, and work history issues can create plenty of reasons, in an employer's mind, to exclude a candidate from being invited to a job interview.

If you have any concerns with your work history, do not despair. There are many subtle and effective ways to minimize these issues on your resume. Continue to work through this chapter, and in step 5 you will find detailed information about how to effectively manage specific issues related to your work history on your resume.

Positive perceptions that can be created by your work history:

THIS PERSON WAS AN EFFECTIVE, PRODUCTIVE MEMBER OF HIS OR HER PREVIOUS COMPANY.

Have you earned progressive responsibility over the length of your career? If you have earned promotions or have gradually been given more responsibility for key projects or tasks at work, you must communicate this fact on your resume. A resume that clearly indicates that you have earned increased responsibilities over time demonstrates to an employer that you were a valued member of your previous company who could be trusted with important tasks.

THIS PERSON HAS EXACTLY THE TYPE OF EXPERIENCE I NEED.

If you communicate your experience, responsibilities and achievements in a way that clearly indicates how your past work experience has prepared you to be excellent at the type of work you are currently seeking, your resume will make a strong, positive impression on the employer.

Do remember, you must communicate this experience in a clear way. It is not enough to write down a job title and a very limited description of what you did on the job with the assumption that all employers in your industry should know what you have done based on your job title.

Employers need to know what you did as well as *what was special or outstanding about the way you do your job compared with others who have similar work experience.* Continue to work through this chapter to learn how to describe your work experience in a way that shows you are a superior candidate for the specific type of job you are seeking.

Step Three
Understand What Information Should be Included in Your Work History

To write this section of your resume, begin by listing the job you currently hold or the job you most recently held. Write down the following:

- Your current job title, or the last job title you had if you are not currently employed

- The name of the company

- The city where you worked

- The dates you worked there - Include years only. It is not necessary to include months in this section, and, for many people, including months in this section can create gaps in the employment history.

- A description of the work you performed – Writing a description of your job-related duties and achievements is the toughest part of this chapter. You will find details about how to describe your work effectively in step 3 in this chapter.

Repeat this process for each job you have held, going back approximately ten years (fifteen years, maximum) in your work history. You should almost never include more than the most recent ten years of work experience on your resume. Employers are most interested in what you have done recently, not what you did twenty-five years ago, and including more than about ten years of work experience can reveal your age and set you up for possible age discrimination.

In extremely rare cases, there may be a good reason to include on a resume a job that was held more than fifteen years ago. If that job provides very strong evidence that you have important skills that are relevant to the job you are currently seeking, and there is absolutely no other way to demonstrate those skills on your resume, you may consider including an older job.

Do keep in mind, though, if you cannot demonstrate that you have used a skill in the past decade, many employers would question whether you still possess that skill.

Another reason why you might go back more than ten years on your resume is if you have worked at the same company for more than ten years. If, for example, you have worked for your current employer for twenty years, you will need to include your full dates of employment on your resume. If you are in this situation, and you are concerned about including such a long employment history on your resume, please review the strategies for minimizing the dates on your resume, which you will find later in this chapter.

The need to go back more than about ten years on a resume is rare, and in the majority of resumes that I have written with clients, there was no reason for including more than ten years of work history on the resume.

An example of a very standard work history section of a resume:

Administrative Assistant, XYZ Company, Any City, State   2013 - present
- List 5-8 points describing your duties and accomplishments here

Customer Service Representative, Any Company, Any City, State   2009 - 2013
- List 5-8 points describing your duties and accomplishments here

Retail Sales Associate, ABC Company, Any City, State   2006 - 2008
- List 5-8 points describing your duties and accomplishments here

Please be aware that this formatting works well when your resume will be reviewed by a human reader. If your resume will be reviewed by an applicant tracking system, there are some different, and very specific recommendations you should follow. Please refer to chapter 13, *Write an Applicant Tracking System Optimized Resume,* any time you need to format a resume that will be screened by an ATS.

STAY ON TRACK

If you have questions about how to deal with specific areas of concern, such as gaps in your work history or holding several jobs in a short period of time, you will find information about handling common areas of concern in step 5 of this chapter.

If you are looking for more detailed information about formatting the work history section of your resume, keep in mind, you should not focus on fully formatting your resume until you have written out all of the content. You will find some information about formatting your resume to minimize specific concerns in step 5 of this chapter, and you will find full details about formatting the work history section, as well as other sections of your resume in chapter 12.

If you are writing a resume that will be screened by an applicant tracking system, you need to be particularly careful about how you format the work history section of your resume. You will find a few comments about that topic in this chapter, but for full details on formatting your resume to pass an ATS screening, please refer to chapter 13.

Step Four
Understand How to Describe Your Work Experience to Make a Great Impression

There are a few key points to remember to ensure that the descriptions of each job you held make a strong, positive impact on employers.

Describe your work history in bulleted point form, not full sentences and paragraphs.

Employers do not read every resume they receive. They will quickly scan your resume in a matter of seconds, and if they feel, based on a quick scan, that you might have the skills they need, then they will review your resume in more detail. No matter how qualified you may be, if your resume cannot be read at a glance, it will not be reviewed by the vast majority of employers.

If you write about each job you have held in bulleted point form, instead of full sentences and paragraphs, employers will be able to read your resume quickly.

EXAMPLE - NOT RECOMMENDED: WORK HISTORY WRITTEN IN FULL PARAGRAPHS

Music Teacher, Anytown Music Academy, City, State   2011-2014

Developed lesson plans for and taught private and group piano, flute, clarinet and early childhood music for approximately 60 students annually. Developed and implemented successful summer music programs which increased summer enrollment by 20%. Created, implemented and evaluated multifaceted lesson plans to accommodate multiple learning styles in a group setting.

Fostered a respectful learning environment and developed positive partnerships with parents and students to ensure student success. Prepared students for participation in recitals, competitions and examinations; 80% of students completing examinations earned first class honors. Organized quarterly student recitals and co-directed a musical production. Assisted with lesson scheduling, accounts receivable and inventory control.

EXAMPLE - RECOMMENDED: WORK HISTORY WRITTEN IN BULLETED POINT FORM

Music Teacher, Anytown Music Academy, City, State   2011-2014

- Developed lesson plans for and taught private and group piano, flute, clarinet and early childhood music for approximately 60 students annually
- Developed and implemented successful summer music programs which increased summer enrollment by 20%
- Created, implemented and evaluated multifaceted lesson plans to accommodate multiple learning styles in a group setting
- Fostered a respectful learning environment and developed positive partnerships with parents and students to ensure student success
- Prepared students for participation in recitals, competitions and examinations; 80% of students completing examinations earned first class honors
- Organized quarterly student recitals and co-directed a musical production
- Assisted with lesson scheduling, accounts payable and inventory control

Compare the two examples above. The information provided in both examples is exactly the same, but the second example is far more readable. The first example presents the reader with several large blocks of text that are not easy to read at a glance. Any employer skimming through the information would easily miss important points and may not even be inclined to read through the long paragraphs.

On the other hand, notice how easy it is to quickly skim through the second example. Each key idea is clearly separated with bullets. This structure pulls the reader through the information on the resume and encourages him or her to continue to read the points.

Include about five to eight points under each relevant job title.

Five to eight points are typically enough to describe your work in sufficient detail without providing so much detail that your resume becomes difficult to read.

If you include more than about eight points in your job description, this section of your resume will become difficult to read at a glance, and crucial accomplishments or experiences may get buried in the long list of points. If you feel you must include more than eight points to describe your work adequately, consider whether some points could be moved into a skills summary.

You may include more points under a job title if your resume will be screened with an applicant tracking system.

You may include fewer points under a job title if you feel the job is completely unrelated to the type of job you are currently seeking.

"Don't just think about what you did at your job. Ask yourself what makes you GREAT at your job."

Under most circumstances, it will be important to include a thorough description of your experience and achievements with each job listed on your resume. Occasionally people include jobs on their resumes that are completely unrelated to the work they are presently seeking. Usually they will include this type of job on a resume to avoid the appearance of gaps in their work history.

If you are including a job on your resume that is *completely unrelated* to the job you are currently seeking, you do not have to describe the unrelated job in detail.

If you are including a job that is different from the job you are seeking, but that job required skills that are required in the new job you are seeking, you should include a description of that job on your resume to show that you have skills from a previous job that will transfer over to your new job.

Avoid using personal pronouns.

It is standard to avoid using personal pronouns such as I, me, and my on your resume. This convention is simply part of the widely accepted way to write resumes, so a resume that includes personal pronouns looks odd to most employers.

Use the past tense for jobs in the past and the present tense for current jobs.

Write each point using the past tense if you are no longer working at that job. Use the present tense if you are currently working at that job. Therefore, if you are presently working, you will use the present tense to describe your current job, and the past tense to describe any previous jobs. Do not be concerned about switching tenses; from one job to the next. The point is to be accurate about the way you describe tasks you are currently doing and tasks you did in the past.

Describe your accomplishments, not just your job duties.

Do not simply write about what you did at your job. As you are writing this section of your resume, *ask yourself what makes you great at your job*.

This point cannot be stressed enough.

As you write your job description, you are not just communicating the fact that you did the job, *you need to demonstrate that you did the job extremely well.* Think about how you contributed to the success of the company and ask yourself what was special or noteworthy about the way you performed your job.

"You need to communicate reasons why you were excellent at your job."

EXAMPLE - NOT RECOMMENDED: LIST OF JOB DUTIES, NO ACCOMPLISHMENTS

- Developed lesson plans for and taught private and group piano, flute, clarinet and early childhood music
- Taught summer music programs
- Prepared students for participation in recitals, competitions and examinations
- Organized quarterly student recitals and co-directed a musical production
- Assisted with lesson scheduling, accounts receivable and inventory control

EXAMPLE - RECOMMENDED: JOB DUTIES WITH ACCOMPLISHMENTS

- Developed lesson plans for and taught private and group piano, flute, clarinet and early childhood music for approximately 60 students annually
- Developed and implemented successful summer music programs which increased summer enrollment by 20%
- Created, implemented and evaluated multifaceted lesson plans to accommodate multiple learning styles in a group setting
- Fostered a respectful learning environment and developed positive partnerships with parents and students to ensure student success
- Prepared students for participation in recitals, competitions and examinations; 80% of students completing examinations earned first class honors
- Organized quarterly student recitals and co-directed a musical production
- Assisted with lesson scheduling, accounts receivable and inventory control

Carefully compare the two job descriptions above. They both describe exactly the same person at exactly the same job. The first description, however, provides no evidence that the person did the job well. We know what his or her job duties were, but we do not have much information about the quality of the work.

In the second example, there is plenty of information about what this person did as well as the quality of the work. Words like "developed," "implemented" and "created" indicate that the job seeker went beyond teaching and took initiative to build aspects of the business.

We also have some information about the job seeker's teaching style and professional knowledge in the description of "multifaceted lesson plans to accommodate multiple learning styles in a group setting" as well as "respectful learning environment" and "positive partnerships with parents and students." This type of detail goes beyond simply describing the job duties of a music teacher and indicates why this particular music teacher was good at his or her job.

Think - Action and Result.

Here is a simple strategy you can use to write effective statements about the jobs you have held. Think in terms of actions and results. Ask yourself what specific action did you take on the job, and then ask yourself what was the positive result of your action.

The point "Developed and implemented successful summer music programs which increased summer enrollment by 20%" is a perfect example of this action and result approach.

WHAT ACTION DID I TAKE?

I developed and implemented successful summer music programs.

AND WHAT WAS THE POSITIVE RESULT?

It increased summer enrollment by 20%.

The second half of the statement (the positive result) provides evidence that your action was beneficial to the company and makes the statement far more powerful than it would be without the result.

> *Remember: Don't just think about what you did at your job. You need to communicate why you were excellent at your job.*

BE SPECIFIC AND QUANTIFY (PROVIDE NUMBERS) WHENEVER POSSIBLE.

The more specific you are when you describe your work, the more impressive and memorable your resume will be. For example, if you were a salesperson, instead of simply writing that you are an effective, dynamic sales person, you could write:

- Increased sales by 25% every year for five consecutive years
  or
- Earned title of top salesperson in the organization within the first six months on the job

Providing specific data to back up your claims makes your statements stronger.

Referring back to the previous example of the music teacher, compare the following points:

NO NUMBERS INCLUDED IN DESCRIPTIONS

- Developed lesson plans for and taught private and group piano, flute, clarinet and early childhood music
- Developed and implemented successful summer music programs
- Prepared students for participation in recitals, competitions and examinations

SAME POINTS WITH NUMBERS INCLUDED IN DESCRIPTIONS

- Developed lesson plans for and taught private and group piano, flute, clarinet and early childhood music for approximately 60 students annually
- Developed and implemented successful summer music programs which increased summer enrollment by 20%
- Prepared students for participation in recitals, competitions and examinations; 80% of students completing examinations earned first class honors

In these examples, the numbers provide an enormous amount of information about this job seeker's skills and experience. In the first point, the phrase "approximately 60 students annually" indicates that this job seeker was a popular teacher with a full schedule of students. The phrase "increased summer enrollment by 20%" in the next point indicates that this teacher actively contributed to the growth of the business. Finally, in the last point, the phrase "80% of students completing examinations earned first class honors" shows that this teacher's students did well on exams, therefore his or her teaching methods are effective.

In the examples where numbers are not used, we know that the job seeker completed certain tasks, but we have no evidence that he or she did them well.

Sometimes it is not appropriate to provide specific numbers. For example, in some cases, including specific sales figures on your resume may be seen as a breach of confidentiality. If you feel that it is not appropriate to include specific numbers, try to use percentages to communicate the extent of your contribution to a company. Percentages are often effective for quantifying data without giving away specific, confidential company information.

You do not need to include specific numbers for every point you make on your resume. Not all entries lend themselves to quantifying. However, numbers do add an enormous amount of information that can help employers understand your experience and accomplishments, and they should be included whenever they are available and appropriate to use.

Highlight experience and accomplishments that are most relevant to the work you are currently seeking.

This recommendation applies to all job seekers, but it is particularly important for people who are making a career change. You will not be able to include all of your job duties on your resume, so you will have to be selective about the information you do and do not include.

When deciding which information to include, ask yourself if the information is relevant to the work you are currently seeking. A good question to keep in mind through the entire resume writing process is:

HOW DOES THIS PIECE OF INFORMATION HELP PROVE THAT I WOULD BE GREAT AT THE TYPE OF JOB I HAVE LISTED IN MY PROFILE?

If the information helps prove that you would be great at the job you are targeting, it belongs on your resume. If the information does not help prove that you are qualified and suited to the type of job you are targeting, it does not belong on your resume.

This means that you might not highlight some of the tasks you do frequently at your current job, particularly if you are making a career change. Remember, you are not necessarily highlighting what you do most often at your current job (or previous jobs), instead, you are highlighting those job duties that are most relevant and similar to duties you would be required to perform at the job you are currently targeting.

Step Five
Know How to Address Common Concerns With the Work History Section of Your Resume

This step contains a lot of detailed and varied suggestions to organize your work history and address a lot of common concerns. Remember, chapter 15 contains sample resumes that show how these strategies look on a completed resume. You can also find those sample resumes on my website at careerchoiceguide.com/resumeexamples.

Consider having that webpage open on your computer while you read through this chapter, or print the resumes from my site if that works better for you. Seeing the recommendations used on sample resumes will clarify the concepts for you, and having them open on your computer screen, or printed on paper, will let you avoid flipping back and forth in the book.

Please note: If you look closely, you will notice I've made a few slightly different formatting choices on some of the resumes on my website compared with the resumes in this book. That is simply due to differences in the way the information fit on the page in the two different mediums.

When employers review resumes, ideally they want to see the following in your work history:

- No gaps in your work history
- Recent experience doing work that is the same as the type of job you are targeting
- A history of staying at the same job for a few years at a time
- Increased responsibility and progress over the course of your career

Few job seekers have a completely perfect work history. If you need to address any of these issues on your resume, the strategies below will help you to minimize the appearance of specific work history concerns while being honest and not losing the trust of employers who read your resume.

What to do when:
You have gaps in your employment history

First, you need to determine if you even have a gap in your employment history. Remember, a gap in employment is typically considered to be a period of six months or more without paid employment, and gaps in the present are more of a concern to employers than gaps in the past.

- If you have had paid employment at some point in the past six months, you do not have a current gap in your work history.

- If you have not had any paid employment for the past six months or longer, some employers may be concerned with this gap in your work history.

- If you have had paid employment in the last six months, but you experienced a long period of unemployment in the past, your gap will probably not be an issue to employers.

If you have determined that you do, in fact, have a gap in your employment history, consider the following strategies for minimizing gaps:

1. INCLUDE ONLY THE YEARS, AND NOT THE MONTHS IN YOUR EMPLOYMENT DATES.

Including the months in your work history dates can unnecessarily highlight gaps in employment. Most employers expect to see only the years on your work history, and not the months, so omitting the months does not raise concerns in the minds of most employers.

EXAMPLE

Imagine it is currently August 2014 and you are job searching. Your last paid employment was from December 2011 to January 2014, and before that you worked from July 2008 to February 2011. There is a seven month employment gap between January 2014 and August 2014, and a ten month gap between February 2011 and December 2011.

If you include the months on your resume, you will expose those two gaps in your work history. If, on the other hand, you omit the months, the gaps disappear.

2. PLACE THE DATES ON THE RIGHT SIDE OF THE PAGE, NOT THE LEFT SIDE.

Many job seekers make the mistake of putting their employment dates on the left side of the page. Because employers scan resumes very quickly, and because readers tend to process more of the information on the left of the page than the right when scanning documents, whatever you place on the left side of the page will stand out to anyone who is reviewing your resume.

Your job title, not the company you worked for, and not the employment dates, is the most important aspect of your work history. Putting your employment dates on the right makes the job title more prominent and the dates less so.

EXAMPLE - DATES ON THE LEFT - NOT RECOMMENDED

2012 - 2014	**Retail Sales Associate**, Any Company, City, State

- Describe the job in several points here

2010 - 2012	**Retail Sales Associate**, Another Company, City, State

- Describe the job in several points here

EXAMPLE - DATES ON THE RIGHT - RECOMMENDED, ESPECIALLY IF YOU WANT TO MINIMIZE EMPLOYMENT DATES:

Retail Sales Associate, Any Company, City, State	2012 - 2014

- Describe the job in several points here

Retail Sales Associate, Another Company, City, State	2010 - 2012

- Describe the job in several points here

Notice that the dates are the first thing you read when they are placed on the left, but when you place the dates on the right, they blend in more with the rest of the information, and your eye is drawn to the company and job title and not the dates.

3. WRITE YOUR EMPLOYMENT INFORMATION ON A SINGLE LINE.

If all of your employment history information including your job title, company name, city, state and dates will fit neatly on a single line, keep them on a single line. This strategy helps the dates blend in more. When you use a second line for the company name, city and state, the extra spacing causes the dates to stand out a bit more than necessary.

If all of the required information will not fit neatly on one line, you will need to separate the information into two lines. Never sacrifice neatness and readability on your resume.

This strategy is really an extremely subtle, finer point of resume writing. If you are trying to minimize the dates of your work history, but you simply cannot place the information on one line in a way that is attractive, do not fret. As long as you have used the other strategies available, you will have successfully minimized the impact of your employment dates as much as possible.

EXAMPLE - INFORMATION ON TWO LINES - CAUSES DATES TO BECOME SLIGHTLY MORE NOTICEABLE

> Retail Sales Associate
> Any Company, City, State   2011 - 2013
> • Describe the job in several points here

EXAMPLE - INFORMATION ON ONE LINE - CAUSES DATES TO BECOME SLIGHTLY LESS NOTICEABLE

> Retail Sales Associate, Any Company, City, State   2011 - 2013
> • Describe the job in several points here

EXAMPLE - INFORMATION WILL NOT FIT ON ONE LINE - DO NOT SACRIFICE NEATNESS AND READABILITY

> **Retail Sales Associate**
> Extremely Long Company Name, Very Long City Name, State   2011 - 2013
> • Describe the job in several points here

4. USE BOLDED TEXT TO HIGHLIGHT YOUR JOB TITLE.

When you bold the text of your job title, the eye will be drawn to the job title and not the dates. When you do not use bolded text, the eye has fewer cues about where to focus, so the dates become more noticeable.

Please note, as I have mentioned earlier in this book, if a human will review your resume, I prefer to put the job title before the company name. This setup makes the job title stand out more to the human eye, and the job title is often the most important thing for an employer to see. The rules for formatting your work experience when your resume will be read by an applicant tracking system are different. Be sure to refer to chapter 13 if you need to format an ATS optimized resume.

EXAMPLE - NO BOLDED TEXT - NOT RECOMMENDED

> Retail Sales Associate, Any Company, City, State   2012 - 2014
> • Describe the job in several points here

EXAMPLE - BOLDED TEXT ON JOB TITLE - RECOMMENDED

> **Retail Sales Associate**, Any Company, City, State   2012 - 2014
> • Describe the job in several points here

5. INCLUDE THE EDUCATION SECTION BEFORE THE WORK HISTORY SECTION IF YOUR EDUCATION IS MORE CURRENT THAN YOUR PAID WORK EXPERIENCE.

If you are a recent graduate, or if you have left the workforce but have been taking courses that are relevant to the work you are currently seeking, include the education section on your resume before the work experience section. This strategy will minimize the perception of a gap in your work history because employers will see that although you did not have paid employment, you were attending school to develop skills and knowledge relevant to your career.

EXAMPLE - RESUME WITH EDUCATION LISTED BEFORE WORK HISTORY

EDUCATION

Adult Learning Certificate, ABC Community College, City, State   2014
- Include relevant points about your course work and field placements

Bachelor of Arts Degree, English, XYZ University, City, State   2010

PROFESSIONAL EXPERIENCE

Adult Education Teacher, Anytown Learning Academy, City, State   2011 - 2013
- Include descriptive points about your job

Notice the effect of putting the education section before the work experience section (called Professional Experience in this example). As employers scan this resume, the first date they will see is a current one. Their first impression will be that this job seeker has recently been actively involved in developing job related skills. On the other hand, if the work experience section was placed before the education section, the first date an employer would notice is an older date, so the first impression would likely be that this person has been out of work for a while.

6. CONSIDER COMBINING VOLUNTEER WORK WITH PAID WORK IF YOU HAVE A CURRENT, SIGNIFICANT GAP IN YOUR PAID WORK EXPERIENCE, AND YOU HAVE VOLUNTEER EXPERIENCE THAT IS CURRENT AND RELEVANT TO THE JOB.

This strategy is one that I do not use very often. It is always best to keep the work experience section of your resume as simple and straightforward as possible. However, there are times when combining paid experience and volunteer work is the only way to move relevant experience to the top of a resume and limit the appearance of a gap.

This strategy can be particularly useful for a parent who has left the workforce to raise a child for a few years but has done some career-related volunteer work during that time to maintain a connection to his or her profession.

If you do combine volunteer work and paid employment into one section, you must clearly label the volunteer positions as volunteer work; it would be dishonest to try to imply that a volunteer job was actually a paid position.

Similarly, if you combine volunteer and paid work into one section, you cannot label the section Work Experience or Work History because those labels imply that the section contains only paid employment. The heading Relevant Experience is a good and honest title for a section that contains both paid and unpaid positions.

EXAMPLE - PAID AND UNPAID EXPERIENCE COMBINED IN ONE CATEGORY

RELEVANT EXPERIENCE

Music Play Group Leader (volunteer)
Anytown Community Center, City, State   2011 - present
- Include descriptive points about your volunteer work

Music Teacher
Anytown Arts Academy, City, State   2007 - 2010
Include descriptive points about your job
- Make it clear that this job was full-time, paid employment

---

7. CONSIDER OMITTING THE DATES OF YOUR WORK HISTORY ONLY IF YOU HAVE NOT BEEN INVOLVED IN ANY PAID EMPLOYMENT, RELEVANT VOLUNTEER WORK, OR EDUCATION IN THE LAST SEVERAL YEARS.

This strategy is another one that I use only in very rare situations when other options do not solve the issue of a gap in experience. It is not an ideal solution because employers expect to see employment dates on a resume, so this strategy can raise a few red flags in the minds of employers.

Also, this strategy is not recommended if the employer uses an applicant tracking system to screen resumes. An ATS will look for dates to understand each job entry. If there are no dates, the ATS may interpret that to mean there are no jobs shown on your resume. Including older dates may be an issue in ATS screening, but including no dates at all will be a bigger issue.

This strategy should only be used if you have a very large, current gap in your work history, if your resume will be reviewed by a human, and if there is absolutely no education or volunteer work that you could use to fill or reduce the gap.

The problem with omitting dates from your work history is that employers will know you have omitted the dates to mask some issue, and employers will imagine the worst. If you omit the dates from your work history, employers will assume that your work experience is many, many years in the past. Therefore, I would only consider omitting dates if your work history actually is many, many years in the past and you have no recent education or volunteer work to reduce the gap.

If your last paid employment was two or three years in the past, *I would not suggest omitting the dates even if you do not have any education or volunteer work to fill that gap*. Showing a gap of a few years is preferable to omitting dates and causing an employer to wonder if your work experience is, perhaps, ten years in the past, instead of just two or three years in the past. In this situation, omitting the dates would create a larger issue than the one that exists.

If your last paid employment was approximately ten years ago or more, and you have no recent education or volunteer experience to fill the gap, then, and only then, you might consider omitting the dates on your resume.

Please remember, unlike the rest of the strategies presented in this section, this strategy is not ideal and can raise concerns with employers. If you try sending out a few resumes with the dates omitted, and you are not being called to interviews, the problem may be with the missing dates, and you will need to rethink your strategy.

You may also want to look for ways to get current experience whether it is through part-time work or volunteer work. Sometimes returning to work and rebuilding your career when you have been out of the workforce for a while is progressive in that you may start with volunteer or part-time work to build current experience before you find a full-time job.

EXAMPLE - DATES OMITTED BECAUSE WORK EXPERIENCE IS 10 YEARS IN THE PAST

Head Chef, ABC Restaurant, City, State
- Describe the job here

Chef, XYZ Restaurant, City, State
- Describe the job here

Sous Chef, Another Restaurant, City, State
- Describe the job here

What to do when:
You have held many jobs in a short time

Reasonable employers expect some movement from one company to another. Standards vary by industry; some industries expect more staff turnover than others. In general, the more training a job requires and the higher the level of responsibility involved with the job, the longer employers will expect you to stay with a company.

In most cases, if you have stayed at each job for at least a couple of years (longer for more complex or more responsible positions), then "job jumping" will not be a large concern on your resume.

If, on the other hand, you have held something like three different jobs in the past year, you will need to minimize the perception that you will not stay at a job for long. These tips will help you do that.

1. REVIEW AND IMPLEMENT THE TIPS IN THE PREVIOUS SECTION FOR MINIMIZING THE APPEARANCE OF DATES ON YOUR RESUME.

The tip about omitting months from your employment dates is particularly helpful when you have held a lot of jobs in a short period of time. It is rarely helpful for anyone to include the months with the dates of employment. The only time you may want to include months is when doing so would make it clear that you worked at a company for a longer period of time.

EXAMPLE

Imagine an entry on your resume is written as follows:

> **Retail Sales Associate**, Any Company, City, State   2013 – 2014

If you worked at that job from November 2013 to January 2014, then excluding the months works to your advantage. If you included the months, it would become clear to employers that you only stayed at that job for two or three months. If you include the years only, you are providing accurate information, but you are not highlighting the fact that you were with the company for a short period of time.

If, on the other hand, you worked at that company from January 2013 to December 2014, then you would want to consider including the months of employment on your resume because, in this case, including the months indicates to employers that you were at that company for a full two years. In that case, your entry would look something like this:

> **Retail Sales Associate**, Any Company, City, State   January 2013 - December 2014

2. CONSIDER OMITTING A JOB FROM YOUR WORK HISTORY IF YOU WORKED THERE FOR A SHORT PERIOD OF TIME AND IT IS UNRELATED TO THE TYPE OF WORK YOU ARE CURRENTLY SEEKING.

You do not have to include every single job on your resume, and in some circumstances it is in your best interest to omit a job.

EXAMPLE

Imagine it is January 2014, and you are job searching. You held three jobs in 2013. You worked as an early childhood education teacher at one company from June 2009 to January 2013. You were laid off from that job, and in order to earn some income, you took a job as a telephone customer service representative from April 2013 to June 2013. You were hired as an early childhood education teacher at another company in June 2013, and you continue to work at that job, but the hours are limited, so you are still job searching to find a full-time position as an early childhood education teacher.

In this case, the customer service representative job that you held for two or three months is not closely related to the job you are currently seeking. If you include this job on your resume, it will show that you held three separate jobs in 2013, and that can cause concern for some employers. In this case, it would be in your best interest to omit the unrelated job that you held for a short time and also omit the months from your dates of employment. The entries would look something like this:

Early Childhood Education Teacher
ABC Daycare Center, Fake City, State   2013 - present
- Describe your job in point form here

Early Childhood Education Teacher
XYZ Daycare Center, Fake City, State   2009 - 2013
- Describe your job in point form here

---

3. CONSIDER COMBINING RELATED JOBS INTO ONE ENTRY.

If you did the same type of job at different companies, and you worked at each company for a short time, consider combining all of the jobs into one entry. You must include the names of all of the employers in the entry in order maintain honesty on your resume.

Keep in mind, you should not combine different types of jobs. Doing so would only confuse employers and make your resume difficult to read. Also, this strategy may confuse applicant tracking systems, so it is a better option if a human, not an ATS, will review your resume.

EXAMPLE

Imagine you worked as a general laborer for three different companies from 2012 to 2014. You worked at the first company from November 2012 to March 2013, you were at the second company from April 2013 to July 2013, and you worked at the third company from August 2013 to January 2014.

If you list all of these jobs as separate entries in your work history, it will be immediately obvious that you were at all of these jobs for a short time, and that fact will raise concerns for many employers. If instead, you combined all three jobs into one entry, listing all of the employers, you will still present an honest representation of your work history, but the fact that you held several jobs in a short time period will be less immediately obvious.

EXAMPLE - SEVERAL SHORT TERM, RELATED JOBS COMBINED IN ONE ENTRY

General Laborer   2012 - 2014
ABC Company, Any City, State
XYZ Company, Another City, State
Another Company, Any City, State
• Describe the jobs in point form here

4. IF YOU WERE AT SEVERAL COMPANIES FOR A SHORT PERIOD OF TIME BECAUSE YOU WERE WORKING THROUGH A TEMPORARY AGENCY, LIST THE TEMPORARY AGENCY AS THE EMPLOYER, NOT EACH COMPANY.

If you have been working with a temporary employment agency, you may have had several short term contract positions at several different companies. If that is the case, do not list each employer separately. If you list each company separately, at a glance your resume will make you look like you have been job jumping.

Instead, combine all of the jobs into one entry. You will probably have done similar work at each company, so you can use a job title that is a good reflection of the type of work you did at each company. List the temporary agency as the employer, and use the date of your first contract as your start date (exclude months) and the date of your last contract as your end date.

If you completed a contract position at a company that would be impressive to other employers and you want to mention that company name in your resume, do so in the bulleted points section where you describe your work.

EXAMPLE

Imagine you worked at four different contract positions through a temporary agency. You started working with the temporary agency in 2012, and you are currently working in a contract position through the agency. The contracts ranged from three to six months in length, and they involved administrative or reception duties. You worked at a couple of companies that were leaders in your industry, so you want to mention these companies on your resume. Your entry would look something like this:

Administrative Assistant / Receptionist
Anytown Staffing Agency, Anytown, State   2012 - present
- Successfully completed contract positions at ABC Company, Any Company, 123 Company; presently working on contract at XYZ Company
- Add more points to describe your work and accomplishments at each contract position

What to do when:
You have a long work history and are worried about age discrimination

The standard recommendation is that you should not include more than ten years of work experience on your resume. There are two reasons why you typically do not go back more than ten years on a resume:

- Employers are most interested in what you have been doing recently and feel that any skills you have not used in more than ten years are not up to date.

- In some industries there comes a point when age becomes an issue for employers, and job seekers start to experience age discrimination.

Although the age varies by industry, in general, when some job seekers reach about 45 years old, they start to feel that their age may be having a negative impact on their job search. If you limit your work history to the most recent ten years of experience, you can minimize the potential for age discrimination.

Minimizing the potential for age discrimination on a resume is simple for most people; simply omit from your work history any jobs that are more than ten years in the past. Keep in mind, the ten year mark is an approximation, so, if you have to go back eleven or twelve years to include an important job, particularly one that you held for a long time and was highly relevant to your career, that is completely acceptable.

Use the ten year mark as a guideline to determine where to cut off your work history if you have a long work history.

Occasionally people have real difficulty cutting off their work history at the ten year mark.

IF YOU HAVE WORKED AT THE SAME COMPANY FOR THE LAST 20 YEARS, YOU SIMPLY CANNOT LIMIT YOUR WORK HISTORY TO TEN YEARS.

If you worked at a company from 1994-2014, those are your dates of employment. You cannot change the dates just to make yourself look younger on your resume. That would be dishonest.

If you are facing this situation, please review the strategies for downplaying the appearance of dates and simply list the full dates of employment on your resume.

IF YOU HAVE WORKED FOR A FEW DIFFERENT COMPANIES AND THERE IS A LOGICAL PLACE FOR CUTTING OFF YOUR WORK HISTORY, BUT YOU FEEL THAT THE WORK YOU DID MORE THAN TEN YEARS AGO IS IMPORTANT TO INCLUDE ON YOUR RESUME, CONSIDER THE FOLLOWING:

Usually, the most recent ten years of experience is all an employer wants to see, but sometimes, showing a longer history of experience in an industry can be help to demonstrate a depth of knowledge in an industry that is important in some jobs. If you truly think this is the case for the work you do, you may consider putting more than ten years of experience on your resume.

In some industries, experienced workers (this term generally refers to job seekers who are 45 or older) do not experience age discrimination. In fact, age and experience can be seen as a real positive in some industries. If you know for a fact that age and experience is considered a positive attribute in your industry, then you may be less stringent about limiting your work history to the most recent ten years. Do keep in mind, however, even if you do not have to worry about age discrimination, most employers feel that experience that is more than ten years old is not particularly relevant.

IF YOU DECIDE TO INCLUDE MORE THAN TEN YEARS OF WORK HISTORY, BE WILLING TO RETHINK THIS DECISION IF YOU DO NOT GET CALLED TO JOB INTERVIEWS.

If you send out several resumes with your full work history, and you are not invited to any job interviews, the long work history on your resume may be the issue. Keep an open mind and be willing to try shortening your work history on your resume if you are not invited to interviews.

What to do when:
You have a short work history

- If your work experience is limited, ensure you describe any experience you do have in full detail.

- Include every detail that is relevant to the type of work you are seeking.

- If you have relevant volunteer experience, be sure to highlight that experience and describe it in detail. Chapter 11 provides information about how to effectively describe volunteer work on your resume.

- If you have education that is relevant to the type of work you are seeking, be sure to highlight your education. If you are a recent graduate, you will probably benefit from putting the education section of your resume before the work history section. You may also consider describing your education in some detail by including your grade point average (if it was impressive), listing relevant courses you completed and/or by providing details about placements or internships that you completed as a part of your course work. Chapter 10 provides information about how to effectively write about your education.

Do be honest about your work experience. Give yourself full credit for all of the responsibility that you have had, but avoid trying to stretch experiences to make it appear as though they involved a higher level of responsibility than you were actually given. Employers will see through this attempt to stretch the truth and will not react favorably.

If you have limited work experience, you will likely be applying to entry-level jobs. Do keep in mind that when employers are hiring someone for an entry-level position, they understand that the person they hire will not have a fully developed career history. When they review resumes for entry-level jobs, they will be looking for relevant volunteer work and/or education to round out a candidate's experience.

What to do when:
Your most relevant work experience is in the past

If your most relevant work experience is only a year or two in the past, you may consider separating your work experience into the headings Related Experience and Additional Experience in order to move your most relevant experience up to the top of your resume.

EXAMPLE

Imagine it is 2014. You spent the majority of your career working as a speech therapy assistant. In 2013, you were laid off from your job as a speech therapy assistant. After you were laid off, you took a part-time job as a library assistant to earn some income and to avoid having a gap in your work experience. You are still searching for work as a speech therapy assistant. You want to include your job at the library on your resume so employers know that you do not have a gap in your work history, but you also want to ensure that employers notice all of your experience working as a speech therapy assistant. Your resume might look something like this:

RELATED EXPERIENCE

Speech Therapy Assistant, ABC Community Center, Anytown, State   2010 – 2013
- Describe your work in bulleted point form here

Speech Therapy Assistant, XYZ Children's Center, Anytown, State   2008 - 2010
- Describe your work in bulleted point form here

ADDITIONAL EXPERIENCE

Library Assistant, Anytown Public Library, Anytown, State   2013 – present

---

Notice that there is no description included for the library assistant job listed under additional experience. If a job is unrelated to the work you are currently seeking, but you are including the job on your resume to avoid gaps in your work history, it is not necessary to describe the job in detail.

Do use this strategy with care. Although it can be helpful in some situations to use this strategy to rearrange the order of your work experience, you can get into murky territory when you start to rearrange the order of your work experience.

If, for example, your relevant work history was a few years in the past, and you moved it up to the top using the strategy described above, you could create the appearance of a gap in your work history where none existed because the first date the employer would see is an older date.

If your most relevant work is more than a year or two in the past, you are typically better off if you leave the work history section in standard reverse chronological order (most recent job first), and do not spend time describing the job that is not relevant to the work you are currently targeting. Also, a combination style resume instead of a chronological resume would work well in this situation because it puts more focus on your skills and less focus on your work history.

EXAMPLE

Imagine you are in a situation similar to the one noted above. It is 2014. You spent the majority of your career working as a speech therapy assistant, but you were laid off from your job in 2011, and you have been working as a library assistant since 2011. You would like to return to work as a speech therapy assistant.

You need to include your job at the library on your resume so employers know that you do not have a gap in your work history, but you also want to ensure that employers notice all of your experience working as a speech therapy assistant. Your resume would be a combination style resume, and the work history section might look something like this:

WORK EXPERIENCE

Library Assistant, Anytown Public Library, Anytown, State   2011 - present

Speech Therapy Assistant, ABC Community Center, Anytown, State   2010 - 2011
- Describe your work in bulleted point form here

Speech Therapy Assistant, XYZ Children's Center, Anytown, State   2008 - 2010
- Describe your work in bulleted point form here

Notice that there is no description of the library assistant job because you want employers to think of you as a speech therapy assistant, not a library assistant. The library assistant job is listed first even though it is not the target job because the relevant speech therapy assistant job is too far in the past, and you do not want employers to think you have such a large gap in your work history.

In a situation like this one, if you have completed any training related to speech therapy or been involved in any volunteer work related to speech therapy since you left the field in 2011, it would be very important to highlight that training or volunteer work on your resume to demonstrate that you have been recently active in the field.

What to do when:
Your most relevant experience was obtained through volunteer work and not paid employment

Point number six under the section titled "How to Minimize Gaps in Your Employment History" describes how to combine paid employment and volunteer work into one section to move the volunteer work up to the top of your resume.

If you are looking for a job that you have done in the past but is different from the type of work you are currently doing, and you are currently doing volunteer work that is related to the type of job you would like to be doing, you may want to consider using the headings Relevant Experience (as described in part 6 of the section "How to Minimize Gaps in Your Employment History") combined with a section called Additional Experience.

EXAMPLE

Imagine it is 2014. You have spent most of your career working as a music teacher. Your last job teaching music was from 2007 to 2011. In 2011, you accepted a job as an office manager because you wanted to work more regular hours. You are still at that job, and you have also been volunteering as a music play group leader since 2011. You would like to return to teaching music, so you need to find a way to highlight your experience related to teaching music, and you also need to include your job as an office manager on your resume to show that you do not have a large gap in your work history. Your resume would be a combination resume, and the work history section might look something like this:

RELEVANT EXPERIENCE

Music Play Group Leader (volunteer)
Anytown Community Center, City, State   2011 - present
- Include descriptive points about your volunteer work

Music Teacher
Anytown Arts Academy, City, State   2007 - 2011
Include descriptive points about your job
- Make it clear that this job was full-time, paid employment

ADDITIONAL EXPERIENCE

Office Manager, ABC Company, City, State   2011 – present

Notice that the office manager position was not described in detail because, in this case, you want the employer to see you as a music teacher, not an office manager. You could include a few points that describe skills that would transfer over into teaching music.

Ideally, the name of the city and state would be on a single line with the job title and company to minimize the appearance of the dates, but because the information would not fit neatly on one line in the entry describing the volunteer position, the city and state were added to a second line.

Note that the city and state were included on one line under the new heading, Additional Experience. It is fine to switch to a slightly different format like this when you start a new section, but the format must be consistent within sections, and the format change in a new section should not be dramatically different from other sections of the resume.

What to do when:
You are making a career change

When you are making a career change, you will need to highlight your transferable skills (the skills you developed at one job that can be used in a new job), and possibly your education and volunteer work. For that reason almost all career changers will benefit from choosing a combination resume format.

If your education and/or volunteer experience is more relevant to the job you are seeking and your work history is less relevant to the type of work you are currently seeking, consider the strategies described previously for moving your volunteer work and/or your education to the top of your resume.

Be sure to describe your current work (in the unrelated industry) in terms that would be clear to someone outside of the industry. Avoid using industry jargon or acronyms.

Highlight aspects of your job that are relevant to the new job you are targeting, and minimize descriptions of tasks that are completely unrelated to your new career. It may seem odd to omit tasks that you manage on a regular basis and are crucial to your current job; however, it is important to highlight the similarities between your current career and the new career. Therefore, when you write a career change resume, you will highlight tasks that are most relevant to your new career, even if those tasks are not the central focus of your current job.

What to do when:
You've held the same job at different companies, and your resume is becoming repetitive

If you have held basically the same job at a few different companies, it can be very difficult to avoid repetition on your resume. If you describe each job in detail in the work history section of your resume, you may end up with the same information in each entry, which is not a good use of space on your resume and can leave an employer wondering why you were not given progressively more responsibility in each job you held.

Instead of describing each job in detail in the work experience section, consider using a combination resume. Describe your job duties, skills and accomplishments in a skills summary that is broken down into sections that describe major skill areas, and then list your jobs in the work history section of your resume, providing only a brief description of each job.

Keep in mind, you do not have to be concerned about being repetitive if your resume will be screened with an applicant tracking system. In fact, repeating major responsibilities held in similar jobs may help your resume score better in an ATS screening because it will show a longer history of experience with that task, and it will allow you to include more relevant keywords that the software will be looking for. Therefore, the strategy described here is most effective when a human, and not an ATS will review your resume.

EXAMPLE

Imagine over the past ten years you worked as an administrative assistant for three companies. The companies were all part of the same industry, and there was a lot of overlap in the responsibilities you were given at each job. To avoid repetition, your resume might look something like this:

ACCOMPLISHMENTS
- List five to eight of your key professional achievements

OFFICE ADMINISTRATION
- Describe administrative responsibilities that you managed in your jobs

TECHNICAL SKILLS
- Describe technical skills, such as computer software programs you are familiar with

PROFESSIONAL EXPERIENCE

Administrative Assistant, ABC Company, Anytown, State   2012 - present
- Briefly describe this job in one or two points

Administrative Assistant, XYZ Company, Anytown, State   2007 - 2012
- Briefly describe this job in one or two points; avoid repeating points from other jobs

Administrative Assistant, Another Company, Anytown, State   2005 - 2007
- Briefly describe this job in one or two points; avoid repeating points from other jobs

---

The sections in the skills summary example were selected because they represent groups of skills that are commonly developed in and required for administrative assistant jobs. You are not required to use these specific heading in your own resume. Instead, if you use this strategy for describing your jobs, you should choose headings that reflect the types of skills that are normally required in the specific type of job you are targeting. Please refer back to chapter 8 for details about how to write an effective skills summary section for your resume.

What to do when:
You need to show a career progression with increased responsibility at one company

If you have worked at one company for a significant period of time and have been promoted over that time, it is important to show this progression of responsibility on your resume. Employers like to see that job candidates have earned progressively more responsibility throughout their careers because it indicates a level of competence and trustworthiness.

If you are not careful with the way you structure your resume when you have worked at the same company for many years, it may appear that your career has stagnated for a period of time. You must separate out each job you have held at a single company to show career progression.

EXAMPLE

Imagine it is 2014. You have worked at the same company for ten years, and that company had several locations throughout North America and Europe. You started working as a lab technician. You moved out of the lab and became the health, safety and environment (HSE) coordinator for your site. Eventually you became the HSE manager for all of your company's North American plants. You need to make it clear on your resume that you have spent several years at one company, and you have earned progressively greater responsibility at that company.

DOCUMENTING SEVERAL JOBS AT ONE COMPANY - NOT RECOMMENDED - COMBINING ALL JOBS TOGETHER

Health, Safety and Environment Manager, North America
ABC Company, Anytown, State   2005 – present
- Describe your responsibilities here

Notice that only the most recent job is listed in this entry. None of the more junior positions are included, so there is no evidence of career progression at this company.

DOCUMENTING SEVERAL JOBS AT ONE COMPANY - RECOMMENDED - SEPARATE JOBS TO SHOW CAREER PROGRESSION

Health, Safety and Environment Manager, North America
ABC Company, Anytown, State   2012 - present
- Describe your responsibilities here

Health, Safety and Environment Coordinator
ABC Company, Anytown, State   2008 - 2012
- Describe your responsibilities here

Laboratory Technician
ABC Company, Anytown, State   2005 - 2008
- Describe your responsibilities here

Notice in this example, each job has been separated to show a progression of increased responsibility within the company. If the oldest job (the laboratory technician in this example) is not particularly relevant to the job you are currently pursuing, you do not need to describe that job in a lot of detail. However, including it as a separate entry on your resume does show that you earned progressive responsibility and trust from your previous employer.

What to do when:
Your education is your strongest selling feature

If you are a recent graduate, and your paid work experience in the type of job you are seeking is very limited or non-existent, list your education before your work history. That way, the first thing employers will notice on your resume is your education, which is your biggest asset.

In this situation, you will need to highlight the skills you can offer as opposed to your work history, and a combination resume is the best type of resume to achieve that goal.

Make the most out of your education on your resume by noting any specific courses you have completed that are directly related to the job you are currently seeking. If you completed internships during your studies, be sure to list these on your resume. Please review chapter 10 for more instructions about writing the education section of your resume.

If you have volunteer experience that is relevant to the type of work you are seeking, be sure to highlight that experience and describe it in full detail. Please review chapter 11 for more instructions about writing the volunteer experience section of your resume.

Keep in mind, if you do not have experience in the type of work you are seeking, but you do have a strong educational background in that field, you will probably be looking for an entry-level job. Employers who are filling entry-level positions understand that the candidates for those jobs are probably not going to have prior experience, so when they review resumes for this type of job, they are typically looking for strong education, experience gained through internships or volunteer work, and evidence that a job candidate has performed well in school, in placements or internships and in volunteer work.

Step Six
Determine What Heading to Use for the Work History Section of Your Resume

There are several different headings you may choose to use for the work history section of your resume. Some have already been noted previously in this chapter. The following list contains headings that are commonly used on resumes; you will need to choose the heading (or headings) that is most appropriate for your specific situation.

While it is fine, and sometimes helpful, to use a variety of headings on a human-reviewed resume, please note that it is important to stick with common, traditional headings in each section of your resume if it will be screened with an applicant tracking system. You will find more information about the types of headings to use for an ATS optimized resume in chapter 13.

Headings you may use for the work history section of your resume:

Work Experience

or

Work History

The headings work experience or work history can be used interchangeably. These headings are most appropriate for job seekers who are looking for entry-level jobs and jobs that do not involve a high level of training.

Professional Experience

This heading is a better choice for job seekers who have established careers and are seeking jobs that require some experience and for job seekers who are seeking jobs that require specialized training or education.

Related Experience

or

Relevant Experience

These two headings are also interchangeable. They can be used when job seekers want to list paid work experience and unpaid experience in a single section. Reasons why you might choose to combine paid and unpaid experience and tips for doing this honestly and effectively can be found earlier in this chapter.

Using this technique to change the standard organization of information on a resume requires some care. Please review step 5: "Know how to address common concerns with the work history section of your resume" in this chapter before using one of these headings on your resume.

Additional Experience

This heading is used when you want to include a job (or jobs) on your resume, but you do not want them to be prominent. It usually follows the heading Relevant Experience or Related Experience and is used to list jobs that are unrelated to the type of work you are currently seeking.

Again, using this heading to change the standard organization of information on a resume requires some care. Please review step 5, "Know how to address common concerns with the work history section of your resume" in this chapter before using this heading on your resume.

There are other headings that can be used for the work history section of your resume, but the ones listed above cover the needs of the vast majority of job seekers. They are fairly standard headings, which means that employers will know exactly what type of information to expect in that section of your resume.

There is no need to get fancy and inventive when determining how to label the work history section of your resume. The standard headings are easily understandable, so they allow employers to review your resume quickly and intelligently.

Step Seven
Write Your Work History

Use a form to get started and organize your thinking.

You can download from my website a form that you may print and use to write out the work history section of your resume (as well as the rest of your resume) at careerchoiceguide.com/resumeform. If you are feeling unsure about how to get started with writing this section of your resume, the form can help to organize your thinking.

Most people feel it is easiest to begin by writing down all the basic information about the jobs they have held in the past including job title, company name, city, state and employment dates before they start describing each job. Describing the jobs takes more thought and can be a bit of a challenge, and starting with the basic details can help get you focused on the task before you get to the more challenging material.

When you do describe your jobs, expect to write several drafts of each section. Your first attempt at describing your duties and accomplishments can be treated as a brainstorming session. Write down all of the thoughts that come to mind. Do not worry whether the points are worded in the best way possible.

Once you have brainstormed all of your job duties, go back and edit your writing to make sure your points are as descriptive and persuasive as possible. Review step 4 of this chapter if necessary to remind yourself how to write about your jobs in a way that is compelling. Also, review chapter 8 if you need more reminders about how to effectively write content for your resume.

Constantly refer back to the job you have specified in your profile. For each point that you write to describe your jobs, ask yourself how that point helps to prove that you would be great at the job you have specified on your profile.

Use additional resources if necessary.

If you are having real difficulty describing your jobs, there are a few online resources you can use that will help you think through the job duties for many different types of jobs. These sites are free and provide thorough job descriptions for thousands of different types of jobs.

If you chose to use these sites for inspiration for your job descriptions, keep in mind that you will still need to rephrase the information to make it your own. Be sure to thoroughly reword any points from these sites so that the concept is expressed in your own words. Also, because these sites provide general job descriptions, you will need to ensure that you make your points specific to your own work.

Before you go to an outside source for inspiration for writing your job description, do your very best to write your own descriptions yourself. It is extremely important to write these descriptions in your own words, and it can be challenging to put things into your own words after you have read someone else's description of the same thing. Use these sites as a final check to ensure you have not missed anything important or as a last resort if you are extremely stuck and unable to write your job description.

SITES WITH JOB DESCRIPTIONS

AMERICAN

Occupational Outlook Handbook - www.bls.gov/ooh/home.htm

O*NET OnLine - www.onetonline.org

CANADIAN

National Occupation Classification (NOC) -

www5.hrsdc.gc.ca/NOC/English/NOC/2011/Welcome.aspx

OTHER SOURCES OF JOB DESCRIPTIONS

You may be able to access a database of thorough job descriptions at your local library or an employment resource center, if you have one in your area.

If you have any difficulty using the sites mentioned above (they have great information, but they are not all intuitive to use), please refer to chapter 16 at the end of this book for further instructions on how to find information on these websites.

Do not worry too much about formatting.

It is easy to start to get hung up on formatting your resume at this stage of the resume writing process. As you are typing up this section of your resume, feel free to begin to use some of the formatting suggestions described in this chapter, but do not become too focused on formatting at this point.

If something is not sitting just right on the page, leave it. You will focus on fully formatting your resume after you have written all of the content for your resume. Until you have written all of the information that you want to include on your resume, you will not know exactly how much and what type of information you need to fit on the page or pages. There is no point trying to fully format your resume when you do not yet know the full scope of what you need to format.

Once you have finished writing your work history...

Open up the document where you have saved the draft of your resume, and write the work history section. Your resume will have some differences compared with the example depending upon choices you have made along the way, but when you are finished writing up the work history section of your resume, your document will look something like this:

Jane Somebody
123 Any Street, Faketown, State, Zip Code
janesomebody@emailprovider.com
(000) 000-0000

Profile
Administrative professional with seven years of experience in the nonprofit sector. Able to prioritize and manage conflicting demands. Exceptional technical skills including proficiency with Word, Excel, PowerPoint and Prezi; type 80 words per minute.

Summary of Skills*

Proven ability to meet strict deadlines, ensure accuracy of work and manage conflicting demands effectively**
Thorough knowledge of and ability to research community resources developed over 7 years working at local, non-profit community organizations

Able to resolve common computer hardware issues for staff and clients in resource center
Exhibit a professional and welcoming demeanor to clients and co-workers; earned reputation as a resourceful problem solver with high degree of integrity
Bilingual in English and Spanish

Professional Experience

Administrative Assistant, ABC Organization, City, State 2012 - present
Provide administrative support to two workshop facilitators; assist additional team of counselors as required
Prepare correspondence and training materials for facilitators
Contact clients by telephone on a weekly basis to ensure participation in workshops, and promote agency programs; telephone contact improves workshop attendance by 20%
Accurately manage client data for up to 1000 clients per year using Excel and complete monthly, quarterly and annual reports for counselors, executive director and funding partners
Developed new database system to efficiently compile and analyze large volume and variety of client data; new system significantly reduced time required to complete monthly, quarterly and annual reports
Liaise with community partners to determine additional resources for clients and colleagues and to promote agency programs

Administrative Assistant, XYZ Organization, City, State 2006 - 2012
Provided administrative support for a team of six counselors, each managing a case load of 100+ clients per year
Prepared confidential correspondence and scheduled meetings for counselors
Independently researched and developed teaching resources and community resource packages for counselors and clients
Cross trained to provide assistance to receptionist as well as administrative support for executive director

Receptionist, Another Organization, City, State 2003 - 2005
Provided professional and friendly telephone and in person assistance for clients; answered approximately 50 incoming calls per day on a multi-line phone system and greeted and assisted up to 30 clients per day in a resource center environment
Received and distributed incoming mail and responded to routine inquiries by mail and email
Ensured office equipment was in working order and rectified common computer hardware problems for clients and colleagues
Prepared confidential correspondence for colleagues
Scheduled appointments for staff of seven counselors and organized monthly team meetings and charity events
Maintained office supply inventory; tracked and ordered supplies on a monthly basis

*You will include this section if you are writing a combination resume. You will not include a summary of skills section if you are writing a chronological resume.

**Each point is not bulleted in the example because it is not necessary to format your resume until you have written all of the content of your resume. If you find it difficult to read without the bullets, feel free to add them at this stage.

Assignment

Write up the work history section of your resume.

Moving Forward

You are ready to move on to the next chapter if you...

- Understand how to write about your work in a way that is compelling and specific.

  1. Know how to use specific strategies to show your work history in the best possible light and minimize and potential concerns with your work history.

  2. Have written your work history.

CHAPTER TEN
EDUCATION

YOUR TASKS FOR THIS CHAPTER:

1. Determine how to structure the education section to make the best impression possible.
2. Determine what information you will include in this section and what you will omit.
3. Write the education section of your resume.

ACTION STEPS FOR THIS CHAPTER

Step One: Understand the features of the education section of your resume.

Step Two: Know what education information should be included and what should be omitted.

Step Three: Know how to address specific situations related to your education.

Step Four: Determine whether the education section should be placed before or after the work experience section.

Step Five: Write the education section of your resume.

"The more that you read, the more things you will know. The more that you learn, the more places you'll go." Dr. Seuss

Before getting into the specifics of writing the education section of your resume, you will need to decide whether you will be including this section on your resume or not.

If you have decided to write a combination resume or a chronological resume (see chapter 4), you will include an education section on your resume. If you have decided to write a functional resume (see also chapter 4), you will not include an education section.

As noted earlier in this book, the vast majority of employers expect to see education listed on each resume they review, and many employers do not trust functional resumes. Combination or chronological resumes are almost always the best choice for job seekers in all different situations.

Step One
Understand the Features of the Education Section of Your Resume

Although there are exceptions, which we will explore in this chapter, the education section of a resume normally contains the name of the degree, diploma, certificate or course you completed, the name of the school you attended, the city and state where you attended school, and usually the date when you completed the program.

Your education should be listed in reverse chronological order (most recent education first); however, you must be careful to ensure any higher level education does not get buried under more recent but less challenging or less relevant coursework that you have completed. You will find information about how to organize your education information when you have completed a lot of professional development later in this chapter.

STANDARD EDUCATION ENTRY ON A RESUME

Bachelor of Arts Degree, English
Anytown University, City, State   2011

Step Two
Know What Education Information Should Be Included and What Should be Omitted

It is not always necessary to include your high school diploma on your resume.

If you have completed a college or university diploma or degree, it is not necessary to include information about high school on your resume. The rationale is that if you can successfully complete college or university level work, then employers know you can manage high school level work, so listing your high school information is not necessary.

If you have not attended college or university, or if you are in the process of completing a college or university diploma or degree, but you have not fully completed any degree or diploma, then you should include your high school information on your resume.

You do not have to include all of your professional development on your resume.

If, for example, your employer sends you on a lot of professional development courses, and you are pressed for space on your resume, you do not have to include all of these courses as long as the courses are not particularly relevant to the type of job you are seeking.

If you have to make some decisions about omitting part of a lengthy list of professional development courses, be sure to include any coursework that is impressive, demonstrates valuable skills, or is crucial to the type of job you are seeking. Consider omitting any courses that do not help to prove that you would be great at the type of job you are currently seeking.

Recent graduates will generally include more details about education than job seekers who have established careers.

IF YOU HAVE AN ESTABLISHED CAREER...

If you have an established career, you will almost never include details about courses you completed while in school because your work experience will be more important than your coursework at this stage in your career. The majority of job seekers who are not recent graduates will write the education section of their resume just like the Standard Education Entry on a Resume example shown earlier in this chapter.

One exception to this guideline is when you are applying to a job that specifically requires the successful candidate to have completed specific courses. If, for example, you were applying to an advertised job, and the job ad stated that the successful candidate must have completed a college level counseling course, an ethics course and a psychology course, and you completed those courses several years ago in college, you can list those courses in a single bulleted point. The entry would look something like this:

Social Services Worker Diploma
Anytown College, City, State   2010
- Courses completes include: Counseling Skills I and II, Cognitive Psychology, Abnormal Psychology and Counseling Ethics

---

IF YOU ARE A RECENT GRADUATE...

If you are a recent graduate, your education may be stronger than your work experience; therefore, it will be important to showcase your academic achievements more than you would if you had an established career.

In addition to the standard information, you may also include:

- A list of courses you completed if they are relevant to the work you are seeking

- Your GPA if it is high

- A description of internships you completed while in school

- Any special honors you received while in school

An entry on the education section of your resume might look something like this example:

Education

Social Services Worker Diploma
Anytown College, City, State   2014
- Received Anytown College award for Commitment to the Field of Social Work

Internships

XYZ Youth Center, City, State   2014
- Co-facilitated seminars concerning study skills and career planning
- Conducted individual and group homework assistance sessions for high school students

Community Resource Center, City, State   2013
- Completed initial intake evaluations and assessed clients' needs
- Assisted clients using print and computer resources within the resource center

---

Notice the internships have been given a completely separate section; they have not been listed under the diploma. Internships can provide powerful, relevant experience for recent graduates who otherwise do not have relevant work experience. Therefore, when you are a recent graduate, it is smart to do everything you can to highlight your internships or school placements on your resume. Giving them a separate section instead of lumping them in with your degree or diploma helps them to stand out and gives them added importance on your resume.

Also, as mentioned previously, if you are a recent graduate, it is very likely that your education is a stronger selling feature than your work experience. If that is the case for you, then your education and internships should come before your work history on your resume.

Step Three
Know How to Address Specific Situations Related to Your Education

What to do when:
You started, but did not complete a diploma or degree

If you started but did not complete a diploma, degree or certificate program, you have a few options:

1. COMPLETELY OMIT THE PROGRAM FROM YOUR RESUME.

If the program is not relevant to the job you are currently targeting, and if omitting the program does not create a large and current gap in the timeline of your work and educational history, it is perfectly acceptable to omit the courses from your resume.

2. USE THE WORDS "DEGREE EXPECTED."

If you are enrolled in a degree, diploma or certificate program, you are working to complete the program, but you haven't completed it, use the words degree expected or diploma expected.

EXAMPLE

Imagine you are currently enrolled in an environmental technology diploma program. It is 2014, you are in the second year of a three year program, and you are on track to graduate in 2015. The entry on your resume would look something like this:

Education

Environmental Technology Program
Anytown College, Anytown, State   diploma expected April 2015
  • List important school-related achievements (optional, but smart for new graduates)

Grade 12 Diploma
Anytown High School, Anytown, State   2012

Notice that the high school diploma was included in this example because this job seeker has not yet completed the college program. Once the college program is completed, the high school diploma may be deleted from the resume.

3. USE THE WORDS "PROGRAM" OR "COURSES."

If you have not completed a diploma or degree, and you are not in the process of completing it, but you want to include the program on your resume because the courses you did complete were highly relevant to the work you are currently seeking, use the words program or courses to describe the program. You may not use the words diploma or degree because you did not earn the diploma or degree.

EXAMPLE

Imagine you completed three semesters of a four semester environmental technology diploma program in 2012. You did not complete the diploma, and you are not in the process of completing the diploma, but you are seeking work in a related field, so you want to include these courses on your resume. The entry on your resume would look something like this:

Environmental Technology Program   2012
Anytown College, Anytown, State
- List important school-related achievements (optional)

or

Environmental Technology Courses   2012
Anytown College, Anytown, State
- List important school-related achievements (optional)

What to do when:
You completed your education many years ago, and you are concerned about age discrimination

If your highest level or most recent education was completed more than ten or fifteen years ago, you may consider omitting the dates from this section of your resume. While it is often helpful to include dates on the education section of your resume, if you are concerned that including the dates will open you up to age discrimination, you may decide to omit them.

Including dates on the education section of your resume can be problematic, particularly if you are including your high school diploma on your resume, and you are concerned about age discrimination. Employers will see the year that you graduated from high school, they will assume you were approximately 18 when you graduated, and they will easily do the math to work out your age.

The decision to omit or include dates from the education section of your resume is a bit of a judgment call. Omitting dates on this section does not cause concern in the minds of employers to the extent that omitting dates from the work history section can. Some employers like to see the dates for your education, and for others, it is less important.

If you are unclear about whether you would be better off with or without the dates in this section of your resume, choose one option, but closely monitor the number of interviews you are invited to, compared with the number of resumes you send out. If you find you are submitting resumes to good job leads and not getting invited to interviews, then you may want to change to the other option.

What to do when:
You have completed a lot of relevant education, and your education section is very long and difficult to read at a glance

One way to address this issue may be to omit some of your less relevant professional development, as discussed earlier in this chapter.

If it is not possible to omit any coursework because it is all highly relevant to the job you are currently seeking, or if you omit some of your courses, and you still have a long list of education to include on your resume, you can separate your education into two headings such as Education and Professional Development.

Using these two headings will allow you to include your more formal training, such as degrees and diplomas under the education section and more short term training under the professional development section. Separating a long list of education into two headings makes this information easier to read at a glance and ensures that your higher level degrees or diplomas do not become buried in a long list of relevant, but less formal training.

EXAMPLE

If you decided to separate your education into two sections, your resume might look something like this:

Education	
Social Service Worker Diploma, Anytown College, City, State	2010
Bachelor of Education Degree, Anothercity University, City, State	2007
Bachelor of Arts Degree, English, Anothercity University, City, State	2006
Professional Development	
Counseling Ethics, ABC Home Study, via correspondence	2014
Spanish 1 and 2, XYZ College, City, State	2012
Crisis Intervention, Mental Health Association, City, State	2011
Social Work Forum, Association of Social Workers, City, State	2011

Step Four
Determine Whether the Education Section Should be Placed Before or After the Work Experience Section of Your Resume

When to place your work history before your education:

Most job seekers will place their work history before their education on their resumes.

If you have established work experience that is relevant to the job you are currently seeking, and your work history is a more important factor than your education, then your work history should be placed before your education because that is what you want employers to notice first.

When to place your education before your work history:

A few job seekers will benefit from placing the education section before the work history section.

- If you are a recent graduate, and you have not established work experience in your field of work, your education should come before your work history.

- If you are a career changer who had established a career in one field, and you returned to school to gain skills and knowledge in a new field, your education should come before your work history.

Step Five
Write the Education Section of Your Resume

Open up the document where you have saved the draft of your resume, and write the education section. Your resume will have some differences depending upon choices you have made along the way, but when you are finished writing up the education section, your document will look something like this:

Jane Somebody
123 Any Street, Faketown, State, Zip Code
janesomebody@emailprovider.com
(000) 000-0000

Profile
Administrative professional with seven years of experience in the nonprofit sector. Able to prioritize and manage conflicting demands. Exceptional technical skills including proficiency with Word, Excel, PowerPoint and Prezi; type 80 words per minute.

Summary of Skills*

Proven ability to meet strict deadlines, ensure accuracy of work and manage conflicting demands effectively**
Thorough knowledge of and ability to research community resources developed over 7 years working at local, non-profit community organizations
Able to resolve common computer hardware issues for staff and clients in resource center
Exhibit a professional and welcoming demeanor to clients and co-workers; earned reputation as a resourceful problem solver with high degree of integrity
Bilingual in English and Spanish

Professional Experience

Administrative Assistant, ABC Organization, City, State 2012 - present
Provide administrative support to two workshop facilitators; assist additional team of counselors as required
Prepare correspondence and training materials for facilitators
Contact clients by telephone on a weekly basis to ensure participation in workshops, and promote agency programs; telephone contact improves workshop attendance by 20%
Accurately manage client data for up to 1000 clients per year using Excel and complete monthly, quarterly and annual reports for counselors, executive director and funding partners
Developed new database system to efficiently compile and analyze large volume and variety of client data; new system significantly reduced time required to complete monthly, quarterly and annual reports
Liaise with community partners to determine additional resources for clients and colleagues and to promote agency programs

Administrative Assistant, XYZ Organization, City, State 2006 - 2012
Provided administrative support for a team of six counselors, each managing a case load of 100+ clients per year
Prepared confidential correspondence and scheduled meetings for counselors
Independently researched and developed teaching resources and community resource packages for counselors and clients
Cross trained to provide assistance to receptionist as well as administrative support for executive director

Receptionist, Another Organization, City, State 2003 - 2005
Provided professional and friendly telephone and in person assistance for clients; answered approximately 50 incoming calls per day on a multi-line phone system and greeted and assisted up to 30 clients per day in a resource center environment
Received and distributed incoming mail and responded to routine inquiries by mail and email
Ensured office equipment was in working order and rectified common computer hardware problems for clients and colleagues
Prepared confidential correspondence for colleagues
Scheduled appointments for staff of seven counselors and organized monthly team meetings and charity events
Maintained office supply inventory; tracked and ordered supplies on a monthly basis

Education

Business Administration Diploma, ABC College, City, State 2007

*You will include this section if you are writing a combination resume. You will not include a summary of skills section if you are writing a chronological resume.

**Each point is not bulleted in the example because it is not necessary to format your resume until you have written all of the content of your resume. If you find it difficult to read without the bullets, feel free to add them at this stage.

Assignment

Write up the education section of your resume.

Moving Forward

You are ready to move on to the next chapter if you...

- Understand how to write the education section of your resume in a way that is clear.

  1. Know how to use specific strategies to show your education in the best possible light.

  2. Have written the education section of your resume.

CHAPTER ELEVEN
VOLUNTEER WORK

YOUR TASKS FOR THIS CHAPTER:

1. Determine whether you should include your volunteer work on your resume.
2. Decide how to structure the volunteer work section.
3. Determine what information you will include in this section and what you will omit.
4. Write the volunteer section of your resume.

ACTION STEPS FOR THIS CHAPTER

Step One: Determine whether you should include your volunteer work on your resume.

Step Two: Understand the features of the volunteer work section of your resume.

Step Three: Know what types of volunteer work should be included and what information should be omitted.

Step Four: Determine what heading to use for this section.

Step Five: Determine where this section should appear on your resume.

Step Six: Write the volunteer work section of your resume.

"The value of a man resides in what he gives and
not in what he is capable of receiving."
Albert Einstein

Please note that while this chapter focuses on volunteer work specifically, you may also use the information in this chapter to determine whether you should include information about your hobbies on your resume. Hobbies have not been given a specific chapter in this book because they rarely add helpful information to a resume. However, occasionally people do have hobbies that help to demonstrate they would be a great fit for the type of job they are seeking.

If you think your hobbies say something positive about you as a potential employee, use the information in this chapter to determine whether you should include them on your resume.

Step One
Determine Whether You Should Include Your Volunteer Work on Your Resume

Including information about your volunteer work on your resume is completely optional. To decide whether you should include this information or not, ask yourself whether your volunteer work is relevant to the type of job you are targeting and says something positive about you as a potential employee.

Employers do not consider this information to be essential, so it is completely acceptable to omit it from your resume if your volunteer work is not relevant to the type of work you are seeking.

Volunteer work and hobbies are normally given less importance than paid employment in the minds of employers, but they can provide powerful opportunities to gain practical experience if you are just starting out in a new field. Therefore, if you are new to a field of work and have little or no paid experience, but you do have some volunteer experience that is relevant to the job you are seeking, you will benefit from including your relevant volunteer work on your resume.

On the other hand, if you have a strong, established career doing the type of work you are currently seeking, you will probably not include volunteer work on your resume. In fact, if you have a well-established career, your resume is already packed full of relevant skills and experience, and you need to omit some information to make room on your resume, the volunteer work section is almost always the first section to go.

One exception to this guideline would be if you have a well-established career, but you have completed some volunteer work that demonstrates a crucial and relevant skill that cannot be demonstrated anywhere else on your resume. In that case, consider including volunteer work on your resume.

Job seekers who often benefit from including volunteer work on their resumes:

- Students
- Recent graduates
- People returning to the work force after a long period of time without paid employment
- Career changers

Job seekers who often do not benefit from including volunteer work on their resumes:

- People who have a well-established career doing the type of work they are currently seeking

Step Two
Understand the Basic Features of the Volunteer Work Section of Your Resume

Volunteer work is typically structured in the same way the work experience section is structured. Include a job title that accurately reflects the volunteer work you do, the name of the organization, the location (city and state) where you volunteer and the dates that you have been an active volunteer. If this volunteer work forms an important part of your relevant, practical experience, include a few points to describe your duties and accomplishments in your role as a volunteer.

Please refer to chapter 9 for more information about how to describe your volunteer experience in terms that are memorable and meaningful to employers. All of the tips in chapter 9 on how to describe your paid work experience can be applied to writing about your volunteer experience.

EXAMPLE OF A STANDARD ENTRY IN THE VOLUNTEER SECTION OF A RESUME

Music Play Group Leader, Anytown Children's Center, City, State   2012 - 2014
- Team taught music play group for group of 8 to 10 children aged 6 to 12
- Developed and taught activities to build social skills, impulse control and self-esteem using music therapy-based strategies

Step Three
Know What Types of Volunteer Work Should be Included and What Information Should be Omitted

Consider including volunteer work or hobbies on your resume if...

1. THE EXPERIENCE IS RELEVANT TO THE TYPE OF WORK YOU ARE CURRENTLY SEEKING.

For example, if you volunteered at a local company or community organization to gain practical experience doing the type of work you would like to do, that volunteer work should be included on your resume.

2. THE EXPERIENCE DEMONSTRATES SOMETHING POSITIVE ABOUT YOU AS A POTENTIAL EMPLOYEE.

For example, if you are applying to a job that requires a high degree of physical fitness, and you volunteer at the local gym or your hobby involves competing in some type of fitness competitions, that information may be included on your resume.

Avoid including volunteer work or hobbies on your resume if...

1. THE EXPERIENCE DOES NOT HELP DEMONSTRATE THAT YOU WOULD BE GREAT AT THE JOB YOU ARE CURRENTLY SEEKING.

For example, if your hobbies are reading and going for walks, those are, for the most part, not hobbies that are out of the ordinary. The majority of people who include hobbies on their resume list reading and going for walks, so those hobbies do not stand out as being special in any way.

Common activities do not demonstrate that you do something that would give you the edge over the competition, so it is rarely helpful to include them on your resume.

2. THE EXPERIENCE COULD BE CONSTRUED IN A NEGATIVE WAY IN THE MINDS OF EMPLOYERS.

For example, if you participate in high risk hobbies like sky diving or hang gliding, and the job you are seeking is in a conservative field, it is safer to omit that information from your resume.

Be careful about including volunteer work or hobbies on your resume if...

1. THE ENTRY MAY REVEAL PERSONAL INFORMATION THAT YOU DO NOT WANT TO REVEAL TO POTENTIAL EMPLOYERS.

Some volunteer work will immediately give away aspects of your personal life that you may not want to share with potential employers. For example, if you volunteer at your child's school, and you include that volunteer work on your resume, many employers will assume you have young children (unless you are seeking a job working with children). If you volunteer at your church, and you include that information on your resume, potential employers will know about your religious affiliation.

Many job seekers choose to keep certain aspects of their personal lives, such as family status or religious affiliations, private during the job search process because they are concerned that they might experience discrimination based on those aspects of their lives.

Occasionally job seekers decide that they are not concerned about revealing that type of personal information to an employer. A few of my clients have subtly, but purposely included hobbies like home renovation or volunteer work at a child's school on resumes because they did not want to work for an employer who would take issue with the fact that they were family oriented. They knew they may have lost out on a few job opportunities, but they made a strategic choice that they were not interested in pursuing those opportunities anyway.

The bottom line is that in order to determine whether certain hobbies or volunteer work should be included on your resume, you need to ask yourself what, if anything, does that experience imply about aspects of your personal life, and then ask yourself whether you want potential employers to know about those aspects of your personal life.

Step Four
Determine What Heading to Use for This Section

There are a few headings that are appropriate for this section of your resume. You may simply label this section **Volunteer Work** if you are listing volunteer work only, or **Hobbies** or **Interests** if you are listing hobbies only.

I have a personal preference for the heading **Community Involvement**. This heading is clear and professional sounding; it highlights the idea that you are a person who is involved in your community, and it is a flexible heading that allows you to include all types of activities and interests. This heading allows you to include volunteer work and hobbies in one section.

You may also include internships or school placements under the heading Community Involvement if, for example, you graduated several years ago and have an established career, so you do not want to expand too much on the education section of your resume, but you do want to mention your internships (perhaps you had placements with some impressive companies).

Step Five
Determine Where This Section Should Appear on Your Resume

When to place your volunteer work at the end of your resume:

Most job seekers who include volunteer work on their resumes will place this section at the end of the resume. If you have any work experience that is relevant to the job you are currently seeking, and/or you have completed education that is relevant to the job you are seeking, then your work experience and/or education will be a more important factor than your volunteer work. In that situation your volunteer work should be placed at the bottom of your resume because you want employers to notice other aspects of your career first when they review your resume.

When to place your volunteer work closer to the top of your resume:

A few job seekers will benefit from placing the volunteer section before the work history and/or education sections.

If you do not have work experience or education that is related to the job you are currently seeking, but you do have significant volunteer experience that is related to the job, then you may consider placing the volunteer experience section closer to the top of your resume. If your volunteer experience is your strongest asset, you will typically benefit from writing a combination style resume, so your volunteer work would be listed immediately after your summary of skills.

If you have relevant work experience, but it is a couple of years in the past, and your most recent relevant experience was gained through volunteer work, you may benefit from combining your work experience and your volunteer work on your resume. You will find information about how to combine work experience and volunteer experience in chapter 9 under the heading How to Minimize Gaps in Employment History.

Step Six
Write the Volunteer Work Section of Your Resume

Open up the document where you have saved the draft of your resume, and write the volunteer section. Your resume will have some differences depending upon choices you have made along the way, but when you are finished writing up the volunteer section, your document will look something like this:

Jane Somebody
123 Any Street, Faketown, State, Zip Code
janesomebody@emailprovider.com
Phone: (000) 000-0000

Profile
Administrative professional with seven years of experience in the nonprofit sector. Able to prioritize and manage conflicting demands. Exceptional technical skills including proficiency with Word, Excel, PowerPoint and Prezi; type 80 words per minute.

Summary of Skills*

Proven ability to meet strict deadlines, ensure accuracy of work and manage conflicting demands effectively**
Thorough knowledge of and ability to research community resources developed over 7 years working at local, non-profit community organizations
Able to resolve common computer hardware issues for staff and clients in resource center
Exhibit a professional and welcoming demeanor to clients and co-workers; earned reputation as a resourceful problem solver with high degree of integrity

Bilingual in English and Spanish

Professional Experience

Administrative Assistant, ABC Organization, City, State 2012 - present
Provide administrative support to two workshop facilitators; assist additional team of counselors as required
Prepare correspondence and training materials for facilitators
Contact clients by telephone on a weekly basis to ensure participation in workshops, and promote agency programs; telephone contact improves workshop attendance by 20%
Accurately manage client data for up to 1000 clients per year using Excel and complete monthly, quarterly and annual reports for counselors, executive director and funding partners
Developed new database system to efficiently compile and analyze large volume and variety of client data; new system significantly reduced time required to complete monthly, quarterly and annual reports
Liaise with community partners to determine additional resources for clients and colleagues and to promote agency programs

Administrative Assistant, XYZ Organization, City, State 2006 - 2012
Provided administrative support for a team of six counselors, each managing a case load of 100+ clients per year
Prepared confidential correspondence and scheduled meetings for counselors
Independently researched and developed teaching resources and community resource packages for counselors and clients
Cross trained to provide assistance to receptionist as well as administrative support for executive director

Receptionist, Another Organization, City, State 2003 - 2005
Provided professional and friendly telephone and in person assistance for clients; answered approximately 50 incoming calls per day on a multi-line phone system and greeted and assisted up to 30 clients per day in a resource center environment
Received and distributed incoming mail and responded to routine inquiries by mail and email
Ensured office equipment was in working order and rectified common computer hardware problems for clients and colleagues
Prepared confidential correspondence for colleagues
Scheduled appointments for staff of seven counselors and organized monthly team meetings and charity events
Maintained office supply inventory; tracked and ordered supplies on a monthly basis

Education
Business Administration Diploma, ABC College, City, State 2007

Community Involvement

Secretary-Treasurer, Anytown Community Organization, City, State 2013-present
Manage all website updates, and write and distribute meeting minutes and newsletters to staff and volunteers
Receive donations, issue receipts for cash received and maintain records of cash paid out
Manage budgets, accounts and financial statements and present financial data to the management committee
Prepare Treasurer's Report for annual general meeting and advise management committee on funding requirements for future projects

*You will include this section if you are writing a combination resume. You will not include a summary of skills section if you are writing a chronological resume.

**Each point is not bulleted in the example because it is not necessary to format your resume until you have written all of the content of your resume. If you find it difficult to read your rough draft of your resume without the bullets, feel free to add them at this stage.

Assignment

Write up the volunteer experience section of your resume.

Moving Forward

You are ready to move on to the next chapter if you...

1. Understand when to include volunteer work on your resume and when to omit that information.

2. Understand how to write the volunteer experience section of your resume in a way that is clear.

3. Have written the volunteer experience section of your resume if you chose to include that information.

If you are writing a combination resume, and you skipped writing your summary of skills, return to chapter 8 to write your summary of skills before you proceed to chapter 12.

CHAPTER TWELVE
FORMATTING YOUR RESUME FOR HUMAN READERS

YOUR TASKS FOR THIS CHAPTER:

1. Format your resume so it is visually pleasing and easy to read.
2. Carefully proofread your resume.

ACTION STEPS FOR THIS CHAPTER

Step One: Review and revise the content of your resume.

Step Two: Make final decisions about the order of sections.

Step Three: Choose font and heading styles, and add bullets.

Step Four: Format your contact information.

Step Five: Format your employment, education and volunteer information.

Step Six: Apply formatting rules for two-page resumes if necessary.

Step Seven: Assess how your content fits on the page and apply strategies to help it fit better if necessary.

Step Eight: Print, proofread and revise.

> *"Simplicity is the ultimate sophistication."*
> *Leonardo da Vinci*

Before we dive into this information, please note that the formatting recommendations in this chapter are relevant to resumes that will be read by a human. If you are submitting a resume that will be screened by an applicant tracking system (ATS), you will need to format your resume to please a computer "reader."

There are several important differences between formatting your resume for a human reader and formatting your resume for an ATS. If you need to format your resume to be screened by an ATS, please refer to chapter 13 for that information.

Step One
Review and Revise the Content of Your Resume

You have carefully thought through and written out the content for each section of your resume. Now it is important to take the time to read through everything you have written and make any necessary revisions.

It is a good idea to put your resume aside for a day or at least a few hours after you have finished writing the rough draft. If you are not working against a tight deadline, begin the process of reviewing and revising your resume after you take a bit of a break.

As you write your resume, you become very involved in the process. When you are in that mindset, it can be very difficult to assess your work. If you have been staring at the same page for a long time, errors that may normally be very obvious to you can be easily missed.

Unless you are working on a deadline and must submit your resume immediately, give yourself a break before you dive into reviewing, revising and formatting your resume.

Edit your resume.

CHECK YOUR GRAMMAR

Carefully review each phrase or sentence you have written to look for grammatical errors. Most word processing software programs have a grammar checking tool. Use this tool when you review your resume, but do be aware that grammar checking tools are typically limited to pointing out common errors. You need to apply your own knowledge of grammatical rules to assess whether the punctuation, or word or phrase you have used is correct.

If you are unsure about a grammar rule and cannot determine whether something on your resume is correct or not, have a look at the writing resources listed in chapter 16. If the phrase or grammar rule is particularly complex, and you just cannot determine how to fix it to ensure it is grammatically correct and easy to read, see if you can reword the phrase to completely avoid the grammar rule that is causing the problem.

If you are still unsure about some aspect of grammar, or if you know that grammar is not one of your strengths, ask a friend who has strong grammar skills to review your resume.

Avoid two grammatical errors commonly found on resumes.

There are two errors that I find constantly on resumes, including resumes that have been written by people who have strong writing skills. Be sure to avoid these mistakes.

1. CAPITALIZING JOB TITLES AND DEPARTMENT NAMES

People tend to use capitals on job titles and department names when there should be no capital. This issue is complicated by the fact that sometimes it is correct to capitalize job titles.

Job titles on resumes should almost never be capitalized when they are not part of a heading.

EXAMPLES

The job title should not be capitalized in this job objective.

> To obtain a position as an administrative assistant.

Only the first word of the job title is capitalized in this next professional profile because it is at the beginning of a sentence (actually a sentence fragment, but fragments are allowed in profiles because personal pronouns like I and me are omitted from resumes).

> Customer service manager with seven years of progressive professional experience. Results oriented with a proven ability to improve customer retention and increase team productivity.

The job title should not be capitalized in the bullet point that occurs within the body of the resume.

> As a legal administrative assistant, developed new database system to efficiently compile and analyze large volume and variety of client data

WHEN TO USE CAPITALS FOR JOB TITLES ON YOUR RESUME

Capitalize the first word in your job title when the job title is at the beginning of a sentence or bullet point such as:

> Customer service manager with seven years of progressive professional experience. Results oriented with a proven ability to improve customer retention, and increase team productivity.

Capitalize the full job title when the job title is a heading on your resume such as:

> **Administrative Assistant**, ABC Organization, City, State   2012 – present

THERE ARE OTHER TIMES WHEN A JOB TITLE MAY BE CAPITALIZED.

If a job title is used as part of someone's name, it is capitalized.

If you wrote, "I'm happy Professor Jones is teaching ancient history," the word professor would be capitalized because it is used as part of the person's name. If you wrote, "Sam Jones is an ancient history professor," professor would not be capitalized because it is not used as a name.

This type of capitalization rarely occurs on resumes because you usually do not refer directly to people when writing a resume.

VANITY CAPITALIZATION

Sometimes people capitalize words that are important to them even though the words do not require capitals. Vanity capitalization is often seen on resumes when people capitalize job titles.

Vanity capitalization used in a profile can effectively draw attention to a job title and help employers read your resume faster. For example:

PROFILE

Customer Service Manager with seven years of progressive professional experience. Results oriented with a proven ability to improve customer retention, and increase team productivity.

The capitals on the job title, combined with the bold text, on this profile will draw the eye to the job title and allow employers to quickly determine the type of job you are seeking.

The decision to use vanity capitals for your job title within a profile is a bit of a judgment call. While they are not grammatically correct, they do effectively draw attention to the right place on your resume.

I tend to avoid vanity capitals on resumes because they are not grammatically correct. However, I do know some skilled resume writers who use them. Also, I have never personally heard of an employer who took issue with the use of vanity capitals in a profile.

2. PLURAL POSSESSIVES AND APOSTROPHES

Deciding when and where to place an apostrophe in a word can become a bit confusing when you are dealing with a word that is both plural (there's more than one of the thing) and possessive (something belongs to the thing). This issue comes up all the time on resumes when someone wants to note the number of years of experience they have in a specific type of job.

I have read countless resumes that have some variation of the following grammatically incorrect statement.

INCORRECT

- Five years experience working as a sales associate

CORRECT

- Five years' experience working as a sales associate

An apostrophe should come after the s in the word years because it is plural (there are five years) and possessive (the experience belongs to the years). Unfortunately, the incorrect version is almost always used on resumes.

To further complicate this issue, there is a problem with using the grammatically correct version of this phrase on your resume. Although it is correct to write "five years' experience" it looks wrong to a lot of people.

When I write resumes for clients, I avoid the issue completely by using the following phrase:

- Five years of experience working as a sales associate

Adding the word "of" to the phrase eliminates the need to add an apostrophe to the end of the word years. This alternative wording is slightly less elegant, but it allows you to write a phrase that is grammatically correct and does not look odd to anyone.

Ensure you have followed standard resume writing conventions.

There are a few stylistic rules for resume writing that are not grammar rules but are expected on resumes. Review your resume to ensure you have followed these conventions in your writing style:

PERSONAL PRONOUNS ARE NEVER INCLUDED ON RESUMES.

Avoid using words like I, me, or we on your resume. Similarly, do not refer to yourself in the third person as he or she. Your resume will be written in point form, and employers know that you are referring to yourself, so personal pronouns are not necessary.

Even your profile (if you include one) should not contain personal pronouns. If you cannot easily remove a personal pronoun from a phrase on your resume, try rewording the entire phrase so you can remove the personal pronoun more easily.

USE OF ARTICLES (A, AN, THE) SHOULD BE LIMITED ON RESUMES.

Words like a, an, and the do not add any new information, and they make point form phrases longer than necessary. While there will be some phrases that do require the use of an article, you should be able to remove the majority of them from your resume.

Each time you come across the words a, an, or the on your resume, ask yourself whether the phrase would still be easy to understand if you removed the word. If the answer is yes, delete it.

USE POINT FORM PHRASES, NOT COMPLETE SENTENCES THROUGHOUT YOUR RESUME.

Every entry on your resume should be written in bulleted point form, which allows you to write a resume that is easy to read at a glance. The only exception is your professional profile, if you include one, which should be two or three sentence fragments grouped together and not bulleted.

As mentioned earlier, the phrases in a profile are sentence fragments (incomplete sentences) and not complete sentences because you do not include personal pronouns like I, me or my on your resume.

Therefore, a profile would be written like this (notice the sentences are not complete):

> Customer service manager with seven years of progressive professional experience. Results oriented with a proven ability to improve customer retention and increase team productivity.

It would never be written in complete sentence form like this:

> I am a customer service manager with seven years of progressive professional experience. I am results oriented with a proven ability to improve customer retention and increase team productivity.

BE ACCURATE WITH YOUR VERB TENSES.

Verb tense rules for resumes are quite simple.

- If you are describing something you did in the past and you no longer do now, use the past tense.

- If you are describing something you do now, use the present tense.

These guidelines confuse some people because they feel bothered by the fact that they are switching from past tense to present tense within the resume. There is nothing wrong with having both past and present tense verbs on your resume.

Be consistent, and use present tense every time you describe something you do now and past tense every time you describe something you did in the past and no longer do.

WRITE IN YOUR OWN VOICE.

Do not over do it when it comes to language on your resume. When you write your resume, do use words that sound professional and clearly describe your skills and experiences, but avoid writing words that you would never use in real life. Your resume must reflect you at your very best.

AVOID ABBREVIATIONS AND CONTRACTIONS.

Abbreviations are too informal for resumes. Use the full version of words on your resume. This rule includes contractions. All contractions should be written out in full on your resume. For example, didn't must be did not, and who'd must be who would.

You can make an exception to this rule when writing industry-related terms. Particularly if your resume will be screened by an applicant tracking system and searched for keywords, you must include both the full spelling of a term as well as the abbreviation.

For example, if you are a registered nurse, your resume should include the phrase "registered nurse" as well as the abbreviation "RN." Including both registered nurse and RN on your resume will ensure your resume is found in a keyword search whether the term registered nurse or RN is used as a search term. You will find more information about using effective keywords to score well in an applicant tracking system screening in chapter 13.

OMIT THE PHRASE "REFERENCES AVAILABLE UPON REQUEST"

While including this phrase at the bottom of a resume was quite common a few years ago, it is not necessary because it does not add any useful information. Employers know they can ask for references if they want them.

Using the phrase "references available upon request" can make your resume appear dated in the eyes of some employers. Including the phrase certainly should not be a deal-breaker if you are an excellent candidate for the job, but the phrase really serves no important purpose. You might as well omit the line "references available upon request" and use that space to add some more helpful, relevant information.

CHECK YOUR SPELLING.

Most popular word processing programs come with a spell checking tool. This tool is a great starting point, but it should not be your only strategy for spell checking your resume.

SOME THINGS TO BE AWARE OF WHEN YOU USE SPELL CHECKING TOOLS:

You can set your spell checker to use different versions of the same language. For example, if you set your spell checking tool to use American English, it would tell you that the word "colour" was spelled incorrectly. However, if you had your spell checker set to Canadian or British English, it would consider that spelling of the word "colour" correct. Therefore, you must be certain that your spell checking tool is set to the correct version of the language you are using, or you may miss errors.

A LITTLE-KNOWN FACT ABOUT SPELL CHECK PROGRAMS:

The default setting on many spell check programs ignores words written in all capitals. Therefore, if you have written the headings of your resume in all capitals, you must be extra careful to ensure there are no spelling errors in these words because your spell checking tool may ignore them. You can also change the settings on most spell check programs to check words written in all capitals.

Read each word individually and out loud, not silently and as a part of a phrase. It is easy to skim over words when you are reading full phrases and sentences silently. To check for spelling errors, read each word on its own out loud, and be particularly careful with words that have more than one spelling such as who's and whose or their, there and they're.

Step Two
Make Final Decisions About the Order of Sections

You have made several decisions about the sections that will be included on your resume and the order in which they will appear as you worked through each chapter of this book. Now that you have written the rough draft of your resume, review the overall content and determine whether you need to make any changes to the order that sections appear on your resume.

Keep in mind that the top of the first page of your resume must include the most crucial information that will show employers you are qualified to do the job. The first few lines of your resume must draw in employers and cause them to read further. If your most crucial and impressive information is not near the top of your resume, you need to rearrange your resume.

Step Three
Choose Font and Heading Styles, and Add Bullets

Choose an appropriate font.

Stick with a fairly standard serif font (the kind with small decorative lines like Times New Roman or Georgia) or sans serif font (the kind with no extra lines like Arial) for your resume. The rule most people follow is serif fonts are most appropriate for printed documents, and sans serif fonts are used for documents that will be read on a screen.

Avoid fancy fonts; they can make your resume difficult to read and give it an unprofessional look. Also, uncommon fonts can cause problems if applicant tracking system software will be used to screen your resume.

If you are emailing your resume to employers, be aware that if you use an uncommon font, an employer may not have that font installed on his or her computer. If that happens, the employer's computer will open your resume document in another, more standard font, and that change may completely ruin the formatting of your resume.

Avoid changing fonts throughout your resume. If you use more than one font on your resume, it can start to look busy, unprofessional and difficult to read.

Although I have seen a few attractive resumes that used one font for headings and another font for the body of the resume, most job seekers are not professional designers, and there is just too much possibility to create an unprofessional looking resume when you start to get creative with fonts. Your best bet is to simply avoid this issue and stick to a single font on your resume.

You can experiment a little bit with font sizes to help your resume fit well on the page. For example, the standard size for Times New Roman is 12 point, but if you need just a little more room on your page, you can use Times New Roman at 11 point (but no smaller). Do not make your font too small or it will be unreadable. If you cannot fit everything on two pages in 11 point Times New Roman font, your resume is too long, and you need to do some editing.

Choose a heading style.

You can use several different styles for your resume headings. I would suggest trying a few different styles to determine which style looks best on your own resume. Just be sure to remain consistent throughout the document.

EXAMPLE RESUME HEADING STYLES

Lower case with bold font:

Professional Experience

Lower case with bold and italicized font:

Professional Experience

Upper case with bold font:

PROFESSIONAL EXPERIENCE

Use standard bullets.

Do not get fancy with your bullets. Stick to the standard circular bullet and avoid using fancy checkmarks, stars or other bullet styles. The fancier bullet styles look unprofessional. They generally make a poor impression and detract from the words on the page.

Step Four
Format Your Contact Information

Your contact information can be formatted in a few different ways. Later in this chapter I will show you ways to adjust the contact information to help your resume fit better on the page. For now, we will get into some overall guidelines for formatting your contact information.

Keep in mind; if you have a two-page resume, your contact information will be included on both pages of your resume. You will need to take this into consideration when you are determining how to space things on your resume.

It is crucial to have your contact information on both pages of a two-page resume so an employer could contact you even if the first page of your resume somehow went missing. Also, by including your contact information in the same format on both pages of a two-page resume, you create a letterhead effect that helps your resume look like a very pulled together and professional document.

ADD A LINE UNDER YOUR CONTACT INFORMATION.

It is always helpful to insert a line under your contact information. You can use a single solid line or a double line. Just avoid anything too fancy because it will not look professional. Adding a line under your contact information sets that section apart from your resume so the employer's eyes can jump directly to the content. The line also creates a header effect and makes your contact information look like your own professional letterhead.

MAKE YOUR NAME STAND OUT.

Your name should have a strong presence on your resume. It should be in bold font and slightly larger than the rest of the text on your resume. The font size you use will vary depending on the font you have chosen. If, for example, you are using Times New Roman throughout your resume, a 14 or 16 point font size is ideal for your name.

EXAMPLE

Jane Somebody
123 Any Street, City, State, Zip Code
_____

janesomebody@emailprovider.com   Phone: (000) 000-0000

Step Five
Format Your Employment, Education and Volunteer Information

Your employment, education and volunteer information can be formatted in a few different ways. Later in this chapter I will show you ways to adjust the set up of these sections of your resume to help your words fit better on the page. For now, we will get into some overall guidelines to follow when formatting your employment, education and volunteer information that do not affect the spacing of your resume.

Set up your resume to highlight the most important information.

Employers need to be able to read your resume quickly, so you need to set up your resume in a way that helps employers to see the most important information first.

The chart below shows what piece of information is most important in each section of your resume:

Section of Resume	Most Important Information
Employment	Job title
Education	Name of degree or diploma
Volunteer	Volunteer job title

For most people, most of the time, it is wise to set up your resume so your job titles, diploma or degree, and volunteer job titles are highlighted.

Because we read from left to right, people tend to notice things that are on the left of a document more than things that are on the right. Therefore, when you set up each of these three sections of your resume, your job titles, the name of your diplomas, and your volunteer job titles should be placed on the left side of the page, and the dates should be on the right.

Also, it is wise to use a bold font on your job titles, the names of your diplomas, and your volunteer job titles to highlight this information.

EXAMPLE

EMPLOYMENT

Administrative Assistant, ABC Organization, City, State   2012 - present
- Include information about your work in bulleted point form

EDUCATION

Business Administration Diploma, ABC College, City, State   2008
- Include information about your school in bulleted point form if appropriate

VOLUNTEER EXPERIENCE

Secretary-Treasurer, Anytown Community Organization, City, State   2013 - present
- Include information about your volunteer work in bulleted point form

---

If you review sample resumes from other sources, you will find different ways to organize these sections of your resume. Some people put the dates on the left side of the page, and others bold the company name instead of the job title. In my opinion, those variations are not as effective as the set up I have described above with the job titles, names of school programs and volunteer job titles in bold font and on the left of the page.

The one time I would make an exception to this set up would be if you worked for a very impressive employer or you went to an extremely impressive school and you truly felt that your employer was more important than your job title or the school you attended was more important than the degree you earned. This situation is rare, and most job seekers would be best served by following the examples above for setting up the employment, education and volunteer sections of their resumes.

Please do be aware that the recommendations for formatting this type of information are slightly different when an applicant tracking system will screen your resume. You can refer to chapter 13 for a detailed description of how to format your experience and education to be read by an ATS.

Step Six
Apply Formatting Rules for Two-Page Resumes if Necessary

There are a few formatting rules that are specific to two-page resumes. If you have a one-page resume, these rules will not apply to your resume.

Include your contact information on the second page.

Contact information should be included on the second page of your resume, so an employer would be able to contact you even if he or she misplaced the first page of your resume.

My recommendation is to copy the contact information from the first page of your resume and paste it on the second page of your resume. If you use exactly the same setup for your contact information on both pages of your resume, the contact information looks like your own professional letterhead and creates a very attractive, pulled together resume.

Include a page number on the second page.

Be sure to insert a page number on the second page of your resume noting that it is page 2. You can include a page number at the top right corner of the page or the bottom right or bottom middle of the page. Because the page number is helpful but not crucial information, I typically switch to a smaller font so the page number does not draw attention away from important aspects of the resume. For example, I would use a 9 or 10 point font for "page 2" if I had written the resume using 11 or 12 point font.

It is not necessary to number the first page of your resume.

Avoid breaking sections between pages whenever possible.

Moving from the first page to the second page without creating an awkward break can be the most difficult aspect of formatting a two-page resume.

If you must break a section between pages, be sure to label the second page clearly.

EXAMPLE

Imagine you have written a combination resume, and your most recent job is included on page one of your resume under the heading "Professional Experience." You have two more jobs to include on your resume, but there is no more space on the first page. In that case, begin the second page of your resume with your contact information, followed by the heading "Professional Experience Continued" so it is clear that you are continuing the section from the previous page. Then proceed to describe the next two jobs.

DO AVOID BREAKING INDIVIDUAL JOB ENTRIES UP BETWEEN PAGES ON YOUR RESUME.

EXAMPLE

Imagine you have used seven bulleted points to describe a job that you once held. You are in the process of formatting your resume, and only five of the seven points fit on page one. In this case, do not allow the last two points about the job to go over onto page two. Breaking up an entry onto two pages can make the resume confusing to read.

Apply the strategies in step seven of this chapter to make adjustments to the layout of your resume to create the space required to allow the full job entry to fit on the first page, or stretch out the spacing on the first page to cause the full job entry to move over to the second page.

Make your decision about whether to try to move the entry entirely to the first page or entirely to the second page based on the amount of information in the entry that is crossing over to the second page. In the example above, there are only two points that do not fit on the first page, so it will probably be easiest to get the job entry to fit on the first page.

Also, when dealing with the page break on a two-page resume, try to create two balanced pages with an approximately equal amount of text on each page. The two pages do not have to be perfectly balanced, and your most crucial information needs to be on the first page, but do aim for as much balance as possible when you determine where to break the information from the first page to the second page of a two-page resume.

Step Seven
Assess How Your Content Fits on the Page and Apply Strategies to Help it Fit Better if Necessary

Keep in mind, your resume should be one or two pages. Some people incorrectly believe that one-page resumes are always better than two-page resumes, and they try to jam two pages worth of information onto a single page.

Do not try to pack too much information on a single page; it makes your resume difficult and frustrating to read. If you have a very full one-page resume that is crammed full of information and difficult to read, you are better off going to a two-page resume.

One of the trickiest aspects of resume formatting is getting the resume to sit well on one or two pages. If you have just a little bit too much information, or not quite enough information to fill a page, you will need to make a few adjustments.

Use some simple tricks to make your resume fit on the page.

1. ADJUST THE STYLE OF THE CONTACT INFORMATION SECTION

Your contact information can be formatted in a few different ways. I never format contact information on a resume until the resume is almost complete because it is necessary to know how the rest of the resume is fitting on the page to determine the best way to set up the contact information.

WHAT TO DO IF YOU HAVE A FULL RESUME

If you have a very full resume, and you need to preserve space on your resume, keep your contact information fairly compact by stretching the information across a couple of lines.

EXAMPLE

Jane Somebody
123 Any Street, City, State, Zip Code   Phone: (000) 000-0000

janesomebody@emailprovider.com

WHAT TO DO IF YOU HAVE A SHORT RESUME

If your resume looks a bit sparse, and you need to fill out a little space, set up your contact information across several lines so it takes up more space. This style of contact information looks best when it is centered on the page. Notice I used a slightly larger font (18 point instead of 16 point) for the name, which makes the contact information section take up just a little more room.

EXAMPLE

Jane Somebody

123 Any Street,
City, State, Zip Code
Phone: (000) 000-0000
janesomebody@emailprovider.com

2. CHANGE THE ARRANGEMENT FOR YOUR JOB AND/OR SCHOOL INFORMATION

The way you structure your job and education information can have a huge impact on the way your resume fits on the page.

If you have a very full resume, and you need more space, try to fit all of the information on a single line. If you have a very long job title or company name, you may not be able to fit all of your employment information on a single line, but if the information will fit, this strategy is an easy way to gain a few extra lines on your resume.

EXAMPLES

Administrative Assistant, ABC Organization, City, State	2012 - present
Business Administration Diploma, ABC College, City, State	2008

If your resume does not quite fill the page, use two lines when you note your job title and company name and/or your diploma and school. This setup takes up a few extra lines, and can help fill out the page.

EXAMPLES

Administrative Assistant
ABC Organization, City, State   2012 - present

Business Administration Diploma
ABC College, City, State   2008

---

3. ADJUST THE FONT

You can make small adjustments to the font size to make room for extra information on a resume. Do not go more than one size smaller than the standard font size (for example, Times New Roman should be no smaller than 11 point) because if the font is any smaller, it will be too difficult to read.

Be consistent with font sizes in the body of your resume. Do not use 12 point font for 75% of the resume and then switch to 11 point to fit in some extra information at the end of your resume. With the exception of your name (which should be a slightly larger font size) you must use a single font size throughout the text of your resume.

I would not recommend using the opposite strategy and increasing the font size to fill out a sparse resume. Increasing the font size is more obvious than decreasing it and can give your resume and unprofessional look.

4. ADJUST THE PAGE MARGINS

If you need a little extra space to fit a lot of information on your resume, you can make small adjustments to the page margins. Do not decrease the margins too much, or your resume will look too full and you may have difficulty printing the document, but decreasing the margins just a bit may be enough to give you the little bit of extra space you need to make your resume sit well on the page.

If your resume is not as full as you would like, you can increase the margins on the page. Do not increase the margins too much because it will make your resume look sparse, but a small change in the margins can help improve the spacing of a resume that does not fully fill out a page.

5. REWORD PHRASES TO ADJUST THE LENGTH

If your resume is too full and you need more space, look for places on your resume where you could change the wording of a phrase to gain an extra line. Look for lines on your resume where your phrase has run over into a second line, but there is only one or two words on the second line. Try to rephrase that line to eliminate a word or two and make it fit on a single line instead of two lines. However, do not compromise clarity to find an extra line or two on your resume.

EXAMPLE

Imagine you have the following point on a very full resume:

> • Proven ability to resolve common computer hardware issues for staff and clients in resource center

To gain an entire extra line of space, simply omit a word or two without changing the meaning of the point:

> • Resolve computer hardware issues for staff and clients in resource center

This strategy works in reverse. If you need to fill out a resume that does not cover an entire page, look for lines that come right to the end of a line and ask yourself whether you could add a single word (perhaps an adjective describing how you performed the task) to cause the point to go over onto a second line. Take care to avoid padding your resume with meaningless words. The point is to add a word or two to help your resume sit well on the page and add meaningful information, not to pad your entire resume full of meaningless phrases.

7. CONSIDER ADDING OR OMITTING SOME INFORMATION

If you have tried the strategies described above, and your resume still does not fit well on a page, ask yourself whether there is any more information you can add (if you resume does not fill the page) or remove (if you have too much information to fit on a page or two).

By the time you are at this stage of writing your resume, you should have included all of the important information and omitted anything that is not relevant, so you will need to be careful to ensure you are not simply adding filler if your resume is a bit thin or removing something important if your resume is too full. However, sometimes a single line added or removed can make all the difference in making a resume look great and fit well on the page.

8. ADJUST THE SPACES BETWEEN LINES

This strategy is the last thing I do when trying to fit a resume on a page. I only use this strategy when nothing else has solved the problem of the resume not fitting well on the page.

IF YOUR PAGE IS TOO FULL...

If you have a very full resume, and you have tried all of the other strategies, but you still need another line or two to make your resume fit on the page, consider changing the font size of the blank lines on your resume. So, for example, if you have used 11 point font throughout your resume, but you need a little more room, place your cursor at each blank line on your resume, and change the font size to 10 point. Sometimes this little change is enough to give you that last bit of space you need.

Do be very careful about using this strategy. It works, but remember, if you have gone through all of the other strategies to fit your resume on a page or two, and you still need more room, it is very likely that you have too much information on your resume, and you need to make a decision to omit something.

White space is important on a resume because it makes it more readable at a glance. Do not make the blank lines on your resume more than one point smaller than the text on your resume, or you will risk creating a resume that is too jam packed to be read quickly.

IF YOUR PAGE IS NOT FULL ENOUGH...

If your resume does not completely fill out a full page or two, you may increase the size of the blank lines on your resume just a bit. Avoid making the spaces too big (one point larger than the font size is a good option) or your resume will look sparse.

Step Eight
Print, Proofread and Revise

Once you feel your resume is sitting nicely on the page, print out a hard copy of your resume to proofread.

Avoid proofreading on your computer screen. Reading from a screen is 25% more difficult than reading from paper. Therefore, if you proofread from paper, you will catch errors more easily than you will if you proofread from your computer screen.

Whenever possible, take a break before you proofread. It will be much easier to find errors if you avoid proofreading immediately after writing and formatting your work.

Tips for proofreading your resume:

- Read the document through once to get an overview of your resume.

- Read through the text a few times. One read through is usually not enough to catch all errors.

- Check for inconsistencies in the style of headings and the way you have structured information.

- Cover the lines below the one you are currently reading with a blank piece of paper to help you focus carefully on one word at a time and prevent your eyes from jumping ahead to the next section.

- Use a spell check and grammar check tool to catch some spelling and grammatical errors. Do remember, though, that spell check and grammar check tools will not find every type of error in your writing.

- Read the document out loud to help ensure each phrase you have written is understandable.

- Read the text backwards to look for spelling errors. Reading the text backwards will help you avoid skimming over the text.

- Check dates for accuracy.

- Carefully check your contact information, especially your phone number and email address to ensure they are correct.

Ask someone who is a strong writer to proofread your resume for you. Another person can find your errors and bad writing habits more easily than you can find your own.

Make any revisions necessary based on this review. Print the document, and complete one final review yourself.

Your Resume is Complete!

Your resume will have some differences compared with the example depending upon choices you have made along the way, but when you are finished formatting your resume, your document will look something like this:

Jane Somebody

123 Any Street, Faketown, State, Zip Code

janesomebody@emailprovider.com   Phone: (000) 000-0000

Profile

Administrative professional with seven years of experience in the nonprofit sector. Able to prioritize and manage conflicting demands. Exceptional technical skills including proficiency with Word, Excel, PowerPoint and Prezi; type 80 words per minute.

Summary of Skills

- Proven ability to meet strict deadlines, ensure accuracy of work and manage conflicting demands effectively
- Thorough knowledge of and ability to research community resources developed over 7 years working at local, non-profit community organizations
- Able to resolve common computer hardware issues for staff and clients in resource center
- Exhibit a professional and welcoming demeanor to clients and co-workers; earned reputation as a resourceful problem solver with high degree of integrity
- Bilingual in English and Spanish

Professional Experience

Administrative Assistant

ABC Organization, City, State   2012 - present

- Provide administrative support to two workshop facilitators; assist additional team of counselors as required
- Prepare correspondence and training materials for facilitators
- Contact clients by telephone on a weekly basis to ensure participation in workshops, and promote agency programs; telephone contact improves workshop attendance by 20%
- Accurately manage client data for up to 1000 clients per year using Excel and complete monthly, quarterly and annual reports for counselors, executive director and funding partners
- Developed new database system to efficiently compile and analyze large volume and variety of client data; new system significantly reduced time required to complete monthly, quarterly and annual reports
- Liaise with community partners to determine additional resources for clients and colleagues and to promote agency programs

Jane Somebody

123 Any Street, Faketown, State, Zip Code

janesomebody@emailprovider.com   Phone: (000) 000-0000

Professional Experience Continued

Administrative Assistant

XYZ Organization, City, State   2008 - 2012

- Provided administrative support for team of six counselors, each managing a case load of 100+ clients per year
- Prepared confidential correspondence and scheduled meetings for counselors
- Independently researched and developed teaching resources and community resource packages for counselors and clients
- Provide reception assistance and administrative support for executive director

Receptionist

Another Organization, City, State   2007 - 2008

- Provided professional, friendly telephone and in person assistance for clients; answered approximately 50 incoming calls per day on a multi-line system and greeted and assisted up to 30 clients per day in a resource center environment
- Received and distributed incoming mail; responded to mail and email inquiries
- Ensured office equipment was in working order and rectified common computer hardware problems for clients and colleagues
- Prepared confidential correspondence for colleagues
- Scheduled appointments for staff of seven counselors and organized monthly team meetings and charity events
- Maintained office supply inventory; tracked and ordered supplies monthly

Education

Business Administration Diploma, ABC College, City, State   2007

Community Involvement

Secretary-Treasurer

- Anytown Community Organization, City, State   2013 - present
- Manage all website updates, and write and distribute meeting minutes and newsletters to staff and volunteers
- Receive donations, issue receipts for cash received, maintain payment records
- Manage budgets, accounts and financial statements and present financial data to the management committee
- Prepare Treasurer's Report for annual general meeting and advise management committee on funding requirements for future projects

Assignment

Format and proofread your resume. Remember, this process takes some work. Be prepared to spend some time experimenting with different strategies to get your resume to sit well on the page. Take the time necessary to proofread your resume effectively. Employers think of your resume as an example of your very best work, so it must be error-free.

Moving Forward

You are ready to move on to the next chapter if you...

1. Have formatted your resume so it fits well on one or two pages.

2. Have carefully proofread your resume and are convinced your resume is error-free.

CHAPTER THIRTEEN
WRITE AN APPLICANT TRACKING SYSTEM OPTIMIZED RESUME

YOUR TASKS FOR THIS CHAPTER:

1. Understand how applicant tracking systems (ATS) are used in the job search process and know how to write and format your resume to score as well as possible in ATS screening.
2. Research relevant keywords to include on your ATS optimized resume.
3. Ensure all relevant keywords and synonyms have been included on your ATS optimized resume.
4. Format your resume to be read by ATS software
5. Know how to correctly save and submit your resume when the employers uses ATS software.

ACTION STEPS FOR THIS CHAPTER

Step One: Understand how applicant tracking systems are used to screen resumes.

Step Two: Discover the general best practices for writing resumes for ATS screening.

Step Three: Learn what you must avoid when writing an ATS optimized resume.

Step Four:	Add relevant keywords to your ATS optimized resume.
Step Five:	Write and format each section of your resume for optimal ATS screening.
Step Six:	Save your ATS optimized resume.
Step Seven:	Submit your ATS optimized resume.
Step Eight:	Know where to find information for formatting ATS-reviewed resumes vs. human-reviewed resumes.

"Acquiring preemptive knowledge about emerging technologies is the best way to ensure that we have a say in the making of our future." Catarina Mota

PLEASE DO NOT SKIP CHAPTER 12.

Before we get into the information about writing and formatting your resume for review by an applicant tracking system, please be sure you have not completely skipped chapter 12, Formatting Your Resume for Human Readers. If you skipped that chapter because you knew you were formatting your resume for an ATS, please go back and read the first section of chapter 12, which describes how to review your work, before you begin working on the formatting described in this chapter. Reviewing your work is important whether you are formatting your resume for a human reader or for an ATS.

IS THIS CHAPTER RELEVANT TO YOU?

Please be aware that not all job seekers will encounter applicant tracking systems. Generally, people who are targeting larger companies and jobs that are advertised online are more likely to encounter ATS screening. People who are applying to jobs with smaller companies and unadvertised jobs are less likely to encounter ATS screening.

There are really two components to writing an ATS optimized resume:

- Formatting for the ATS
  and
- Targeting the resume with keyword-rich content (good research is part of this component)

Of course, if you are pursuing jobs with companies that do use ATS screening, both components will be relevant to you.

If you will never need to write an ATS optimized resume, the information about *formatting* will not be relevant to you, but the information about *targeting your resume* and *researching jobs* will be relevant. Scoring well in ATS screening requires a higher level of excellence and clarity when writing content for your resume. That higher level of excellence in research, targeting and writing can also be applied to human-reviewed resumes. Improving your writing skills and better targeting your resumes is useful no matter how your resume will be screened.

SOME CLARIFICATION ON KEYWORDS AND PHRASES:

Finally, please note that I write a lot about keywords in this chapter. Whenever I mention keywords, I am referring to a single word, or an exact phrase consisting of a few words that might be used to search for qualified job candidates. Please assume I am referring to both single words and to phrases anytime you see the word "keywords."

Step One
Understand How Applicant Tracking Systems Are Used to Screen Resumes

Applicant tracking system screening is becoming a more important part of the hiring process. Unfortunately, many job seekers are still unaware of the importance of optimizing a resume when it will be screened by an ATS, and sometimes very qualified candidates are never considered for jobs because they did not understand how to create a resume that works with this type of software.

The use of applicant tracking systems has raised the bar in terms of the need to write highly targeted resumes for each job you apply to.

We have covered a lot of information in the past few chapters, so before we get into the details, I would like to quickly refresh your memory from chapter 3 about ATS basics.

Review applicant tracking system basics.

An applicant tracking system is software that allows employers to post jobs, receive resumes, analyze resumes for their degree of fit with the job to be filled, and track applicants through the rest of the hiring process. Applicant tracking systems are more than just resume screening software, but their resume screening function is the part of the process you need to understand.

IN THE RESUME SCREENING STAGE OF THE JOB SEARCH PROCESS AN APPLICANT TRACKING SYSTEM WILL:

- Receive resumes submitted by job applicants

- Interpret the information on all resumes submitted for a job opening

- Organize the information, putting it into specific categories like work experience, education and contact information

- Analyze the content of resumes, looking for specific criteria such as amount of experience, type of education and relevant skills

- Score resumes based on how well they match the criteria for the job

- Return only a few top-scoring resumes for the employer to review

"Scoring well in ATS screening requires a higher level of excellence and clarity when writing content for your resume."

If an employer uses an ATS, your resume must be optimized to score well in that type of screening in order to have a chance of moving on to the next phase of the hiring process. There are many applicant tracking systems with different capabilities. In general, though, an ATS can search by:

- Keywords or phrases on your resume that match keywords or phrases describing the requirements of the job

- Job titles you have included on your resume, noting whether they match with the job title of the position being filled

- Length of experience and recentness of experience based on the dates in the work history section of the resume

- Percent the resume matches the job posting

- Rare keywords, giving extra weight to relevant skills and qualifications that many job seekers do not possess

In addition to writing a resume that contains enough keywords and phrases to score well in ATS screening, you also must format your resume correctly to be read by this software. ATS software is still somewhat limited and flawed, and incorrect formatting can "choke" the software causing it to interpret your resume incorrectly or completely fail to read sections. When incorrect formatting chokes the ATS software, excellent, well-qualified candidates can be eliminated from competition for the job.

The increasing use of ATS software to screen resumes does add an entirely new dimension for job seekers to consider. However, the good news is, once you complete this chapter, you will have a solid understanding of how to write and format your resume to score as well as possible in ATS screening. That knowledge will give you a big advantage over a lot of job seekers.

APPLICANT TRACKING SYSTEMS AND ADVERTISED JOBS

As you read through this chapter, you will notice that I refer to advertised jobs frequently. That is because often, when you are writing an ATS optimized resume, it will be in response to a job you found advertised online.

I am a huge advocate of taking full advantage of the hidden job market and doing everything you can to find unadvertised jobs, so in the rest of the book, I have not assumed you are writing a resume for an advertised job. The comments in this chapter about job ads should not dissuade you from looking for unadvertised jobs. In fact, accessing the hidden job market is one way to help avoid or reduce the need to go through ATS screening because your resume is more likely to be seen by a human reviewer when the job has not been advertised.

Step Two
Discover the General Best Practices for Writing Resumes for ATS Screening

Here are several general best practices that can help your resume score as well as possible in the ATS screening stage of the hiring process.

YOU *MUST* WRITE A TARGETED RESUME

I have always encouraged clients to write a targeted resume for each job they pursue. Before employers started using applicant tracking systems, writing a targeted resume was a good strategy to help you stand out just a bit better than the average applicant. With the growing use of applicant tracking systems, targeting your resume has become more than just a good strategy for getting ahead of the competition. Targeting your resume is an absolute necessity to get through the initial phase of the hiring process when an ATS is used to screen resumes.

You really need to match your resume to the job ad and the company as much as possible. Be sure to include keywords throughout your resume, do not simply fill your most recent job with keywords and ignore the rest of your resume. Including relevant keywords throughout your resume helps to communicate the idea that you have a solid depth of industry experience.

USE REASONABLY SIZED, SIMPLE AND COMMON FONTS

- Stick to a single font and size

- Use common fonts. Standard sans serif fonts like Arial or Verdana are safe choices. Remember, sans serif fonts (fonts that do not have decoration like Arial and Verdana) are easier to read online than serif fonts (fonts that do have decoration, like Georgia). Serif fonts are often used for documents that will be printed (for example, a paper copy of your resume), while sans serif fonts are often used for documents that will be read on a screen.

- Do not go too extreme with font sizes. Keep your font size between 11 and 16 point. 12 point font is safe and fairly standard. Remember, you do not have to fit an ATS optimized resume perfectly on a page, so there really is no reason to be manipulating font sizes.

USE ONE-INCH MARGINS

Keep your margins to one inch at the top and bottom of each page. Again, you do not need to fit an ATS optimized resume perfectly on a page, so there is absolutely no need to manipulate the margins on your page.

YOUR RESUME MUST BE ERROR-FREE

This advice is also true for the traditional, human-reviewed resume, but when an ATS reads your resume, it will not recognize a misspelled word, so you will not get points for that skill if you have spelled the word incorrectly.

A misspelled word will cause a negative impression if a human reviews your resume, and it can be enough for the employer to decide not to bring you in for an interview. However, that human will usually know what you meant, and if the rest of your resume is impressive, and there are not a lot of other strong candidates for the job, the employer may still decide to bring you in for an interview in spite of the misspelled word.

On the other hand, the ATS is not capable of interpreting what you intended to write if you misspell a word. If that misspelled word happens to describe a crucial skill, your score will be lower because the ATS will not recognize the skill for what it is.

Errors on resumes are always problematic, but they can be doubly problematic when your resume is screened by an ATS.

USE BLANK LINES TO SEPARATE SECTIONS

Use blank lines before heading titles to separate sections, but ensure there are no blank lines separating information that belongs together. For example, include a blank line before the heading for a new section like this:

Business Administration Diploma
ABC College
City, State
2007

VOLUNTEER

Notice the blank line between the educational information and the heading "volunteer." This blank line helps the ATS to understand that it has reached a new section of the resume.

Do ensure any related chunk of information, such as all components of a job description, remain together with no blank lines, like this:

XYZ Organization
City, State
Administrative Assistant
2008 - 2012
- Provided administrative support for team of six counselors, each managing a case load of 100+ clients per year
- Prepared confidential correspondence and scheduled meetings for counselors
- Provide reception assistance and administrative support for executive director

---

Notice there is no blank line separating any part of this chunk of information. Keeping related information all together as shown in this example helps the ATS understand this information is describing a single item.

KEEP YOUR CONTACT INFORMATION SIMPLE

Include your name and nothing else on the top line. Do not add degrees or certifications after your name. Put those in the body of your resume. ATS software is programmed to expect certain information in certain places. At the beginning of your resume, it is looking for your name and your contact information. It is not necessarily looking for professional designations or degrees, so including that information at the top can cause some applicant tracking systems to misinterpret your resume.

USE POINT FORM LISTS WITH STANDARD BULLETS

Avoid writing in full paragraph form. The ATS may not recognize different points if they are written in paragraph form.

When you describe your skills, accomplishments and experience, use bulleted point form. Bullets help the ATS differentiate between points. Do use the standard round bullet, and avoid using any of the other fancy bullets. Fancy bullets are non-standard characters, and they may choke the ATS.

REMEMBER THE HUMAN READER

You will make a lot of formatting and content choices that are designed to please the ATS. Do remember, however, if you make it through the ATS screening process, your resume will be viewed by a human reader, so your resume does need to be readable by a human.

You need to avoid fancy formatting, and employers who use applicant tracking systems do know your resume will be formatted differently than traditional, human-reviewed resumes. However, you can make your ATS optimized resume as attractive as possible for human readers by using bold fond, capitals and bullet points to organize your material.

YOUR RESUME CAN BE LONGER WHEN IT IS BEING FILTERED THROUGH AN ATS

While it is advisable to keep your resume to a maximum of two pages when a human will review it, an ATS resume can be longer. In fact, if you need the extra space to include important, relevant keywords, it *should* be longer.

The ATS does not care how long your resume is, and by the time your resume is seen by a human, that person is only looking at the top few resumes that have been prescreened by that ATS. Once your resume gets to the employer, that person is not reading through hundreds of resumes.

Employers know it is very likely you are a reasonably good fit for the job because you passed the ATS test, so they can spend a little more time with your resume than they would if they were hand-sorting hundreds of resumes.

Do not take this recommendation to the extreme. Avoid stuffing your resume, but also do not sacrifice showing great experience just because your resume is getting longer. If you need more than two pages to include all of your relevant information on a resume that will be screened by an ATS, do not worry about the extra length. Your goal here is to find a balance between pleasing the ATS and pleasing the human reader.

AN ATS RESUME DOES NOT HAVE TO FIT PERFECTLY ON THE PAGE

You do not have to worry about using all kinds of fancy formatting tricks to make an ATS optimized resume fit nicely on the page. Save those tricks for human-reviewed resumes. In fact, fancy formatting can choke an ATS, so it must be avoided.

Summary of ATS Optimized Resume Writing Best Practices

- Target your resume to the job and the employer.
- Use a standard font and standard font size.
- Use one-inch margins.
- Your resume must be error-free.
- Use blank lines to separate sections, and do not use blank lines between information that belongs together.
- Keep contact information simple.
- Use standard round bullets.
- Remember, a human will eventually read your resume if it scores well in ATS screening.
- Your ATS optimized resume can be more than two pages if necessary.
- Your ATS optimized resume does not have to fit well on the page.

Step Three
Learn What You Must Avoid When Writing an ATS Optimized Resume

AVOID FANCY FORMATTING INCLUDING:

- Headers
- Footers
- Templates
- Borders
- Shading
- Lines
- Text boxes
- Symbols
- Accents on words or other special characters (standard round bullets are acceptable)

All of this fancy formatting can cause the ATS to have difficulty reading and interpreting your resume.

AVOID LARGE FONTS

Some applicant tracking systems do not read font larger than 16 point.

AVOID ITALICS AND UNDERLINES

Reading italics and underlined text can be problematic for some applicant tracking system software. Instead, use words in all capitals and bold font to highlight sections of your resume.

AVOID EXTRA SPACES BETWEEN WORDS, AND LEFT ALIGN EVERYTHING

Some applicant tracking systems are not designed to handle extra spaces between words. Avoid using more than one space between words. Also, left justify everything, and avoid full justifying text. If you are not familiar with the term "full justified" it refers to text that is even on both the left and right sides of the page like the text in this book. ATS optimized resumes should have text justified (with an even edge) on the left only; the right side should be ragged (not justified).

DO NOT "GAME THE SYSTEM"

Avoid simply stuffing in piles of keywords. Remember, if you pass the ATS screening process, a human will eventually review your resume. You need to write for the software screening and for a human review.

Summary of Things to Avoid on Your ATS Optimized Resume

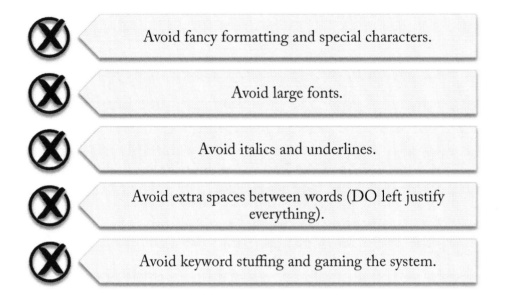

Avoid fancy formatting and special characters.

Avoid large fonts.

Avoid italics and underlines.

Avoid extra spaces between words (DO left justify everything).

Avoid keyword stuffing and gaming the system.

Step Four
Add Relevant Keywords to Your ATS Optimized Resume

Including relevant keywords in your resume is crucial to passing the ATS screening process. To get the keywords right, you need to understand two things:

- How applicant tracking systems assess keywords on resumes

- How to find the right keywords to include on each resume you submit

How applicant tracking systems assess keywords:

Different applicant tracking systems will assess keywords in slightly different ways, and newer ATS software is generally better at analyzing keywords in more complex ways. However, there are some standard guidelines you can follow when thinking about how to include keywords on your ATS optimized resume.

MIRROR THE LANGUAGE IN THE JOB AD, BUT AVOID SIMPLY COPYING THE ENTIRE AD

It is important to include keywords and keyword phrases from the job ad in your resume. In fact, it is advisable to write keyword phrases *exactly as they are written in the ad* because these phrases are the ones the ATS will most likely search for when scoring your resume. You may have exactly the type of experience an employer needs, but if you do not use the language used in the job ad to describe that experience, your resume may not score well in the ATS screening process, and human eyes may never see your resume.

On the other side of this coin, you also must avoid simply copying and pasting the job ad into your resume. Instead, you need to naturally work the relevant keywords and phrases into the descriptions of your skills, experience and accomplishments.

INCLUDE ALL OF YOUR SPECIALIZED, RELEVANT SKILLS

Ensure you include all skills that are specialized and relevant to your work. Do not assume the employer will know that you used a specific skill or have a specific body of knowledge simply because you have experience in your field.

A human who is screening a resume may be able to read between the lines and realize that someone with experience in a certain job likely has skills that are not listed on the resume. ATS software cannot make these types of inferences. An ATS can only score the actual information on the page, so you must include on your resume all skills that are relevant and specialized in your field. Do not assume anything.

USE SYNONYMS, ACRONYMS, AND THE FULL VERSION OF IMPORTANT KEYWORDS

There are ways to research and predict the keywords an ATS is most likely to use to score your resume, which will be discussed later in this chapter. However, even with excellent research, you will not know with absolute certainty all of the keywords the ATS will use to score the resumes that are submitted. For that reason, you need to include variations of relevant keywords to increase the likelihood of hitting the most important keywords.

EXAMPLE

- Be sure to use both the complete, spelled out version of a skill or qualification as well as the acronym. For example, if you have completed an MBA degree, use both the phrase "Master of Business Administration Degree" and the acronym "MBA Degree" in your resume.

- Skills that are frequently grouped together should be listed in the group and individually. For example, if you are skilled with Microsoft Office, mention Microsoft Word, Excel, PowerPoint, and Access individually, but also use the phrase Microsoft Office somewhere on your resume.

USE KEYWORDS IN CONTEXT

This recommendation is a bit controversial. Some professional resume writers recommend you include a list of keywords near the top of your resume, while other resume writers recommend you avoid simple keyword lists, and instead, write phrases that use the keywords in context to describe your skills and accomplishments.

I prefer to use keywords in context, but I can see the reasoning behind the recommendation to use keyword lists. Keyword lists provide an easy place to fit a lot of relevant keywords near the top of your resume, and a human reviewer can read single keywords easily, at a glance.

However, keywords in lists do not demonstrate your level of skill. Remember, when you write a resume, you are not just trying to show an employer that you have a specific set of skills, you are also trying to show the employer that you are more proficient with those skills than all of the other job seekers who have the same set of skills. A keyword list does not allow you to explain your proficiency with a skill.

"You are not just trying to show an employer that you have a specific set of skills, you are also trying to show the employer that you are more proficient with those skills than all of the other job seekers who have the same set of skills."

Weaving keywords in context into point form phrases that describe your accomplishments allows you to "prove your brags" better. It gives you opportunities to quantify and provide more information. Anyone can write a list of buzzwords, but the added information you can include when you use keywords in context helps to back up your claims to each skill.

Also, newer ATS software has an improved ability to interpret the context in which a keyword is used. That means it is not enough to simply stuff your resume with long lists of keywords. Instead, you need to include the keywords within the context of your professional experience and accomplishments.

In previous chapters in this book you learned how to effectively write about your accomplishments and experience. In order to make those points ATS-friendly, you will simply need to work relevant keywords and keyword phrases into the points you have already written. In my opinion, this approach to adding keywords to your resume is more effective for the more sophisticated ATS software, and it is more effective for the human reader.

RARE, RELEVANT SKILLS ARE IMPORTANT

Applicant tracking systems do not necessarily weight all relevant keywords equally. They can give extra points to rare, relevant skills. So if you have a skill that is relevant to the job, and a lot of other job seekers do not have that skill, your rare skill can help your resume score better in ATS screening.

COMPETING COMPANY NAMES MIGHT HELP

An ATS might search resumes for competitors' names. Look for ways to include these names on your resume if you have experience with industry competitors.

How to find important industry keywords:

You understand why and how you should include keywords on your resume when it will be screened by an ATS. Now you need to know where to find these keywords.

You can look for important keywords on three different levels. *You should look for keywords that are relevant to:*

- The specific job you are seeking
- The company that is hiring
- Your industry

FIND KEYWORDS THAT ARE RELEVANT TO THE SPECIFIC JOB YOU ARE SEEKING

Start by looking for keywords in the job ad. This step is the easiest and most important way to determine which keywords and phrases need to be included on an ATS optimized resume.

Some people recommend copying and pasting the text of the job ad into software that automatically analyses text to determine which words are most common and relevant. Taking this step can't hurt, but I would suggest you read through the job ad manually to look for important keywords yourself. Job ads are not terribly long, and reading through an ad carefully, looking for keywords and determining what is most important to the employer will give you a deeper understanding of the job, which will help you write a better resume. An automated scan of the text would not provide that level of understanding.

Either copy and paste the job ad into your favorite word processing software, and use the highlight tool to highlight important words, or print up a paper copy of the ad, and use a highlighter to highlight important words. Those words and phrases that you highlight are the beginning of the list of words you will want to consider including on your resume.

As you work through your analysis of the job ad, try to determine which keywords are most important to the employer. You may end up with a very long list of keywords, and prioritizing the most important ones will help you to decide which ones absolutely must be on your resume at least once, and maybe more than once.

To determine which keywords are most important, look for words that are mentioned frequently. These words may indicate skills that are particularly important to the employer. Similarly, look for a distinction between crucial skills and not necessary, but nice-to-have skills. Certainly, if you possess the nice-to-have skills, you will include them on your resume, but the crucial skills must absolutely be included on your resume whenever it is possible to do so honestly.

You can't say you have a skill that you do not have simply for the sake of adding an important keyword or phrase to your resume. However, you should think very carefully about each skill mentioned in the job ad, and ask yourself whether there is any way at all you could honestly include

"Targeting your resume is an absolute necessity to get through the initial phase of the hiring process when an ATS is used to screen resumes."

that skill on your resume.

Once you have analyzed the job ad thoroughly, take some time to think through the job. Imagine you are an employer who is hiring someone to fill this position. Ask yourself what skills you would be looking for in a candidate and what keywords you would use to try to search for resumes of qualified candidates. Make a list of all of the keywords you come up with.

FIND KEYWORDS THAT ARE RELEVANT TO THE COMPANY THAT IS HIRING

Next, look for information about the company that is hiring. Start by visiting their website, and look them up on social sites like LinkedIn and perhaps Facebook and Twitter if they have a social media presence.

Gather as much information as you can about the company, the work that they do, the customers or clients they serve and their corporate values. The "about us" or "mission statement" section on a company's website is often a good place to start. Also, the "about us" statement on any social media accounts often contains good, concise information about what the company does, who they serve, how they differentiate themselves from the competition, and how they view themselves as an organization. As you read about the company, make note of any words, phrases or ideas that stand out to you. These words and phrases may also be good keywords to include on your resume if you can add them in a natural, meaningful way.

FIND KEYWORDS THAT ARE RELEVANT TO YOUR INDUSTRY

It is wise to build a list of industry keywords and add to it as you job search. You can start this process by collecting several ads for the type of job you are seeking and reviewing all of the ads to look for the skills employers are requesting. Five or six ads should be enough to provide you with the information you are looking for. These ads do not have to be for perfect jobs. For example, the job might be too far away for you to consider pursuing. That is fine, as long as the job ads show a good representation of the type of job that interests you.

You can either print up the job ads and highlight important keywords in each ad, or you can copy and paste them all into a Microsoft Word document and analyze them there. Use whichever strategy works best with your own working and thinking style.

Once you have highlighted all of the important keywords, make lists of them. Be sure to notice which skills are mentioned in almost all of the ads, and which are mentioned only occasionally or in certain niches of your industry. Note these observations on your list of keywords; it will help you to gauge the importance of specific skills in your industry.

As I mentioned earlier in this chapter, some people recommend analyzing job ads by pasting the text of the ads into a program that automatically analyzes text. While this strategy is faster than analyzing each ad manually, it does not give you the same insight. I would recommend going through each ad the old fashioned way - reading and understanding each point. It will take a little longer, but you will have a deeper understanding of what employers are looking for if you analyze the ads yourself.

Once you have analyzed a few job ads that are representative of the type of job you are seeking and made a list of common keywords used in those ads, you can go back to the points you have written for each section of your resume and look for places to naturally add in those keywords and phrases.

Yes, this industry analysis is an investment of time, but it provides valuable information, and you will only have to do it once. You can save this information and use it on subsequent jobs that interest you.

This type of analysis can also help you find holes in the information you have included on your resume. If employers in your field frequently request a skill you possess, and you have not included that skill on your resume, you will need to find a way to add that skill to your resume. If employers in your field frequently request a skill you do not possess, try to find a way to develop that skill so you can honestly include it on your resume.

FIND SYNONYMS

Once you have completed all of the research described above, you will have a thorough list of keywords and phrases to consider including on your resume. Your final step is to consider any common synonyms an employer might use to express a specific skill. Look at your list of keywords and phrases, and ask yourself whether any of the words or phrases on the list are commonly stated in a different way in your industry. If there is a commonly used synonym for an important keyword or phrase, add that synonym to your list.

Step Five
Write and Format Each Section of Your Resume for Optimal ATS Screening

Use a few standard section headings in a predictable order.

Headings are important because they help direct the ATS software to each section of your resume and interpret the information accurately. Stick with common headings like:

Summary
Profile
Work Experience
Education
Certifications
Volunteer Work

AVOID USING NON-STANDARD HEADINGS

It is important to avoid non-standard headings and avoid combining resume sections under one heading. Applicant tracking systems use headings to help interpret and categorize the rest of the information on your resume, so if you use a non-standard heading that the ATS software does not recognize, your resume may not be interpreted correctly.

For example, a section called Education and Certifications can confuse an ATS that has been designed to look for the standard heading, Education.

For the same reason, you should avoid breaking a skills summary into sub-sections if you think your resume will be read by an ATS. You learned in chapter 8, if your resume is going to be screened by a human, and you have a long list of skills to include, that long list would be more readable if you divide it into smaller sections with subheadings. This strategy is not recommended for ATS optimized resumes because there is a good chance the ATS will not understand any non-standard subheadings you would use to categorize your skills. If you have a long list of skills, and your resume will be screened by an ATS, simply keep that list of skills under a standard heading such as Summary.

USE STRAIGHTFORWARD, PREDICTABLE RESUME ORGANIZATION

In other sections of this book, you will find suggestions for reorganizing parts of your experience to help you move the most crucial information to the top of your resume. For example, in chapter 9 you saw how to move older work experience to the top of your resume if your most recent experience is not your most relevant, and in chapter 9, you also learned how to move your volunteer experience to the top of your resume if it was more relevant than your current work experience.

While these recommendations can be very effective when a human reader will review your resume, they may be problematic when your resume will be screened by an ATS. Applicant tracking systems have limitations, and some applicant tracking systems may not interpret your information correctly if you stray from the most standard, straightforward resume organization. A safe way to organize the sections of your ATS optimized resume is as follows:

Contact Information
Profile
Summary
Work Experience
Education
Volunteer Work (if it is relevant)

There may be other sections you will include, such as certifications, or publications if they are relevant to you, but the list above represents the most common sections in a resume.

USE CAPITALS AND BOLDED TEXT TO VISUALLY ORGANIZE AND HIGHLIGHT INFORMATION

Typing section headings in all capitals and using bold font can help the applicant tracking system categorize your information. Capitalized and bolded section headings can also make the resume more readable to the human eye once it reaches the human review stage. Your section headings will look something like this:

PROFILE

SUMMARY

WORK EXPERIENCE

EDUCATION

Do be careful when you type anything in all capital letters. The spell check function on most word processing programs is set up by default to ignore any words that are typed in all capitals. That means you cannot rely on spell check to catch any errors you may have made while typing a word in all capitals. Please be extra careful when you proofread anything typed in all capital letters.

INCLUDE A BLANK LINE BETWEEN SECTIONS

Including a single blank line between sections can help the ATS determine where one section ends and a new section begins. It can also make your resume more readable for human eyes. Do not add any more than a single line between sections, and do not add extra spaces between words.

OMIT THE PHRASE "REFERENCES AVAILABLE UPON REQUEST"

This phrase is really not necessary on your resume. Employers typically do not need your references until after you have attended an interview. If they want references before the job interview stage, they will ask for them. The phrase "references available upon request" is not necessary and does not add any helpful information to your resume.

Edit and format your contact information for the ATS.

Here are some guidelines for formatting your contact information for a resume that will be screened by ATS software.

- Put each piece of contact information on a new line.

- Consider labeling your name, address, phone number and email address with the words "name" "address," "phone" and "email," particularly if you are concerned the ATS may not recognize each piece of information for what it is.

- Avoid special characters in your email address. The @ symbol is fine because it is necessary and expected in an email address. Most email addresses do not contain any other special characters, but if yours does, consider setting up a new email address for job searching.

- Do not repeat your contact information on the second page if you are submitting a two-page resume that will be read by an ATS.

- Do not list your credentials on the same line with your name. Include them on a separate line.

- Do not put your contact information (or any other information) in a header in Word. Type it in the normal body of the page because some applicant tracking systems do not read headers well, and your contact information could be lost if you put it in a header.

EXAMPLE OF CONTACT INFORMATION:

Jane Somebody
123 Any Street, Faketown, State, Zip Code
(000) 000-0000
janesomebody@emailprovider.com

EXAMPLE OF CONTACT INFORMATION WITH EACH PART LABELED:

Name: Jane Somebody
Address: 123 Any Street, Faketown, State, Zip Code
Phone: (000) 000-0000
Email: janesomebody@emailprovider.com

CONSIDER OMITTING YOUR MAILING ADDRESS

Sometimes an the ATS software will be set to filter out applicants who live outside of a certain distance from the company. So, if you live far from the job, no matter how qualified you are, you will not get called for an interview if the employer is filtering applicants by location.

If you are applying to jobs that are far from your home, consider omitting your address from your resume. You can refer back to the more detailed discussion of this topic in chapter 6 if you would like more information to help you make the decision about whether to include or omit your mailing address.

EXAMPLE OF CONTACT INFORMATION WITH ADDRESS OMITTED:

Name: Jane Somebody
Phone: (000) 000-0000
Email: janesomebody@emailprovider.com

Edit and format your profile for the ATS.

Your profile will be basically the same as the profile you created for a traditional, human-reviewed resume in chapter 7 with a few extra considerations to help your resume score better in the ATS screening process.

INCLUDE IN YOUR PROFILE THE EXACT JOB TITLE OF THE POSITION YOU ARE SEEKING

Including the exact job title should help your resume score better because ATS software often searches for an exact match of the job title listed in the job ad. If you currently hold a position with this job title, simply include your current job title in your profile.

If you hold the same position, but your job title is different, you can still use the job title in the job ad *as long as it is an honest reflection of your professional experience.* For example, imagine you are a quality, health, safety and environment coordinator, but your company calls people in this position integrated management systems coordinators. The company-specific job title, integrated management systems coordinator, is fairly meaningless outside of your company, so it is completely acceptable to call yourself a quality, health, safety and environment coordinator in your profile as long as that job title is an honest reflection of the work that you do.

If you cannot honestly use the exact job title that is listed in the ad, you can still include the exact match for the job title in your profile. You may write something like, "Seeking a position as a (include the exact job title here)." Then add one or two sentences that describe key strengths that make you an ideal candidate for the job.

This strategy may seem a bit tricky, but it can help your resume to score better and make it through the ATS screening process. You have not been dishonest about your experience, and, in my opinion, it does not cross the line into the kind of keyword stuffing that would put off most employers.

LOOK FOR OPPORTUNITIES TO INCLUDE OTHER IMPORTANT KEYWORDS IN YOUR PROFILE

The more keyword-rich your resume is, the better chance you will have of passing the ATS screening process. Look at the list of keywords you have developed, giving extra weight to important keywords from the job ad, and find ways to include those keywords in your profile. Remember, you are writing to please both the ATS and a human reader, so you need to avoid nonsensical keyword stuffing. Instead, find logical, natural ways to blend important keywords and phrases into your profile.

CONSIDER INCLUDING THE HIRING COMPANY'S NAME IN YOUR PROFILE

Some people have found resumes score better in ATS screening when the hiring company's name is on the resume. Obviously, you cannot include the company's name in your work experience if you have no experience with that company. If you do have experience with the hiring company in any capacity, be sure to mention it.

You can also include the hiring company's name in your profile by writing something like this, "Seeking a position as a (include the exact job title here) at (include the company's name here)." Then add one or two sentences that describe key strengths that make you an ideal candidate for the job.

INCLUDE A JOB REFERENCE NUMBER IF THERE IS ONE

If there is a job reference number, you can include it in your profile also. If you would like to include a job reference number in your profile, you could write something like this, "Seeking a position as a (include the exact job title here) at (include the company's name here), job reference number (include the reference number here)." Then add one or two sentences that describe key strengths that make you an ideal candidate for the job.

Edit and format your skills summary for the ATS.

Write your skills summary using the recommendations in chapter 8. When you have completed that task, go through your list of important keywords, and find ways to naturally weave those keywords into your summary.

Remember, you need to limit yourself to using only standard section headings, so avoid breaking this section into smaller sections with non-standard headings. If your resume will be screened with an applicant tracking system, you do not need to worry so much about having a single, long list of skills.

Edit and format your work experience for the ATS.

To write your work experience for an ATS optimized resume, start with the information you completed back in chapter 9. You will need to take that information and slightly revise the content and the format to make your resume as ATS-friendly as possible.

REVISING THE CONTENT OF YOUR WORK EXPERIENCE

Look for opportunities to add keywords.

Work through each point you have written to describe your work experience and look for opportunities to naturally weave in important keywords and phrases.

Next, look at your list of important keywords, and see if there are any important skills or qualifications the employer has requested that you have not included in the work experience section of your resume. If you find you have missed anything important, add that information to your resume.

Repetition is acceptable, and even desirable.

Remember, if you have done similar jobs at different companies, you can, and should include all of your relevant responsibilities under each job even if that means your resume will be repetitive. This approach is different to the approach you would take for a human-reviewed resume because you would normally try to avoid repetition if a human was screening your resume. However, if an ATS is screening your resume, it is important to include all of your relevant experience under each job because it shows the full length of time you have worked in a field, and it also provides valid opportunities to repeat important keywords and add synonyms for those keywords.

Include all of your job-specific skills.

Take a look at what you have written for each job, and ask yourself whether you have included every relevant, work-specific skill. Remember, ATS software cannot read between the lines to assume you have a certain skill just because you have a number of years of relevant experience. Ensure you have included all of your job-specific skills under each job that is relevant to the one you are currently seeking.

The bottom line is, the content of the work experience section will be more thorough and possibly more repetitive when you write for an ATS than it would be if you were writing for a human reviewer.

Keep your resume relevant.

You can include jobs that are not relevant to the job you are seeking in order to avoid creating gaps in your work history and show career progression. However, do not describe those irrelevant jobs in detail. Applicant tracking systems may assess what percent of the content of your resume matches their criteria and give a higher score to resumes that have a higher match. That means, the more irrelevant job duties you include, the lower percent match your resume will score. It is not recommended to fill your resume with a lot of details about jobs that are not relevant to the job you are pursuing.

FORMATTING YOUR WORK EXPERIENCE

It is absolutely crucial to format your work experience correctly if your resume will be screened by an ATS. There are some standard approaches to formatting a human-reviewed resume that are not recommended if your resume will be reviewed by an applicant tracking system, so do read this section carefully.

The most important thing to remember when formatting the work experience section of your resume is to *never put your employment dates before your job title and / or company name.* Putting your employment dates before the rest of your employment information can cause the ATS software to skip that entire job on your resume or otherwise interpret your resume incorrectly.

A safe way to structure your employment information is as follows:

Company
Location
Position
Dates
Description

> **"When formatting an ATS optimized resume, never put your employment dates before your job title, company name or location."**

NOT RECOMMENDED - WORK EXPERIENCE FORMATTED WITH EXTRA SPACES, AND DATES ARE NOT LAST

Administrative Assistant   2012 - present
ABC Organization Incorporated, City, State

There are two problems with the formatting above. First, there are extra spaces between the word "Assistant" and the employment dates. It is not recommended to include extra spaces between words (or other characters) on a resume that will be screened by an ATS because the extra spaces can cause the software to have difficulty reading your resume.

Second, if you look closely at the example, you will see that the employment dates come *before* the name of the employer. When you format your work experience, the employment dates must come last because this format is what an ATS is typically programmed to expect, and any other format can cause the software to misinterpret the information on your resume.

The example above would work perfectly well for a human-reviewed resume, but it is not recommended formatting for an ATS-reviewed resume.

RECOMMENDED - WORK EXPERIENCE FORMATTED WITH NO EXTRA SPACES, AND DATES ARE LAST

ABC Organization Incorporated
City, State
Administrative Assistant
2012 – present

In the example above, there are no extra spaces between words. Each piece of information has its own line, making it easier for the software to interpret, and the employment dates are the last part of the entry.

This example is less attractive to the human eye than the previous example, but remember, if your resume will be screened by an ATS, you must write to please the ATS first, or a human will never see your resume.

Use the words "current" or "present" for your current job.

If you are currently working, use the words "current" or "present" to describe your employment dates. Avoid any other word because the ATS may not recognize anything else. For example, if you started working at a job in 2012, and you still work there, your employment dates would be 2012 - Present.

Use your company's formal name.

Use the full, formal name of any company you have worked for to help the ATS understand that it is the company name. For example, if the words "incorporated" or "corporation" "company" or "LLC" are part of your company's full name, you might not normally use those words when referring to your company, but you should include the full, formal company name on your ATS optimized resume because it can help the software interpret those words as being a company name.

If it is not possible to include a word that clearly defines the name as a company name, consider labeling the information on your work experience like this:

Company:
Location:
Position:
Dates:
Description:

You can use this strategy if you are concerned for any other reason that the ATS will not recognize your employment information for what it is.

Avoid adding extra spaces between words on your resume.

On a human-reviewed resume, you would commonly tab over to line up your employment dates on the right side of the page. **Like this:**

Administrative Assistant   2012 - present
ABC Organization Incorporated, City, State

Adding extra spaces can choke the system, so it should be avoided if your resume will be screened by an ATS. Instead, you should left justify everything, and keep the information together without added spaces. **Like this:**

ABC Organization Incorporated
City, State
Administrative Assistant
2012 – present

Use an exact match job title whenever possible.

Sometimes qualified people do not pass the ATS screening process simply because their job title is different from the one in the ad even though it is essentially the same job. If you have held jobs that are basically the same as the job you are applying to, but your job title is different, list your job title, and the title of the job in the ad. For example, imagine you work as an employment coach, and your official job title is career development facilitator. You want to apply for a similar job, and the exact job title is employment coach. In that case, you could write the following:

> ABC Company
> City, State
> Career Development Facilitator / Employment Coach
> 2009 – 2014

You must be honest if you use this strategy. You cannot give yourself an exact match job title if it isn't a reasonable reflection of the work you do. However, if it is a reasonable reflection of the work you do, this strategy is a perfectly acceptable way to improve your score when your resume will be screened with an ATS.

Avoid using dates in the job description section of your resume.

Sometimes people like to include dates when they describe projects or accomplishments to show they were recent or long term. The problem with using dates within your list of job duties and accomplishments is that it can confuse the ATS into thinking they are referring to a completely separate job. Never use dates inside a job description on an ATS optimized resume.

NOT RECOMMENDED - DATES WITHIN THE JOB DESCRIPTION

> ABC Organization Incorporated
> City, State
> Administrative Assistant
> 2012 – present
> - In 2013 - 2014, developed new database system to efficiently compile and analyze large volume and variety of client data; new system reduced time required to complete monthly, quarterly and annual reports by 20%

In the example above, the dates show that this project was accomplished recently. Including this date in a bulleted point would be perfectly acceptable on a human-reviewed resume. However, including a date in a bulleted point is not recommended if your resume will be reviewed by an ATS. A date that occurs in an unexpected location can cause the ATS to misinterpret your resume.

RECOMMENDED - NO DATES WITHIN THE JOB DESCRIPTION

ABC Organization Incorporated
City, State
Administrative Assistant
2012 – present
* Developed new database system to efficiently compile and analyze large volume and variety of client data; new system reduced time required to complete monthly, quarterly and annual reports by 20%

In the example above, the year has been removed from the bulleted point. It doesn't provide quite as much information, but you will not risk a problem with an ATS with the date omitted.

LIST JOBS SEPARATELY IF YOU HAVE HELD SEVERAL JOBS AT ONE COMPANY.

If you have had several jobs at a company, list each job separately. Associate dates with each job.

EXAMPLE

ABC Manufacturing Company
City, State
Wastewater Operator
2011 - 2014
* Describe this job in several bulleted points here

ABC Manufacturing Company
City, State
Machine Operator
2008 - 2011
* Describe this job in several bulleted points here

ABC Manufacturing Company
City, State
Packer
2006 – 2008
* Describe this job in several bulleted points here

If you do not list each job separately, the ATS will see them all as a single job and will not recognize your career progression within the company.

Please be aware that, in another section of this book, I have shown several jobs at a single company formatted with each job listed under a single, overall entry for the company. If you need clarification, the sample resume labeled Job Seeker Earned Increased Responsibility at One Company in chapter 15 is an example of what I'm referring to. That nested approach is only acceptable for human-reviewed resumes. If your resume will be reviewed by an ATS, list each job separately as shown above.

Edit and format your education for the ATS.

As mentioned earlier in this chapter, do not get fancy with section headings. Call this section education; do not call it education and training or professional development, otherwise the ATS may not recognize the section for what it is.

Structure your education information the same way you structured your work experience information with the dates after the school and program. Do not put the dates before the school and / or the name of the program. For example:

NOT RECOMMENDED - EXTRA SPACES, AND DATES ARE NOT LAST

PROFESSIONAL DEVELOPMENT

Business Administration Diploma   2007
ABC College, City, State

The example above has the same problems the not recommended work experience example had. There are extra spaces between characters, and the date comes before the name of the school. Also, the section heading is labeled "Professional Development," which might confuse some ATS software.

RECOMMENDED - NO EXTRA SPACES, AND DATES ARE LAST

EDUCATION

Business Administration Diploma
ABC College
City, State
2007

This example has no extra spaces after words, the date is the last part of the entry, and the section heading "Education" is a standard heading that any ATS would recognize.

A safe way to organize your education details is as follows:

Degree / Diploma, Subject of specialization (if there is one)
School
Location
Date the degree was received
Details (in bulleted point form) about classes if you intend to include that information

Be sure to use a word like "degree," "diploma," "certificate" or "course" (whatever is appropriate) to describe your education because if a specific type of education is a requirement of the job, the ATS will screen resumes for that word or phrase. For example, if the job requires a Bachelor of Science degree, the ATS may select only resumes that have the phrase "Bachelor of Science degree." You may have a Bachelor of Science degree, but if you omit the word "degree," there is a chance your resume will be filtered out of the competition.

Similarly, if there is an area of specialization, be sure to include that on your resume.

NOT RECOMMENDED - WORD "DEGREE" AND AREA OF SPECIALIZATION MISSING

Bachelor of Science
ABC University
City, State
2007

In the example above, the word "degree" is missing. If the ATS searches for the exact phrase "bachelor of science degree" this resume will not be returned in the search in spite of the fact that this job seeker has completed that degree. Also, the area of specialization is missing, which is a lost opportunity to include another keyword that may be relevant to the job.

RECOMMENDED - WORD "DEGREE" AND AREA OF SPECIALIZATION INCLUDED

Bachelor of Science Degree, Biology
ABC University
City, State
2007

In this example above, the area of specialization, and the word "degree" is included. This resume will be found whether the ATS searches for the phrase "bachelor of science" or "bachelor of science degree." Adding the word "degree" covers both possibilities.

Similarly, if a degree is in progress, call it a degree, and note that it is in progress, so your resume will still come up in a search for that term.

EXAMPLE

Bachelor of Science Degree, Biology
ABC University
City, State
In progress, degree expected December 2015

If you have started an educational program, but you have not completed it, and you are not in the process of completing it, you can still ensure your resume comes up for a search for that phrase while remaining honest about your credentials. If, for example, you have completed 30 credits of a Bachelor of Science degree, but you have not completed the degree, and you are not in the process of completing it, you could write that you have completed 30 credits of a Bachelor of Science degree. That way, you include the important phrase "bachelor of science degree" while being honest that you have not completed that degree. The entry would look something like this:

EXAMPLE

> 30 Credits Toward Bachelor of Science Degree, Biology
> ABC University
> City, State
> 2007

Edit and format your certifications for the ATS.

If you have relevant certifications or professional licenses, list them under a separate heading. You may include the name of the certification and the date you received the certification like this:

> Certified Internal Auditor (CIA) - Certified May 2012

In some cases, it may make more sense to include the name of the certificate, and the date it expires like this:

> First Aid and CPD / AED Certified - Expiration: September 2015

If you are a licensed professional in your field, you may also include your license number in this section if it is relevant. Like this:

> Speech Pathologist License Number 000000 - Effective: September 2014 Expiration: September 2016

Edit and format your volunteer work for the ATS.

The recommendations for making the volunteer work section of your resume ATS optimized are similar to the recommendations for making your work history section ATS-friendly. Structure the information so the dates are listed after the name of the organization, and then type of volunteer role you held. Remember to look for opportunities to include keywords in this section.

EXAMPLE

Anytown Community Organization
City, State
Secretary-Treasurer
2013 - present
- Describe your volunteer work here
- Be sure to find opportunities to naturally weave in important keywords

Ensure you have not missed any important keywords.

Once you have worked through your entire resume, formatted it for an ATS and added important keywords, go through the contents of your resume and compare it to your list of keywords that are important for that job to ensure you have not missed any important keywords.

I would suggest printing your resume and the job ad at this point because most people find it easier to edit on paper instead of on a computer screen. Start with the first word on your list of important keywords, and look for it on your resume. Highlight each occurrence of the word on your resume, then go back to your list of important keywords, and beside that word, make note of the number of times you found that word on your resume. Repeat this process for each word on your list of keywords. If a keyword from your list is not found on your resume, circle that keyword.

Next, take a look at your list of keywords and notice the ones that are circled. These circled words represent the skills or qualifications that you decided were important to the employer, but you have not demonstrated on your resume. Work through each word one at a time, and ask yourself whether you have that skill or qualification. Remember, you must be honest, but if there is any way that you can honestly include that word or phrase on your resume, add that information into the appropriate section.

Yes, this process will take a while, but it will be time well spent. It really is important to weave in as many keywords as possible and to ensure you have not missed including any crucial keywords on your resume.

Proofread your resume.

It is finally time to proofread your resume. You will find tips on how to proofread effectively at the end of chapter 12.

Step Six
Save Your ATS Optimized Resume

Above all else, be sure to read and follow the employer's instructions carefully. Do not skip anything in the application process, and be sure to **save your resume in the exact format the employer requests**. If any of the employer's instructions are different from the information in this book, *follow the employer's instructions*.

Applicant tracking systems cannot handle all document formats. If you do submit your resume in the wrong format, it may never reach a human reviewer. Even if a resume in the wrong format does reach a human, you will give the employer the impression that you do not follow instructions carefully, and hiring managers will not take the time to convert your document to a format that can be read by the ATS.

Some employers will provide thorough instructions and, unfortunately, some will provide none at all. If the employer does not provide information about the file type required, save your resume as a .doc document (.doc is also known as a Word 2003 document). While there are a few file types that certain ATS software can read, the .doc file is the one that works with most applicant tracking systems.

YOU ARE GOING TO SAVE YOUR RESUME IN TWO DIFFERENT FORMATS

In step 6, you are going to end up saving your resume twice in two different formats. To avoid confusion, here is a quick outline of what you will be doing in this step and why you need to save your resume twice:

1. Save Your Resume to Get Rid of Special Characters.

First, you are going save your resume as a .txt file. This file type will help you get rid of any stray special characters that could cause problems with the ATS.

2. Save Your Resume in the Format the Employer Requires.

Next, you are going to save your resume in the file format the employer requires. Usually an ATS optimized resume will be saved as a .doc file.

1. *Save your resume to get rid of special characters.*

As you wrote your resume, you were careful to avoid special characters because they can cause problems when the ATS reads your resume. No matter how careful you were, there is a chance that a problematic character may have slipped in by accident. The following steps will help you find and remove any stray special characters and avoid problems.

SAVE YOUR RESUME AS A .TXT FILE TO REMOVE SPECIAL CHARACTERS

You will need to open your resume in Microsoft Word and then save it as a .txt file. Saving your resume as a .txt file will get rid of any special characters that may have been in the document.

The specific instructions for saving as a .txt file will vary slightly depending on which version of Word you are using, but the following instructions should provide enough information to take you through the process.

To save your resume as a .txt file, open your document in Microsoft Word. Click on "File" (normally in the top left of the screen) then click "Save As." Next, look for the option to save as .txt or save as plain text. You can save the .txt file to your desktop to make it easy to find. Once you have saved your resume as a .txt file, close your resume document.

LOOK FOR ANY PROBLEMS IN THE DOCUMENT

Find the .txt version of your resume that you just saved, and open it in Microsoft Word.

You will probably notice that your font has been changed to Courier, which is not an ideal font for resume writing. Select all of the text, and change the font to something more appropriate like Arial or Verdana.

Look carefully through your resume for any changes that may have occurred. If there were any special characters in your resume, they will have been changed. This change may result in a different character, or it may cause some spacing or other formatting issues. Review your resume carefully to ensure all of the characters make sense, and fix any formatting issues you find. Also, do a final review of the document to make sure you have followed all of the best practices for formatting your resume for an ATS.

Save the file again as a .txt file to preserve any changes you made. You can keep this .txt file on hand to help you with subsequent ATS optimized resumes you may need to write for other job applications.

Now that you've removed any special characters that could problems, it is time to save your resume in the format the employer requires.

2. Save your resume in the format the employer requires.

Remember to save your resume in the exact format the employer asks for.

Do you need to save your resume again?

- If the employer wants you to send a .txt file, you do not need to save your resume again. You already saved your resume as a .txt file in the previous step, so you can simply use that file.

- If the employer wants any other file type, you will need to save your resume again.

Let's get started saving your resume in the format the employer wants!

Because .doc files are commonly used with ATS software, I will describe in detail how to save your resume as a .doc file. Don't worry if the employer has asked for any other file type, we will cover that information in a moment

To save your resume as a .doc file, open the resume you just saved as a .txt file in Microsoft Word. Click on "File" (normally in the top left of the screen) then click "Save As." Next, look for the option to save as .doc or save as Word 2003, and click on that option.

Avoid giving your resume a generic file name like resume.doc. Use a file name that will be helpful for the employer such as YourNameJobTitle.doc. For example, if I wanted to submit a resume for a job as a career coach, I would name my resume document LisaMcGrimmonCareerCoach.doc. Employers receive a lot of resumes with generic file names, and it is inconvenient for them because that file name is meaningless to them. As a job seeker, it is your task to make things as easy as possible for the employer.

Do be aware that newer versions of Microsoft Word use the extension .docx by default. Do not save your resume as a .docx file unless the employer has specifically asked for that file type. Some applicant tracking systems cannot properly read a .docx file.

Similarly, avoid saving your resume as a PDF file unless the employer has specifically asked for a PDF file. Many applicant tracking systems cannot properly read a PDF file.

If you need to save your resume as a file type other than a .doc file, simply click on "File" then "Save As" and then look for the specific file type you need in the list of options on your screen.

ASK FOR HELP IF YOU NEED HELP

I do realize that these directions may seem quite technical to anyone who does not use Microsoft Word very often. If you are struggling to save your resume correctly, ask a more computer savvy friend or family member for help. The task is not difficult for someone who is comfortable with Microsoft Word, so you should not have trouble finding someone who can help you.

Step Seven
Submit Your ATS Optimized Resume

Above all else, when you submit your ATS optimized resume, be sure to follow the employer's instructions precisely. If any of the employer's instructions are different from the recommendations below, do what the employer has requested.

Some employers will provide you with excellent, detailed instructions for submitting your resume, while others will not provide much information at all. The tips below will help you avoid problems when you submit your ATS optimized resume.

UPLOADING YOUR SAVED RESUME IS BETTER THAN COPYING AND PASTING

If you have a choice between uploading your saved resume document or cutting and pasting it into text boxes, choose to upload your saved resume. An uploaded saved resume will look better to a human reader once it gets to that stage.

RESUMES SUBMITTED THROUGH A PERSONAL CONTACT MAY STILL BE SCREENED THROUGH AN ATS

While business networking can be a great strategy to try to bypass ATS screening and get your resume directly into the hands of a hiring manager, there is still a chance that a resume submitted directly through a personal contact might be entered into the ATS for screening. It is still advantageous to have your resume submitted directly through a personal contact, but do not assume you will completely bypass the ATS screening if you submit your resume in this manner. Ask your personal contact if he or she can tell you whether you need to submit a traditional resume or an ATS optimized resume.

SOME EMPLOYERS SCORE RESUMES BASED ON HOW YOU APPLIED FOR THE JOB

Some employers prefer candidates who submit their resumes directly through the company website because it implies you have been watching the company and have a specific interest in working for them. These employers will give additional points to any resume that has been submitted through the company's website.

If you have found a job somewhere else online, do be sure to check the company's website to see if you have the option to submit your resume directly from their site.

SUBMIT YOUR APPLICATION AS SOON AS POSSIBLE

Some employers stop searching the resumes that have been submitted once they have enough resumes to fill the job. If they receive plenty of resumes from strong candidates, they may stop screening new submissions well before the closing date listed in the job ad. For that reason, you need to submit your resume as soon as possible.

Do take the time you need to write an excellent resume, but make it a priority to complete and submit your resume as quickly as you can.

CHECK YOUR EMAIL'S SPAM FOLDER

Sometimes an ATS will send a confirmation that your resume was received, but it might end up in your spam folder. When you are job searching, be sure to check your spam folder regularly to make sure you do not miss any important messages. If you do find important messages in your spam folder, you can whitelist emails from that source so they do not end up in the spam folder in the future.

If you are not familiar with whitelisting, it is a simple process that ensures emails from certain senders do not go in your spam folder. The procedure for whitelisting email from a specific address varies depending on the email provider you use, so it is not something I can easily explain in this book. If you would like to whitelist emails from a certain source, and you are not sure how to do it, ask a computer savvy friend for help. It is a fairly easy task to do if you are comfortable with email systems, so you shouldn't have too much trouble finding someone who can help you.

Step Eight
Know Where to Find Information for Formatting ATS Resumes vs. Human-Reviewed Resumes

There are some strategies that work well when your resume will be screened by a human that are not recommended when your resume will be screened by an ATS. The reverse is also true. There are some strategies that work well when your resume will be screened by an ATS that are not ideal when a human will review your resume.

To avoid confusion, if you are writing a resume that will be screened by an ATS, please refer to this chapter for answers about how to best format your resume. If you are writing a resume that will be reviewed by a human, please refer to chapter 12 for information about how to format your resume for a human reader.

YOUR ATS OPTIMIZED RESUME IS COMPLETE!

Your resume will have some differences compared with the example depending upon choices you have made along the way, but when you are finished formatting and optimizing your resume for ATS screening, your document will look something like this:

Name: Jane Somebody
Address: 123 Any Street, Faketown, State, Zip Code
Phone: (000) 000-0000
Email: janesomebody@emailprovider.com

PROFILE

Administrative professional with seven years of experience in the nonprofit sector. Able to prioritize and manage conflicting demands. Exceptional technical skills including proficiency with Word, Excel, PowerPoint and Prezi; type 80 words per minute.

SUMMARY

- Proven ability to meet strict deadlines, ensure accuracy of work and manage conflicting demands effectively
- Thorough knowledge of and ability to research community resources developed over 7 years working at local, non-profit community organizations
- Able to resolve common computer hardware issues for staff and clients in resource center
- Exhibit a professional and welcoming demeanor to clients and co-workers; earned reputation as a resourceful problem solver with high degree of integrity

- Bilingual in English and Spanish

WORK EXPERIENCE

ABC Organization Incorporated
City, State
Administrative Assistant
2012 - present
- Provide administrative support to two workshop facilitators; assist additional team of counselors as required
- Prepare correspondence and training materials for facilitators
- Contact clients by telephone on a weekly basis to ensure participation in workshops, and promote agency programs; telephone contact improves workshop attendance by 20%
- Accurately manage client data for up to 1000 clients per year using Excel and complete monthly, quarterly and annual reports for counselors, executive director and funding partners
- Developed new database system to efficiently compile and analyze large volume and variety of client data; new system significantly reduced time required to complete monthly, quarterly and annual reports
- Liaise with community partners to determine additional resources for clients and colleagues and to promote agency programs

XYZ Organization LLC
City, State
Administrative Assistant
2008 - 2012
- Provided administrative support for team of six counselors, each managing a case load of 100+ clients per year
- Prepared confidential correspondence and scheduled meetings for counselors
- Independently researched and developed teaching resources and community resource packages for counselors and clients
- Provide reception assistance and administrative support for executive director

Another Organization LLC
City, State
Receptionist
2007 - 2008
- Provided professional, friendly telephone and in person assistance for clients; answered approximately 50 incoming calls per day on a multi-line system and greeted and assisted up to 30 clients per day in a resource center environment
- Received and distributed incoming mail; responded to mail and email inquiries
- Ensured office equipment was in working order and rectified common computer hardware problems for clients and colleagues

- Prepared confidential correspondence for colleagues
- Scheduled appointments for staff of seven counselors and organized monthly team meetings and charity events
- Maintained office supply inventory; tracked and ordered supplies monthly

EDUCATION

Business Administration Diploma
ABC College
City, State
2007

VOLUNTEER

Anytown Community Organization
City, State
Secretary-Treasurer
2013 - present
- Manage all website updates, and write and distribute meeting minutes and newsletters to staff and volunteers
- Receive donations, issue receipts for cash received, maintain payment records
- Manage budgets, accounts and financial statements and present financial data to the management committee
- Prepare Treasurer's Report for annual general meeting and advise management committee on funding requirements for future projects

Assignment

If you think you will be submitting your resume to employers who use applicant tracking systems, add relevant keywords and format your resume so it is optimized to score well in an ATS screening.

Moving Forward

You are ready to move on to the next chapter if you…

1. Understand how applicant tracking systems (ATS) are used in the job search process to screen resumes.

2. Have researched relevant keywords and phrases to include on your ATS optimized resume and added those keywords and phrases to your resume in a way that reads naturally.

3. Have ensured your resume is formatted optimally for ATS software.

4. Know how to correctly save and submit your resume when ATS software will be used in the screening process.

    or

5. If you have determined that you will not be submitting resumes to employers who use applicant tracking systems, you may move on to the next chapter, knowing that you can always return to this chapter if you need to format your resume for ATS screening some time in the future.

CHAPTER FOURTEEN
BE READY FOR ANY TYPE OF JOB:
CREATE YOUR FOUNDATION RESUME

YOUR TASK FOR THIS CHAPTER

1. Expand on your current resume to create a foundation resume that can be used to quickly prepare a resume targeted to any type of job you are qualified to do.

Writing a foundation resume is optional, and it does require some time and effort. However, it is an excellent document to keep on hand, and in the long run, it can make resume writing much easier.

ACTION STEPS FOR THIS CHAPTER

Step One:	Understand the concept of a foundation resume.
Step Two:	Understand how you will benefit from creating a foundation resume.
Step Three:	Understand how a foundation resume is different from a targeted resume.
Step Four:	Understand how to write a foundation resume.
Step Five:	Understand how you will use your foundation resume.
Step Six:	Write your foundation resume.

"Luck is a crossroad where preparation and opportunity meet" Unknown

Step One
Understand the Concept of a Foundation Resume

DEFINITIONS

The term *"foundation resume"* is a term I use to refer to a resume that describes all of the skills, accomplishments and experiences you have achieved throughout your entire career with nothing omitted. It is a foundation you can use to build all of your targeted resumes.

I will also use the phrase *"targeted resume"* throughout this chapter. The phrase "targeted resume" refers to any resume that has been written to highlight your skills and experience related to a specific job that you are seeking.

Targeted resumes are the resumes you send out to employers. A foundation resume is resume-type document you keep for your own use to document your full career and make it easier to write as many different targeted resumes as you need.

Foundation resume basics:

A foundation resume breaks a lot of the rules that apply to standard, targeted resumes.

- It could easily be three or four pages long.

- It can go back many years in the past.

- It will include every job you have held, every course you have completed, every volunteer position you have held, every major accomplishment you have achieved and every skill you have developed even if they are completely unrelated to the type of work you are currently seeking.

A foundation resume *is for your personal use only*. It should *never* be sent to an employer. It would be far too long and unfocused to make a good impression on an employer.

A foundation resume can be used as the basis for all of the targeted resumes you write. When you need to write a targeted resume for a specific type of job, you will be able to open up your foundation resume and simply choose all of the items that are relevant to the job you are targeting and include those items on your targeted resume.

Step Two
Understand How You Will Benefit From Creating a Foundation Resume

IF A FOUNDATION RESUME SHOULD NEVER BE SENT TO AN EMPLOYER, WHAT IS THE POINT OF WRITING THIS TYPE OF RESUME?

Throughout this book, I have mentioned that it is important to write a specific resume for each type of job you are seeking. The idea of writing several resumes can be extremely overwhelming. A foundation resume makes it fairly simple to write as many different targeted resumes as you need, especially if you are applying to more than one type of job.

When you have a foundation resume, you have a document that describes every aspect of your career in detail.

Benefits of having a foundation resume:

1. YOU WILL BE ABLE TO WRITE TARGETED RESUMES QUICKLY.

If you already have all of your career information in one large resume-type document, you will not have to spend a huge amount of time thinking about how to describe each aspect of your career.

You will complete the hard work of resume writing when you write the foundation resume. When it is time to write a targeted resume, you will be able to simply choose the relevant information from your foundation resume, paste it into your targeted resume, make slight revisions and format the information.

2. YOU WILL BE MORE LIKELY TO WRITE TARGETED RESUMES BECAUSE THE TASK WILL NOT SEEM SO DIFFICULT.

If you had to start from a blank page each time you needed to write a resume for a new job opportunity, you might be more tempted to send a generic resume instead of a targeted one. If you already have everything you need on your foundation resume, and you just need to edit and format the information, you will be far more likely to write a targeted resume for every job.

3. YOU WILL BE ABLE TO APPLY TO JOBS FASTER

If you have a foundation resume, you will be able to write targeted resumes faster than you could if you did not have a foundation resume, which means you will be able to submit your resumes to job leads faster. Employers sometimes stop reviewing resumes before the application deadline if they have received enough resumes from qualified applicants to fill the job. Therefore, it is important to submit your resume as quickly as possible. A foundation resume will allow you to do that.

4. YOU CAN EVEN MAKE SMALL CHANGES TO YOUR RESUME TO TARGET A SPECIFIC COMPANY.

For example, if you had written a targeted sales resume for a sales job in one industry, and you also wanted to apply to a sales job in another industry, you could easily make small changes to your sales resume to highlight experience you have related to each specific industry. A foundation resume makes it possible and reasonable to adapt your resume so it is a perfect fit every time you apply for a job.

5. YOU WILL HAVE A RECORD OF ALL OF YOUR PROFESSIONAL ACCOMPLISHMENTS.

Memories become foggy quickly. Without a written copy of your career history, it is very easy to forget about professional accomplishments.

If you maintain an up-to-date foundation resume, you will always have a record of every course you completed, every start and end date for every job you held, every accomplishment you achieved, and every task you performed.

BOTTOM LINE

The better you target your resumes to the jobs you are seeking, the better chance you have of being invited to an interview and ultimately getting a job. A foundation resume makes it easier to write as many targeted resumes as you need.

Step Three
Understand How a Foundation Resume is Different From a Targeted Resume

A FOUNDATION RESUME:

CAN BE ANY LENGTH

In fact, the longer your foundation resume is, the more useful it will be. When you write your foundation resume, you are attempting to document every aspect of your career.

DOES NOT HAVE TO BE FORMATTED TO FIT WELL ON THE PAGE

This resume will never be sent in full to employers, so there is no point in wasting time making it fit well on a page.

INCLUDES EVERYTHING RELATED TO YOUR CAREER

Do not omit items for any reason.

CAN GO BACK MORE THAN TEN YEARS

It is wise to document your full career on your foundation resume, even if that means going back many years.

INCLUDES ALL DATES

Throughout this book, I have described reasons for omitting dates in certain sections of your resume and in certain situations. Your foundation resume is a full record of your career, so you should include all dates on this document even if you would omit those dates in a targeted resume that you sent out to an employer.

DOES NOT HAVE TO INCLUDE A PROFILE

Your foundation resume is not targeted to a specific job, so there is no need to include a profile. If you have written a great profile for a targeted resume, include it on your foundation resume so you can use it as the basis for future profiles.

ALWAYS INCLUDES A SUMMARY OF SKILLS AND/OR ACCOMPLISHMENTS

Even if you intend to write chronological resumes to submit to employers, it is helpful to include a summary of your skills and accomplishments in your foundation resume.

Your skills and accomplishments are a crucial part of your career history and can be worked into the body of a chronological resume.

At some point, you may change your mind and decide that you need to write a combination resume. If you do decide to use a combination format, you will be happy that you took the time to document your skills and accomplishments in your foundation resume.

CAN INCLUDE A LIST OF RELEVANT KEYWORDS AND PHRASES

Back in chapter 13, Writing an Applicant Tracking System Optimized Resume, you learned how to research important industry keywords that employers might use when screening resumes in your industry. Those keywords will give you valuable insight into the skills that are most important in your industry. It is wise to keep a running list of those keywords as you research them, and your foundation resume is a good place to keep that list.

Simply add a heading called keywords at the beginning or end of the document. That is where you will keep track of those important words and phrases. You will be able to refer back to this keyword list each time you write a resume to ensure you have included the most important skills that are relevant to employers in your industry and woven the most important words and phrases throughout your resume.

Step Four
Understand How to Write a Foundation Resume

If you have completed chapters 1 through 13, you will already have completed a resume that is targeted for a specific type of job. You will use this targeted resume as the starting point for writing your foundation resume.

You may wonder why you did not just start with writing the foundation resume first. Remember, a foundation resume is not targeted to a specific type of job. It is much easier to write a resume when you have a specific job in mind. That is why we started with the specific, targeted resume and now move to the more general, foundation resume.

Open up your resume document, and, before you do anything, save it under a new name so you do not lose your completed targeted resume.

Complete the following tasks for each section:

CONTACT INFORMATION

This information remains the same. There is nothing to add here.

PROFILE

A foundation resume is not focused on a specific type of job, so you may choose to leave this section as is and write a new profile each time you prepare a new targeted resume.

Alternatively, if you know you will be looking for two or three specific types of jobs, you could write a basic profile for each of the types of jobs you are seeking. You will end up with two or three profiles written out in this section, which you can edit to fit each specific job lead you pursue.

SUMMARY OF SKILLS AND ACCOMPLISHMENTS

If you have completed a combination or functional resume, you should have a good summary of skills already. If you have completed a chronological resume, you will be starting from scratch in this section. You can return to chapter 8 to refresh your memory about how to write a good summary of skills.

If you completed the keyword research described in chapter 13, you can use that information to look for important skills employers in your industry require. Simply review your research from that chapter, and look for skills you have that could be added to your foundation resume.

For your foundation resume, instead of noting only skills that are crucial to a specific type of job, you will note all of the marketable skills you have no matter what type of job they relate to. If you deleted points from your targeted resume because they were not relevant to a specific job, you can add those points back in to your foundation resume because they might be relevant to another job you might want to pursue in the future.

For example, imagine you had written a targeted resume for a job as a medical administrative assistant, but you also had experience working as a waitress. When you write your foundation resume, you will add any skills you developed as a waitress that you omitted from your medical administrative assistant resume.

This summary of skills should be quite long, so it is helpful to group your skills into sub-categories that reflect the different types of skills you have.

When a skills summary is written well, a lot of the points start to sound like accomplishments. You may choose to add a sub-category called accomplishments and list all of your professional accomplishments throughout your entire career in this section.

EMPLOYMENT HISTORY

If you omitted any jobs when you wrote your targeted resume, you will need to add them to your foundation resume. Include on your foundation resume every job you have ever held and describe each job in detail.

You may have included certain jobs on your targeted resume without describing them in detail. If that is the case, describe those jobs in detail for your foundation resume.

EDUCATION

Include every degree, diploma, certificate, course and seminar you have attended. Note the name of the program, the school or organization that delivered the program, the date you attended and a few points about the program.

If you completed any internships or other placements during any of your training, describe them in this section.

If you received any special honors or were active in any extracurricular activities, note that information also.

VOLUNTEER WORK AND/OR HOBBIES

Include information about every volunteer position you have ever held.

You do not have to include every hobby in this section. If you have a hobby that could be relevant at a job, include it in your foundation resume. If your hobbies would not be relevant to a job, feel free to omit them.

At this point, you will have documented every single bit of information that could possibly be relevant to your career. Yes, it is a lot of work, but the work you put in on the front end creating a foundation resume will vastly reduce the work necessary later to create as many targeted resumes as you need.

Step Five
Understand How You Will Use Your Foundation Resume

REMEMBER, YOU WILL NEVER SEND YOUR FOUNDATION RESUME TO AN EMPLOYER.

Each time you apply to a new job, you can use your foundation resume to create a targeted resume that is perfect for the job you are seeking.

EXAMPLE

Imagine you have experience working as an adult education teacher and you have recently completed a diploma in drug and alcohol counseling. You are job searching, and you have written a targeted resume for adult education jobs, and you have also written a foundation resume. Now you want to write a resume for an addictions counselor job.

Start with your foundation resume, and work through it carefully one line at a time. Ask yourself which points are relevant to a job as an addictions counselor. Those are the points and sections that will be included on your addictions counselor resume.

Look for items that are directly related to addictions counseling, such as your diploma, and any placements or internships you completed at school.

Also look for items that are indirectly related and demonstrate transferable skills. Transferable skills are skills that you used in one type of job, but they are useful in another type of job. For example, an adult education teacher, would lead groups of adults in a classroom environment. An addictions counselor may need to lead groups of adults in a counseling environment. The tasks are not exactly the same, but they require a lot of the same skills, so that teaching experience should be included on the addictions counselor resume.

DETERMINE THE BEST STYLE OF RESUME FOR THE TYPE OF JOB YOU ARE SEEKING.

Your original, targeted resume may be a chronological resume, but a different style of resume might highlight your skills for the second job more effectively.

For example, if you have worked as an adult education teacher for several years, and you just finished a diploma in drug and alcohol counseling, a chronological resume could be a good choice for your adult education resume if you have a solid work history in that field, but a combination resume would probably be the best option for the addictions counseling resume since you do not have work experience in that field.

DETERMINE THE BEST ORDER FOR THE SECTIONS IN YOUR NEW RESUME.

Follow the guidelines in this book to determine the best order for sections in your resume.

In the example we have been using, it would probably be wise to move education ahead of work experience in the addictions counselor resume because the recently completed diploma is the item that is most relevant to the job.

REPHRASE POINTS AS NECESSARY.

Go through each of the lines that you are including on your resume, and ask yourself whether it needs to be rephrased to make it more targeted to the specific job you are seeking.

For example, if you took the point about teaching groups of adults that was originally written about your adult education job and included it on an addictions counselor resume, you may need to change the wording slightly to fit the expectations of the new work setting. If the original point was very specific and referred to the type of material you taught, you would need to make the point more general so it was clear how it related to working as an addictions counselor.

FORMAT YOUR RESUME.

Finally, set up the information so it sits well on one or two pages, and your resume is complete.

Sample foundation resume:

Here is a sample foundation resume that covers a varied career. It is not formatted, and you would never send all of the information to an employer. It goes back too many years, and it is not targeted to a specific job.

However, it does document all of this person's skills and experiences, and having all of this information in one place makes it extremely easy to write a variety of targeted resumes. In fact, if you look carefully at the sample resumes in chapter 15, you will see some that are based on the information in this foundation resume and used to apply to several different types of jobs.

Whenever this person needs to write a resume, she can simply go to her foundation resume and choose all of the points that are relevant to the specific job she is interested in, reword the profile and perhaps rephrase a few points if necessary to target a specific industry, and then format everything.

That is a lot easier and less daunting than starting with a blank page every time you need to write a different resume!

Joanne Jobseeker (RRP)
12 Any Street, City, State, (000) 000-0000
joannejobseeker@emailprovider.com

PROFILE

Vocational rehabilitation specialist with over 5 years of counseling experience and 5 years of teaching experience. Self-motivated, with proven ability to work independently. Areas of specialization include work with clients who are injured workers, experienced workers, long term unemployed and new immigrants.

ACHIEVEMENTS

- Developed, negotiated, budgeted and managed half million dollar training projects
- Maintained over 80% success rate in job search workshop; consistently met and exceeded program and agency targets
- Individually and as a team, developed and implemented successful marketing strategies, which doubled, program intake numbers
- Instrumental in establishing job search workshop as a new and successful program within the agency, including building community awareness and refining program delivery and data management
- Part of a team that consistently provided welcoming, professional and nonjudgmental client support

WORKSHOP FACILITATION

- Experienced facilitating job search and career management workshops for groups of 8 to 12 individuals; taught groups of up to thirty people
- Developed, implemented and evaluated multifaceted lesson plans to accommodate multiple learning styles in a workshop setting
- Proven ability to address group and individual needs within a diverse group setting; foster a respectful learning environment and develop partnerships with clients to ensure client, program and agency success

COUNSELING

- Effectively assessed needs of clients and assisted clients to develop, implement and evaluate strategies for professional and personal development, emphasizing strengths and overcoming challenges
- Excellent knowledge of and ability to research community resources
- Able to balance needs of clients, funding partners and agency
- Developed, implemented and managed labor market re-entry action plans in partnership with injured workers and insuring agency

- Knowledge of challenges facing a variety of client groups, particularly clients who are new immigrants, experienced workers and long term unemployed; able to assist clients to implement strategies to overcome these challenges

TEACHING

- Developed lesson plans for and taught private and group piano, flute, clarinet and early childhood music for approximately 60 students annually
- Prepared students for participation in recitals, competitions and examinations; 80% of students completing examinations earned first class honors
- Collaborated with students and parents to set long and short-term goals and plans including participation in recitals, competitions and examinations
- Created, implemented and evaluated multifaceted lesson plans to accommodate multiple learning styles in a group setting
- Fostered a respectful learning environment and developed positive partnerships with parents and students to ensure student success
- Developed and implemented successful summer music programs, which increased, summer enrolment by 20%

ADMINISTRATION

- Accurately managed client data for case load of up to 500 clients per year using Excel and in-house software and completed weekly, monthly, quarterly and annual reports
- Developed and managed database to efficiently compile and analyze large volume and variety of client data
- Individually and as a team, developed and implemented successful marketing strategies, which doubled, program intake numbers
- Estimated and tracked costs of labor market re-entry plans, ensured sufficient funds were available and submitted invoices for payment to secondary service providers in a timely manner

COMPUTER SKILLS

- Experienced with Microsoft Word, Excel, PowerPoint and Prezi
- Solid knowledge of self-assessment software including Choices and Career Cruising

PROFESSIONAL EXPERIENCE

Vocational Rehabilitation Case Manager 2011-2014
Anytown Vocational Services, City, State
- Developed and managed safe and suitable return to work action plans for injured workers and the insuring agency

- Problem solved, liaised and negotiated with injured workers, secondary service providers and claims adjudicators to ensure success of return to work action plans
- Liaison between injured workers and claims adjudicators; ensured claims adjudicators were informed of injured workers' progress throughout labor market re-entry plan and any relevant concerns and injured workers were aware of claims adjudicators' expectations as related to the labor market re-entry plan
- In partnership with injured workers and claims adjudicators, recommended appropriate career options and training plans for injured workers
- Supported injured workers in retraining programs, including problem solving in cooperation with insuring agency, injured workers and secondary service providers to resolve a wide variety challenges as they arose
- Maintained contact with secondary service providers to ensure injured workers were receiving appropriate training
- Earned Registered Rehabilitation Professional (RRP) designation, 2012

Job Search Workshop Facilitator 2006-2011
Career Resource Center, City, State
- Facilitated 3 day job search workshop; course material included resume and cover letter preparation, effective interview strategies, maintaining self-esteem, labor market trends and traditional and creative job search techniques
- Facilitated weekly 2 hour workshops on career exploration, resume preparation, interview techniques and job search strategies
- Managed client data for case load of approximately 500 clients per year using Excel and Contact IV and completed monthly, quarterly and annual reports
- Provided ongoing support to all Job Club clients through telephone follow up, individual counseling and/or internal and external referrals
- Responsible for ongoing development of workshop materials and resources
- Hired and supervised part-time workshop support staff

Music Teacher 2002-2006
Anytown School of Music, City, State (part-time 2002 and 2006)
- Developed lesson plans for and taught private and group piano, flute, clarinet and early childhood music
- Collaborated with students and parents to set long and short-term goals and plans including participation in recitals, competitions and examinations

Adult Education Teacher 2001-2003
Anytown Learning Center, City, State
- Facilitated return to work and entry into college of injured workers through development of literacy and numeracy skills
- Ensured maintenance of timelines through effective long and short-term planning and time management

Music Teacher 2000-2001
Faketown Music Academy, City, State
- Developed curricula for and taught private and group piano, flute, theory and early childhood music
- Organized quarterly student recitals and co-directed a musical production
- Assisted with lesson scheduling, accounts receivable and inventory control

Research Assistant 1998-2000
Imaginary University, City, State
- Assisted professor in music department in sourcing print and online resources
- Accurately transcribed recorded interviews

Librarian 1998-2000
Imaginary University, City, State
- Assisted patrons at the circulation desk
- Shelved books, periodicals, CDs and DVDs, located missing items and kept library collection in order

Job Coach Summer 1997
Association for Community Living, City, State
- Supported individuals who were developmentally delayed; developed work, life and social skills

EDUCATION

Career Coach Diploma, Anytown College, City, State 2006
Bachelor of Education Degree, Imaginary University, City, State 2000
Bachelor of Music Degree, Imaginary University, City, State 1999

PROFESSIONAL DEVELOPMENT

Counseling Ethics, Anytown College, City, State 2012
French 1 and 2, Faketown College, City, State 2009
Anti-Racist Social Work, Social Development Council, City, State 2008
Crisis Intervention, Mental Health Association, City, State 2008

COMMUNITY INVOLVEMENT

Intern, Fictitious University Career Services, City, State Fall 2006
- Co-facilitated seminars concerning career management skills, the new economy and accessing resources for career development
- Completed individual resume and cover letter critiques for students, alumni and staff
- Assisted clients in the effective use of print and computer based resources

Intern, Community Employment Resource Center, City, State Spring 2006
- Assisted clients using print and computer resources and preparing resumes and cover letters
- Completed initial intake evaluations and assessed clients' needs and job readiness

Music Play Group Leader, Children's Center, City, State 1997-1999
- Initiated, developed and team-taught activities to build social skills, impulse control and self-esteem using music therapy concepts and strategies

Teacher's Assistant, Anytown High School, City, State 1997-1999
- Assistant teacher in grade nine music class
- Worked with groups of approximately 5 students to develop basic musicianship skills

Tutor, Anytown Children's Center, City, State 1996-1999
- Worked one-on-one with at-risk youth aged 9 to 11 to develop literacy and numeracy skills
- Received literacy tutor training from Anytown Literacy Network

Assignment

Use the targeted resume that you have already written, as well as any brainstorming points you wrote but discarded from your targeted resume as a starting point, and write a foundation resume that describes every aspect of your career to date.

Moving Forward

You are ready to move on to the next chapter if you...

1. **Have written your foundation resume.**

CHAPTER FIFTEEN
SAMPLE RESUMES

THERE ARE NO TASKS FOR THIS CHAPTER. INSTEAD, YOU WILL FIND SEVERAL SAMPLE RESUMES THAT ILLUSTRATE THE IMPORTANT CONCEPTS DESCRIBED IN THIS BOOK.

If you are reading the Kindle version of this book, please note, the resume samples in this chapter are shown as image files to ensure the formatting remains correct on all Kindle devices. I have also posted these resumes on my website, so if you are reading this book on a small screen, you can easily view the resumes more clearly on a larger computer screen.

If you would prefer to view the resume samples online, you will find links to all of the sample resumes in this book on my website at careerchoiceguide.com/resumeexamples. Consider bookmarking the page so you can easily return to it and review resume samples as you write your own resume.

If you do view the resumes online, you will find supplemental information about the formatting decisions made for many of the resumes, which will help you understand:

- Why certain formatting decisions were made

- How each resume was adjusted to fit well on one or two pages

- How you can apply those strategies to your own resume formatting

WHAT YOU WILL FIND IN THIS CHAPTER:

1. Combination Resume with Education First (Recent Graduate)
2. Basic Combination Resume
3. Combination Resume with Skills Grouped Into Several Sections
4. Combination Resume with Accomplishments Section
5. Combination Resume with Gap in Employment History
6. Combination Resume for a Job Seeker Who is Over 45
7. Basic Functional Resume
8. Basic Chronological Resume
9. Chronological Resume with Education Listed First
10. Career Change Resume
11. Combining Several Contracts at a Temporary Agency Into One Entry
12. Job Seeker Has a Short Work History
13. Job Seeker's Relevant Experience is in the Past
14. Job Seeker's Relevant Experience was Obtained Through Volunteer Work
15. Job Seeker Earned Increased Responsibility at One Company
16. Job Seeker Held the Same Job at Different Companies

"A good example has twice the value of good advice"
Author Unknown

Combination Resume with Education First (Recent Grad)

Judy Jobseeker

jjobseeker@emailprovider.com

123 Fake Lane, City, State

Home: (555) 555-5555   Cell: (000) 000-0000

Profile   Registered early childhood education teacher with 5 years of experience working with children from age two to ten in childcare centers and summer camp.

Summary of Skills

- Create and implement fun, educational and developmentally appropriate activities
- Develop positive relationships with parents through clear and consistent verbal and written communication to ensure wellbeing of children
- Resourceful and creative; able to work effectively in a constantly changing environment
- Proficient in Microsoft Word and Excel, with excellent online research skills and ability to quickly learn new software programs and technologies

Education

Early Childhood Education Diploma, XYZ College, City, State   2014
First Aid and CPR Certification, Red Cross, City, State   2014

Co-Op Placements

Anytown Childcare Center, City, State   Spring 2014
- Worked with children age 2-10
- Introduced puppet theater play area to encourage creative play
- Planned and implemented book-based units "Chicka Chicka Boom Boom" and "Guess Again"

ABC Childcare Center, City, State   Fall 2013
- Observed and taught group lessons in two classrooms with children aged 4-5

Work Experience

Assistant Early Childhood Educator, XYZ Center, City, State   2010-2012
- Taught one-on-one and small groups; planned and implemented lessons for children age 2-5
- Provided school-aged children with safe transportation to and from school
- Developed and implemented thematic units on hibernation, autumn and deciduous and coniferous trees

Camp Counselor, Anytown Community Center, City, State   Summers 2009 and 2010
- Lead counselor in summer camp for children aged 8-12
- Organized and implemented weekly field trips

Volunteer Experience

Tutor, Anytown Community Center, City, State   2009-2010
- Tutored at risk youth aged 7-12 in English, mathematics, science and reading

Basic Combination Resume

Joe Teacher
101 Fake Street, City, State
(555) 000-0000
joeteacher@emailprovider.com

PROFILE

Elementary teacher with over 5 years of professional teaching experience. Self-motivated, and deeply committed to creating a dynamic and supportive learning environment.

PROFESSIONAL SUMMARY

- Experienced teaching grades five through seven including multi-age split classes
- Develop, implement and evaluate multifaceted lesson plans to accommodate multiple learning styles
- Proven ability to address group and individual needs within a culturally and socio-economically diverse classroom setting; foster a respectful learning environment and develop positive relationships with students, parents and colleagues
- Dedicated to building a positive school community; active leader and enthusiastic in planning and implementing extracurricular school programs and special events
- Experienced with Microsoft Word, Excel and PowerPoint
- Maintain accurate records and consistently complete all reports and other written communication in a timely manner

EXPERIENCE

Elementary Teacher   2011-present
Anytown Elementary School, City, State
- Teach grades five through seven including two years teaching a grade five-six multiage split class
- Prepare and implement grade appropriate curriculum in all major subject areas including, reading, writing, social studies, mathematics and science
- Work cooperatively with colleagues to share and develop lessons and resources and coordinate class trips and special in-class guests
- Prepare and distribute monthly classroom newsletters, regularly update class information on school website, and encourage open communication with parents in person or via email to develop partnerships in learning and inspire a shared commitment to quality education

Occasional Teacher   2010-2011
Anytown School Board, City, State
- Supply teacher in elementary and high school classrooms
- Successfully completed several long term contracts including one month position in a grade three classroom and three weeks in a split grade four-five classroom
- Demonstrated strong classroom management skills and ability to adapt quickly

Joe Teacher
101 Fake Street, City, State
(555) 000-0000
joeteacher@emailprovider.com

EXTRACURRICULAR LEADERSHIP

- Coach school track and field program; plan and lead training program, organize participation in track meets and coordinate total program for approximately 50 fourth through eighth grade students
- Part of the team that plans and stages school winter and spring school-wide student concerts
- Co-developed and implemented Personal Responsibility after school program for at risk students in grades five to eight

EDUCATION

Bachelor of Education Degree   2010
City University, City, State

Bachelor of Arts Degree, English   2009
City University, City, State

PROFESSIONAL DEVELOPMENT

Instructional Models for the Education of Gifted Students Course   2013
City University, City, State

TESOL Certificate (Teaching English as a Second Language)   2012
City University, City, State

VOLUNTEER EXPERIENCE

Tutor, ABC Community Tutoring Program, City, State   2008-2010
- Worked individually and with groups of up to five students to develop literacy and numeracy skills

Play Group Leader, City Children's Center, City, State   2007-2009
- Initiated, developed and team-taught activities to build social skills, impulse control and self-esteem using play therapy concepts and strategies

Teacher's Assistant, City Elementary School, City, State   2007-2009
- Worked with grade two classroom teacher to prepare materials for use in the classroom and assisted with supplementary reading program

Combination Resume With Skills Grouped Into Several Sections

Sonya Fakename
456 Imaginary Street, City, State

sonyafakename@emailprovider.com
Home: 000 000-0000 Cell: 555 555-5555

PROFILE   Career coach with 5 years of workshop facilitation experience. Areas of specialization include work with clients who are injured workers, experienced workers, long-term unemployed and new immigrants.

ACHIEVEMENTS

- Maintain over 80% success rate in job search workshop; consistently met and exceeded program and agency targets
- Individually and as a team, developed and implemented successful marketing strategies which doubled program intake numbers
- Instrumental in establishing new and successful programs within the agency, including building community awareness and refining program delivery and data management
- Part of a team that consistently provides welcoming, professional and nonjudgmental client support

FACILITATION AND COUNSELING

- Use multifaceted program delivery strategies to accommodate multiple learning styles in a workshop setting
- Proven ability to address group and individual needs within a diverse group setting; foster a respectful learning environment and develop partnerships with clients to ensure client, program and agency success
- Experienced facilitating workshops for groups of 8 to 12 individuals; taught groups of up to thirty people
- Excellent knowledge of and ability to research community resources

ADMINISTRATION

- Accurately manage client data for caseload of up to 500 clients per year using Excel and complete weekly, monthly, quarterly and annual reports
- Develop and manage database to efficiently compile and analyze large volume and variety of client data

COMPUTER SKILLS
- Experienced with Microsoft Word, Excel and PowerPoint, and Prezi
- Solid knowledge of self-assessment software including Choices and Career Cruising

Sonya Fakename
456 Imaginary Street, City, State

sonyafakename@emailprovider.com
Home: 000 000-0000 Cell: 555 555-5555

PROFESSIONAL EXPERIENCE

Job Search Workshop Facilitator, Career Services, City, State   2009-present
- Facilitate weekly three-day job search workshop; course material includes resume and cover letter preparation, interview strategies, maintaining self-esteem, labor market trends, and traditional and creative job search techniques
- Facilitate weekly two hour workshops on career exploration, resume preparation, interview techniques and job search strategies
- Manage client data for caseload of approximately 500 clients per year using Excel and in-house software; complete monthly, quarterly and annual reports
- Provide ongoing support to all clients through telephone follow-up, individual counseling and/or internal and external referrals
- Responsible for ongoing development of workshop materials and resources
- Hire and supervise part-time workshop support staff

Music Teacher, Anytown School of Music, City, State (part-time 2008)   2005-2008
- Developed lesson plans for and taught private and group piano and flute lessons
- Collaborate with students and parents to set long and short-term goals and plans including participation in recitals, competitions and examinations

EDUCATION

Career Coach Program, Anytown College, City, State   2008
Bachelor of Music Degree, ABC University, City, State   2005

PROFESSIONAL DEVELOPMENT

Anti-Racist Social Work, Social Development Council, City, State   2013
Crisis Intervention, Mental Health Association, City, State   2012

INTERNSHIPS

Intern, XYZ University Career Services, City, State   Fall 2008
- Co-facilitated seminars concerning career management skills, the new economy and accessing resources for career development
- Completed resume and cover letter critiques for students, alumni and staff
- Assisted clients in the effective use of print and computer based resources

Intern, Community Employment Resource Center, Anytown, State   Spring 2007
- Assisted clients with resume and cover letter preparation and use of resources
- Completed intake evaluations and assessed clients' needs and job readiness

Combination Resume with Accomplishments

Here's a resume with spacing adjusted because it is too long for one page but doesn't fill two pages.

Jane Fakename

202 Any Street, City, State
Home: (555) 000-0000
Cell: (000) 000-0000
janefakename@emailprovider.com

PROFILE Experienced customer service representative with proven commitment to increasing productivity, customer satisfaction and company productivity. Areas of expertise include client services, troubleshooting and account retention.

PROFESSIONAL SUMMARY

- Efficient, well-organized and able to work in a fast paced environment; resolved approximately 200 inquiries per week
- Results oriented; consistently exceed company targets for quality, accuracy and speed of service by over 20%
- Excellent sales skills; successfully cross sell products on 45% of calls
- Committed to maintaining exceptional product knowledge to effectively resolve customer concerns and up-sell by recommending appropriate products
- Demonstrated ability to effectively assess areas of customer concern and offer appropriate recommendations, resulting in increased productivity, account retention and customer loyalty
- Able to quickly establish positive rapport with clients and work well with all levels of management
- Proficient with MS Word, Excel and PowerPoint, and able to quickly learn industry specific customer service software

ACCOMPLISHMENTS

- Lead trainer for new call center staff; ensured new customer service representatives made smooth transition into new role and were able to provide quality customer service
- Developed training and customer service manuals for four new product lines
- Proven ability to diffuse volatile customer situations; directly responsible for resolving complex issue that resulted in retention of $500,000 contract
- Completely revised product database, which simplified product information searches and increased representative efficiency by an average of 10%

Jane Fakename

202 Any Street, City, State
Home: (555) 000-0000
Cell: (000) 000-0000
janefakename@emailprovider.com

EXPERIENCE

Customer Service Representative   2009-2014
ABC Company, City, State
- Consulted with customers by telephone; provided information about products, processed orders, and resolved customer concerns
- Based on knowledge of recurring customer concerns, recommended changes to packaging, shipping and billing methods, which completely eliminated some issues and reduced customer calls on other issues by 60%
- Maintained accurate and timely records of customer communications and transactions, and followed up to ensure appropriate actions were completed to resolve customers' concerns

Customer Service Representative   2007-2009
XYZ Company, City, State
- Worked with customers to resolve billing related issues and assist sales staff with concerns related to specific transactions and billing
- Advised potential customers, providing information about packages and pricing, plan features and billing processes
- Accurately completed enrollment records and maintained complete and accurate records of customer calls using in-house customer service software

EDUCATION

Customer Service Diploma   2006
City College, City, State

PROFESSIONAL DEVELOPMENT

Cross Selling Strategies Course   2013
ABC Company, City, State

Closing the Sale Course   2011
ABC Company, City, State

Combination Resume with Gap in Employment History

Susan Jobseeker

93 Any Street, City, State

sjobseeker@emailprovider.com

Home: (000) 000-0000   Cell: (555) 555-5555

PROFILE   Children's librarian with eight years of experience working in community and academic libraries.

ACCOMPLISHMENTS

- Established and ran two popular parent and child preschool programs for children 18 month2 to 2 years and for children aged 2 to 3 years, encouraging the development of early literacy skills though songs, rhymes and storytelling.
- Created and implemented popular new summer and March Break children's programs which were consistently fully booked on the first available registration day and increased use of the children's library by 20% during March Break and summer months
- Developed thorough knowledge of children's books, reference materials and computer software
- Implemented and managed library social media marketing strategy, which increased community involvement in and awareness of library programs

EXPERIENCE

Faketown Public Library, City, State   2008-2013
Head Children's Librarian (2011-2013)
Librarian (2008-2011)
- Assisted teachers with research projects and conducted tours of the library for public school classes
- Wrote monthly children's library newsletter
- Developed educational series for parents where local experts presented information about topics such as computer safety for children, early literacy development, and healthy development
- Identified and recommended new materials for purchase
- Assisted patrons at the circulation desk
- Supervised and trained 10-12 library volunteers
- Instructed patrons in the use of online resources

Faketown University Library City, State   2006-2007
Library Assistant
- Assisted patrons at the circulation desk
- Shelved books and other materials, located missing items and kept library collection in order

EDUCATION

Bachelor of Arts Degree, English, Faketown University, City, State   2007

COMMUNITY INVOLVEMENT

Fundraiser, Community Literacy Network, City, State   2010-present
- Part of a team that has raised $20,000 for local literacy organization

Combination Resume for a Job Seeker Who is Over 45

James Manager

jmanager@emailprovider.com
67 Fake Street, City, State   Home (000) 000-0000   Cell: (555) 555-5555

PROFILE   Retail manager with over ten years of progressively responsible fashion retail sales and management experience. Able to motivate staff in a competitive team-based environment.

ACCOMPLISHMENTS

- Consistently meet and exceed monthly store sales targets
- Developed and implemented effective marketing strategy which increased store sales by 15% when stores in other locations were experiencing declines in sales
- Created staff training manual and records system, which streamlined training process and ensured staff received all training relevant to their role in the store
- Achieved lowest staff turnover rate of all store locations though effective employee recognition and training strategies
- Trained store managers on staff recognition and training strategies, which resulted in partner stores reducing staff turnover by an average of 20%
- Experienced with Word and Excel

EMPLOYMENT

Manager, ABC Clothing Company, City, State   2009-present
- Supervise a staff of 3 full-time and 6 part-time employees, and oversee day to day operation of a busy and growing retail clothing store
- Assist customers, with an eye to providing exceptional, personalized customer service and building relationships with long term, loyal customers
- Organize and lead team meetings and training sessions
- Hire and train new staff, create staffing schedules and manage payroll
- Set monthly sales targets and track all sales data and store budget
- Track inventory and analyze product sales and communicate sales trends to company buyer

Retail Sales Associate, XYZ Clothing, City, State   2005-2008
- Handled all aspects of sales including assisting customers with choices, advising on care of products, and processing cash, credit card, and debit payments
- Developed creative window displays to increase walk-in customers and draw attention to featured products

EDUCATION

Grade 12 Diploma, Anytown High School, City, State

Basic Functional Resume

I do not recommend using this resume style. Notice how there is no information to show the employer how or when the jobseeker developed the skills that are described on the resume.

Karen Jobseeker

kjobseeker@emailprovider.com

59 Imaginary Street, City, State

Home: (555) 555-5555 Cell: (000) 000-0000

Profile   Machine operator with 5 years of experience in a resin manufacturing plant. Safe and dependable worker; able to troubleshoot and meet quality standards and production quotas.

Summary of Skills

- Mechanically inclined; able to troubleshoot basic mechanical problems on equipment
- Experienced with safely handling and transferring hazardous chemicals
- Able to work and plan daily tasks independently
- Member of Emergency Team; trained in first aid, spill response and cleanup, fire response
- Health and Safety Committee member
- Cross-trained; successfully qualified to work in a variety of production positions
- Trained and experienced in correct machine lockout techniques for equipment cleaning
- Able to regularly lift and transfer 40 pound bags

Machine Operator

- Monitored and adjusted various aspects of the production process to ensure customer requirements were met, including product inspection
- Maintained expected production rates and met production goals
- Investigated and resolved quality concerns
- As part of 5S team, reorganized production area to create cleaner and more efficient work area; reduced wasted effort and improved housekeeping
- Performed daily equipment safety inspections

Packer

- Packaged finished product coming from production lines for shipment to customer
- Performed final quality inspection on product before sealing and packaging
- Consistently maintained expected pace of work and met daily targets
- Cross trained in a variety of production roles to fill in during breaks and vacations

Basic Chronological Resume

Justin Anyone
58 Any Street, City, State

justinanyone@emailprovider.com
Home: (000) 000-0000 Cell: (555) 555-5555

Profile

Quality assurance lab technologist with six years of experience in the paper industry. Proven track record of reducing customer claims and improving product consistency.

Employment Experience

Paper Quality Technician   2008-2014
ABC Manufacturing Company, City, State
- Successfully maintained paper inspection process at ISO 9001 certified plant; responsible for analysis of 500,000 square meters of paper per week
- Reduced customer claims by 20% through improvements in claim tracking trend analysis and paper inspection process
- Communicated with customers regarding quality related issues, troubleshooting any problems and taking appropriate corrective actions
- Provide internal technical service and support to a broad range of departments, including sales, production and logistics
- Internal auditor for ISO 9001 system; annually perform 6-10 quality system audits in a variety of departments and report findings to management
- Conduct visits to supplier sites for planning and problem resolution
- Used Six Sigma project management techniques to support site Six Sigma projects, which improved product consistency by 10%
- Skilled with a variety of paper quality inspections and tests including weight, strength, color and porosity
- Designed and implemented Access based database to track and analyze paper quality results
- Accurately maintain and calibrate testing equipment

Education

Six Sigma Green Belt, XYZ Corporate Training, City, State   2010

Microsoft Access Course, Faketown College, City, State   2009

Bachelor of Science Degree, Chemistry, Anytown University, City, State   2007

Chronological Resume with Education Listed First

Samuel Jobseeker (RRP)

samueljobseeker@emailprovider.com
45 Fake Street, City, State
Home: (000) 000-0000
Cell: (555) 555-5555

PROFILE

Vocational rehabilitation specialist with 7 years of counseling experience. Self-motivated, and able to work independently. Areas of specialization include work with injured workers, experienced workers and long-term unemployed.

EDUCATION

Master of Vocational Rehabilitation Counseling
Any University, City, State   degree expected spring 2015

Career and Work Counselor Diploma
FakeName College, City, State   2007

Bachelor of Arts Degree, Psychology
Anytown University, City, State   2005

PROFESSIONAL EXPERIENCE

Case Manager
Anytown Vocational Services, City, State   2011-2014
- Developed and managed safe and suitable return to work action plans in partnership with injured workers and the insuring agency
- Estimated and tracked costs of labor market re-entry plans, ensured funds were available and submitted invoices for payment to secondary service providers
- Developed, negotiated, budgeted and managed half-million dollar training projects
- In partnership with injured workers and claims adjudicators, recommended appropriate career options and training plans for injured workers
- Supported injured workers in retraining programs, including problem solving in cooperation with the insuring agency, injured workers and secondary service providers to resolve a variety challenges and ensure success of return to work action plans
- Earned Registered Rehabilitation Professional (RRP) designation 2011

Samuel Jobseeker (RRP)

samueljobseeker@emailprovider.com
45 Fake Street, City, State
Home: (000) 000-0000
Cell: (555) 555-5555

PROFESSIONAL EXPERIENCE (Continued)

Job Club Facilitator
Community Vocational Services, City, State   2007-2011

- Facilitated three day job search workshop; course material included resume and cover letter preparation, interview strategies, labor market trends and traditional and job search techniques
- Managed client data for caseload of approximately 500 clients per year using Excel and complete monthly, quarterly and annual reports
- Provided ongoing support to all clients through in-office and telephone follow-up, and/or internal and external referrals
- Responsible for ongoing development of workshop materials and resources
- Provided welcoming, professional and nonjudgmental client support
- Assess needs of clients and assist clients to develop, implement and evaluate strategies for professional and development, emphasizing strengths and overcoming challenges

PROFESSIONAL DEVELOPMENT

Counseling Ethics
Case Manager Home Study, Online   2011

Crisis Intervention
Mental Health Association, City, State   2009

**Notice this resume does not quite fill two pages. Sometimes, no mater what tricks you use, you will not be able to get your resume to fit perfectly on the page. This resume is too long to fit on one page, and too short to completely fill out two pages. In that case, it is better to use two pages and fill it out as much as you reasonably can because white space makes your resume more readable. Trying to cram all of this information on a single page would make it difficult to read.

Career Change Resume

Emma Fakename

12 Imaginary Street, City, State
Home: (555) 000-0000   Cell: (000) 000-0000
emmafakename@emailprovider.com

PROFILE

Career and Work Counselor program graduate with five years of teaching experience. Thorough knowledge of effective job search strategies. Able to address group and individual needs within a diverse group setting; foster a respectful learning environment and develop partnerships with clients to ensure client, program and agency success.

SUMMARY OF SKILLS

- Develop, implement and evaluate multifaceted lesson plans to accommodate multiple learning styles in a workshop setting
- Excellent knowledge of and ability to research community resources
- Experienced teaching groups of up to 30 individuals
- Effectively assess needs of clients and assist clients to develop, implement and evaluate strategies for personal and professional development
- Experienced with Microsoft Word, Excel and PowerPoint
- Solid knowledge of self-assessment software including Choices and Career Cruising

EDUCATION

Career and Work Counselor Diploma, Anytown College, City, State   2014

Bachelor of Education Degree, Faketown University, City, State   2007

Bachelor of Music Degree, Faketown University, City, State   2006

INTERNSHIPS

Intern, Anytown University Career Services, City, State   Fall 2013
- Co-facilitated seminars concerning career management skills, the new economy and accessing resources for career development
- Completed individual resume and cover letter critiques for students, alumni and staff
- Assisted clients in the effective use of print and computer based resources

Emma Fakename

12 Imaginary Street, City, State
Home: (555) 000-0000   Cell: (000) 000-0000
emmafakename@emailprovider.com

INTERNSHIPS CONTINUED

Intern, Community Employment Resource Center, City, State   Spring 2013
- Assisted clients using print and computer resources and preparing resumes and cover letters
- Completed initial intake evaluations and assessed clients' needs and job readiness

PROFESSIONAL EXPERIENCE

Music Teacher   2009-2012
Anytown School of Music, City, State (part-time 2009-2010)
- Developed lesson plans for and taught private and group piano, flute, clarinet and early childhood music classes
- Collaborated with students and parents to set long and short-term goals and plans including participation in recitals, competitions and examinations

Adult Education Teacher   2009-2010
Adult Learning Center, City, State
- Facilitated return to work and entry into college of injured workers through development of literacy and numeracy skills
- Ensured maintenance of timelines through effective long and short-term planning and time management

Music Teacher   2007-2009
Anywhere Music Academy, City, State
- Developed curricula for and taught private and group piano, flute, theory and early childhood music classes
- Organized quarterly student recitals and co-directed a musical production
- Assisted with lesson scheduling, accounts receivable and inventory control

Job Coach   Summer 2006
Association for Community Living, City, State
- Supported individuals who were developmentally delayed; developed work, life and social skills

Several Contracts at a Temporary Agency

Anna Fakename

456 Imaginary Street, City, State

afakename@emailprovider.com

Home: (000) 000-0000   Cell: (555) 555-5555

PROFILE Bilingual administrative assistant with exceptional computer skills and eight years of experience providing administrative support in nonprofit community agencies.

SUMMARY OF SKILLS

- Type 70 words per minute error-free
- Advanced skill with Word, Excel, PowerPoint, Access and Prezi, knowledge of basic HTML
- Exceptional knowledge of community resources coupled with strong research skills
- Greet all clients in a professional and friendly manner, and maintain poise and clear thinking in a busy, constantly changing work environment
- Bilingual in English and Spanish

EXPERIENCE

Administrative Assistant, Anytown Temporary Agency, City, State   2013-present
- Successfully completed several contract positions including a three month contract at ABC Company, and a six month contract at XYZ Company
- Schedule appointments, prepare correspondence and manage invoices
- Standardized paper and digital filing system
- Answer a multi-line phone system; handle 50 to 60 calls per day

Administrative Assistant, XYZ Resource Center, City, State   2006-2012
- Greeted clients, assisted clients in finding print and online materials in the resource center and scheduled appointments for three counselors
- Scheduled quarterly meetings and handled travel arrangements for 3 senior managers; arranged meal orders, prepared audio-visual equipment, made travel arrangements and maintained documentation for expense reports
- Compiled and prepared presentation visual aids for weekly and quarterly meetings
- Purchased business supplies, maintained cost records and ensured costs remained within budget; negotiated contract with suppliers, which resulted in 20% savings in the cost of all office supplies
- Created volunteer training manual, which streamlined training of 20 volunteers, clarified responsibilities and eliminated duplication of tasks
- Updated company website on a weekly basis and compiled monthly office newsletter
- Organized annual general meetings; researched and booked venues, booked travel and accommodations for guest speakers, and arranged catering

EDUCATION

Advanced Microsoft Office Certificate, XYZ College, City, State   2013
Office Administration Diploma, ABC College, City, State   2006

Job Seeker Has a Short Work History

Joshua Newgrad

62 Any Street, City, State

jnewgrad@emailprovider.com
Cell: (000) 000-0000

Profile   Experienced retail sales assistant manager seeking a full-time position at XYZ Boutique. Areas of expertise include customer retention, social media marketing, and staff training and development.

Accomplishments

- Consistently surpass individual sales targets by 20%
- Promoted to assistant manager within 10 months of working at Anytown Department Store
- Praised by customers and manager for comprehensive product knowledge and ability to communicate product information clearly
- Excellent memory for names and details; have developed positive relationships with repeat customers
- Excellent technical troubleshooting skills; quickly became go-to person for resolving problems with store computers and office equipment
- Developed successful social media campaign which increased overall sales by 10 percent and increased community awareness of and affinity for the business

Experience

Anytown Department Store, City, State   2013-present
Assistant Manager (2013-present)
- Support store manager in management of the store including providing customer assistance, dispute resolution, and staff training and motivation
- Schedule monthly team meetings and, with the store manager, develop and run training workshops to develop staff customer service skills, sales strategies and product knowledge.
- Track data to analyze and improve store performance
- Develop and implement social media marketing strategies
- Train new staff in product knowledge, company policies and effective customer service and sales strategies

Retail Sales Associate (2013)
- Facilitated all aspects of sales and customer assistance including educating customers about relevant products and services, receiving payment and completing warranty documents

Education

High School Diploma, Anytown High School, City, State   2013

Job Seeker's Relevant Experience is in the Past

Chris Fakename
94 Any Street, City, State

chrisfakename@emailprovider.com

Home: (000) 000-0000   Cell: (555) 555-5555

PROFILE   Experienced forklift operator with valid license and seven years of manufacturing experience seeking a full-time position at ABC Widgets.

SUMMARY OF SKILLS

- Over five years of experience working as a forklift operator; possess current lift truck certification
- Work safely and efficiently with minimal supervision loading and unloading trucks
- Detail oriented, self-motivated, and able to work flexible hours

RELEVANT EXPERIENCE

Forklift Operator, XYZ Company, City, State   2009-2013
- Loaded and unloaded trucks and completed packaging quality checks on material
- Reviewed packing slips for inbound loads and completed all necessary paperwork and system updates for inbound and outbound loads
- Completed damage reports as required
- Ensured proper safe loading and unloading procedures were followed
- Maintained clean and safe work environment in warehouse and parking lot areas
- Accurately completed daily log sheet and logged and distributed courier packages
- Completed daily cycle counts and pallet inventory counts when required

Forklift Operator / Machine Operator, ABC Company, City, State   2006-2009
- Transferred material to and from production areas using forklift
- Monitored and adjusted various aspects of the production process to ensure customer requirements were met
- Maintained expected production rates and performed product inspection
- Investigated and resolved quality concerns
- As part of 5S team, reorganized production area to create a cleaner and more efficient work area; reduced wasted effort and improved housekeeping
- Performed daily equipment safety inspections

ADDITIONAL EXPERIENCE

Retail Sales Associate, ABC Building Supply, City, State   2013-present

EDUCATION

Forklift Certificate, XYZ Training, City, State   2013
DOT Training, ABC Training, City, State   2013
HAZCOM Training, ABC Training, City, State   2013
Grade Twelve Diploma, Anytown High School, City, State   2005

Relevant Experience Was Obtained Through Volunteer Work

Anna Fakename

456 Imaginary Street, City, State

afakename@emailprovider.com

Home: (000) 000-0000   Cell: (555) 555-5555

PROFILE   Professional administrative assistant with exceptional client service skills and four years of experience in the non-profit sector.

SUMMARY OF SKILLS

- Type 70 words per minute error-free
- Advanced level skill with Word, Excel, PowerPoint, Access, Prezi, and HTML
- Exceptional knowledge of community resources coupled with strong research skills
- Greet all clients in a professional and friendly manner, and maintain poise and clear thinking in a busy, constantly changing work environment
- Bilingual in English and Spanish

RELEVANT EXPERIENCE

Administrative Assistant (Volunteer), ABC Community Center, City, State   2011-present
- Greet clients, assist clients in finding print and online materials in the resource center and schedule appointments for three counselors
- Assist with organization of quarterly meetings; arrange meal orders, prepare audio-visual equipment, and prepare printed materials
- Compile and prepare presentation visual aids for weekly and quarterly meetings
- Created a volunteer training manual, which streamlined training of 20 volunteers, clarified responsibilities and eliminated duplication of tasks

Administrative Assistant (Volunteer), XYZ Resource Center, City, State   2010-2011
- Updated website on a weekly basis and compiled monthly newsletter
- Scheduled appointments for a team of 6 staff
- Assisted in organizing annual general meetings; researched venues, accommodations for guest speakers, and arranged catering
- Standardized paper and digital filing system
- Answered a busy multi-line phone system; handled 50 to 60 calls per day

ADDITIONAL EXPERIENCE

Server, Hometown Restaurant, City, State   2005-2008

EDUCATION

Advanced Microsoft Office Certificate, XYZ College, City, State   2014
High School Diploma, Anytown High School, City, State   2005

Job Seeker Earned Increased Responsibility at One Company

Andrew Jobseeker

andrewjobseeker@emailprovider.com
84 Fake Street, City, State
Home (000) 000-0000
Cell: (555) 555-5555

Profile

Wastewater operator with 8 years of experience working in a manufacturing environment. Quick learner; cross-trained to work in a variety of production positions.

Skills and Accomplishments

- Operated wastewater treatment system for three years with no environmental violations
- Possess current forklift certification and overhead crane certification
- Experienced with safely handling and transferring hazardous chemicals
- Mechanically inclined; able to troubleshoot basic mechanical problems on equipment
- Able to work and plan daily tasks independently
- Member of Emergency Team; trained in first aid, spill response and cleanup, fire response
- Health and Safety Committee member
- Cross-trained; successfully qualified to work in a variety of production positions
- Trained and experienced in correct machine lockout techniques during equipment cleaning

Work Experience

ABC Manufacturing Company, City, State   2006-2014
Wastewater Operator (2010-2013)
- Managed chemical treatment of wastewater, including filter press operation, movement of chemicals to wastewater area, taking sewer samples, cleaning filter press plates
- Accurately maintained wastewater inventory and treatment logs on a daily basis using in house inventory control software, and maintained clean and safe work area
- Periodically met with city water treatment plant operators as part of standard inspections
- Regularly handled 40 pound bags of treatment chemicals

Andrew Jobseeker

andrewjobseeker@emailprovider.com
84 Fake Street, City, State
Home (000) 000-0000
Cell: (555) 555-5555

Work Experience (ABC Manufacturing Company, Continued)

Machine Operator (2007-2010)
- Monitored and adjusted various aspects of the production process to ensure customer requirements were met, and investigated and resolved quality concerns
- Maintained expected production rates and performed product inspection
- As part of 5S team, reorganized production area, to create cleaner and more efficient work area; reduced wasted effort and improved housekeeping
- Performed daily equipment safety inspections

Packer (2005-2007)
- Packaged finished product coming from production lines for shipment to customer
- Performed final quality inspection on product before sealing and packaging
- Consistently maintained expected pace of work and met daily targets
- Cross trained in a variety of production roles to fill in during breaks and vacations

Education

HAZCOM Training   2014
ABC Manufacturing Company, City, State

Forklift Certification   2013
XYZ Training, City, State

Overhead Crane Certification   2013
XYZ Training, City, State

First Aid and CPR   2013
Red Cross, City, State

Grade 12 Diploma   2006
Anytown High School, City, State

JOB SEEKER HELD THE SAME JOB AT DIFFERENT COMPANIES

Stephen Musician

295 Fake Street, City, State

smusician@emailprovider.com

Home: (000) 000-0000   Cell: (555) 555-5555

PROFILE   Music teacher with 9 years of experience teaching group and private piano, flute and clarinet lessons and 6 years of experience managing busy private music academies. Well organized and able to develop positive relationships with parents, students and teachers to ensure success of students and school.

TEACHING

- Developed lesson plans for and taught private and group piano, flute, clarinet and early childhood music for approximately 60 students annually
- Prepared students for participation in recitals, competitions and examinations; 80% of students completing examinations earned first class honors
- Collaborate with students and parents to set long and short-term goals and plans including participation in recitals, competitions and examinations
- Created, implemented and evaluated multifaceted lesson plans to accommodate multiple learning styles in a group setting
- Fostered a respectful learning environment and developed positive partnerships with parents and students to ensure student success

STUDIO MANAGEMENT

- Managed professional music studio with 20 to 25 teachers and over 800 students
- Developed and implemented marketing strategies which increased student registration by 15%
- Developed and implemented successful summer music programs which increased summer enrollment by 20%
- Scheduled classes, organized quarterly student recitals and oversaw applications to examinations
- Trained and supervised instructors and provided support with instructional challenges
- Established parent and tots music program, and built relationship with local schools to teach group piano lessons in schools; extending teaching hours and increasing enrollment by 10%

PROFESSIONAL EXPERIENCE

Studio Director and Music Teacher, Anytown Academy of Music, City, State   2010-2014
Studio Director and Music Teacher, Faketown School of Music, City, State   2007-2010
Music Teacher, Anywhere Music Academy, City, State   2005-2007

EDUCATION

Bachelor of Music Degree, Anywhere University, City, State   2007

COMMUNITY INVOLVEMENT

Music Play Group Leader, Anywhere Children's Center, City, State   2005-2007
- Initiated, developed and team-taught activities to build social skills, impulse control and self-esteem using music therapy concepts and strategies

CHAPTER SIXTEEN
RESOURCES

There are no tasks for this chapter. Instead, you will find tools and resources for more in-depth research you may need to do while writing your resume.

WHAT YOU WILL FIND IN THIS CHAPTER:

1. Resume Writing Form
2. List of Verbs for Resume Writing
3. List of Descriptive Words (Adjectives and Adverbs) for Resume Writing
4. Websites That Have Thorough Job Descriptions
5. Choosing a Career
6. Grammar for Resume Writing

> *"Knowing is not enough; we must apply.*
> *Willing is not enough; we must do."*
> *Johann Wolfgang von Goethe*

Resume Writing Form

I have posted a free resume writing form on my website. You can download a copy, which you can use to help organize your thoughts as you write your resume.

careerchoiceguide.com/resumeform (this URL will open a pdf document)

List of Verbs for Resume Writing

Use a variety of strong, meaningful verbs to clearly describe your experience and achievements. The list below will give you some ideas to spice up the verbs on your resume. Remember, if you are not happy with the verbs you have used on your resume, you can also use the website thesaurus.com to look up the verbs you have used and find alternative words that might work.

A
Accelerated
Accomplished
Accentuated
Accomplished
Accounted for
Accumulated
Achieved
Acquired
Acted
Activated
Active in
Adapted
Addressed
Adjusted
Administered
Advanced
Advertised
Advised
Advocated
Affected
Aided
Alerted
Allocated
Amplified
Analyzed
Answered
Anticipated
Applied
Appointed
Appraised
Approved
Arbitrated
Arranged
Articulated

Ascertained
Assembled
Assessed
Assigned
Assisted
Assumed responsibility
Assured
Attained
Attracted
Audited
Augmented
Authored
Authorized
Automated
Awarded

B
Balanced
Began
Boosted
Bought
Briefed
Broadened
Budgeted
Built

C
Calculated
Campaigned
Captured
Carried out
Cataloged
Caused
Centralized
Chaired

Championed
Changed
Channeled
Charted
Checked
Clarified
Classified
Closed
Co-directed
Co-managed
Coached
Coded
Collaborated
Collected
Combined
Commanded
Commented
Communicated
Compared
Compiled
Completed
Composed
Computed
Conceived
Conceptualized
Condensed
Conducted
Conferred
Conserved
Considered
Consolidated
Constructed
Consulted
Contacted
Contained

Continued
Contracted
Contributed
Controlled
Converted
Conveyed
Convinced
Cooperated
Coordinated
Corrected
Correlated
Corresponded
Corroborated
Costed
Counseled
Counted
Crafted
Created
Critiqued
Cultivated
Customized
Cut

D
Dealt with
Debated
Debugged
Decided
Decreased
Defined
Delegated
Delivered
Demonstrated
Described
Designated
Designed
Detected
Determined
Developed
Devised
Diagnosed
Diagrammed
Directed

Discovered
Discussed
Dispatched
Dispensed
Displayed
Dissected
Distinguished
Distributed
Diversified
Diverted
Documented
Doubled
Drafted
Drew
Drove

E
Earned
Economized
Edited
Educated
Effected
Elected
Elicited
Eliminated
Emphasized
Employed
Empowered
Enabled
Enacted
Encouraged
Ended
Endorsed
Energized
Enforced
Engineered
Enhanced
Enlarged
Enlisted
Ensured
Entered
Entertained
Established

Estimated
Evaluated
Examined
Exceeded
Executed
Exhibited
Expanded
Expedited
Experienced
Experimented
Explained
Explored
Expressed
Extended
Extracted

F
Fabricated
Facilitated
Familiarized
Fashioned
Filed
Filled
Finalized
Financed
Fine-tuned
Fixed
Focused
Forged
Formalized
Formed
Formulated
Fortified
Fostered
Found
Founded
Fulfilled
Furnished
Furthered

G
Gained
Gathered

Generated
Governed
Graded
Graduated
Granted
Grew
Grossed
Guided

H
Halted
Halved
Handled
Harmonized
Harnessed
Headed
Heightened
Helped
Hired
Honed
Hosted
Hypothesized

I
Identified
Illustrated
Imagined
Implemented
Impressed
Improved
Improvised
Incorporated
Increased
Indexed
Individualized
Influenced
Informed
Initiated
Innovated
Inspected
Inspired
Installed
Instilled

Instituted
Instructed
Insured
Integrated
Interacted
Interpreted
Intervened
Interviewed
Introduced
Invented
Inventoried
Invested
Investigated
Invited
Involved
Issued

J-K-L
Joined
Judged
Kept
Launched
Learned
Lectured
Led
Liaised
Licensed
Lifted
Listened
Located
Logged

M
Machined
Made
Magnified
Maintained
Managed
Manufactured
Mapped
Marketed
Mastered
Matched

Maximized
Measured
Mediated
Mentored
Merged
Met
Minimized
Mobilized
Moderated
Modernized
Modified
Monitored
Motivated
Moved

N
Navigated
Negotiated
Netted

O
Observed
Obtained
Opened
Operated
Optimized
Orchestrated
Ordered
Organized
Originated
Outlined
Overhauled
Oversaw

P
Participated
Perceived
Performed
Persuaded
Photographed
Piloted
Pinpointed
Pioneered

Placed
Planned
Played
Posted
Predicted
Prepared
Prescribed
Presented
Preserved
Presided
Prevented
Printed
Prioritized
Processed
Procured
Produced
Programmed
Projected
Promoted
Proofread
Proposed
Prospected
Protected
Proved
Provided
Publicized
Published
Purchased
Pursued

Q
Qualified
Questioned

R
Raised
Ran
Ranked
Rated
Reached
Realigned
Realized
Reasoned

Received
Recognized
Recommended
Reconciled
Recorded
Recruited
Rectified
Recycled
Redesigned
Reduced
Reestablished
Reevaluated
Referred
Regained
Registered
Regulated
Rehabilitated
Reinforced
Reinvigorated
Related
Remodeled
Rendered
Renegotiated
Reorganized
Repaired
Replaced
Replied
Reported
Repositioned
Represented
Researched
Reserved
Reshaped
Resolved
Responded
Restored
Restructured
Retrieved
Revamped
Reversed
Reviewed
Revised
Revitalized

Routed

S
Saved
Scheduled
Screened
Searched
Secured
Selected
Separated
Served
Serviced
Settled
Shaped
Shared
Showed
Signed
Simplified
Simulated
Sketched
Slashed
Sold
Solicited
Solidified
Solved
Sorted
Sought
Sparked
Spearheaded
Specialized
Specified
Spoke
Sponsored
Staffed
Standardized
Started
Steered
Stored
Streamlined
Strengthened
Stressed
Stretched
Structured

Studied
Submitted
Substituted
Succeeded
Summarized
Superseded
Supervised
Supplemented
Supplied
Supported
Surpassed
Surveyed
Sustained
Synchronized
Synthesized

T
Tabulated
Tackled
Targeted
Taught
Terminated
Tested
Tightened
Totaled
Toured
Traced

Tracked
Traded
Trained
Transcribed
Transferred
Transformed
Transitioned
Translated
Transmitted
Transported
Traveled
Treated
Triggered
Trimmed
Tripled
Triumphed
Troubleshot
Turned
Tutored
Typed

U
Umpired
Uncovered
Understood
Understudied
Undertook

Underwent
Underwrote
Unified
United
Updated
Upgraded
Urged
Used
Utilized

V
Validated
Valued
Verbalized
Verified
Visited
Vitalized
Volunteered

W
Waged
Weighed
Widened
Won
Worked
Wrote

List of Descriptive Words (Adjectives and Adverbs) for Resume Writing

Go beyond simply stating that you completed a task and describe how you completed your work related tasks. Use these descriptive words to help make your phrases more descriptive.

A

able / ably
absolute / absolutely
abundant / abundantly
accommodating / accommodatingly
accurate / accurately
active / actively
adept / adeptly
affirmative / affirmatively
aggressive / aggressively
alert / alertly
alternative / alternatively
ambitious / ambitiously
amicable / amicably
analytical / analytically
annual / annually
appealing / appealingly
appropriate / appropriately
approximate / approximately
ardent / ardently
artful / artfully
articulate / articulately
artistic / artistically
assertive / assertively
assured / assuredly
astute / astutely
athletic / athletically
attentive / attentively
authentic / authentically
authoritative / authoritatively
avid / avidly

B

beneficial / beneficially
brave / bravely
brief / briefly
bright / brightly
broad / broadly

C

calm / calmly
candid / candidly
capable / capably
careful / carefully
casual / casually
cautious / cautiously
central / centrally
certain / certainly
cheerful / cheerfully
clear / clearly
close / closely
coherent / coherently
cohesive / cohesively
collective / collectively
compassionate / compassionately
competent / competently
competitive / competitively
complete / completely
comprehensive / comprehensively
concise / concisely
conclusive / conclusively
confidential / confidentially
confident / confidently
congenial / congenially
conscientious / conscientiously
considerable / considerably

considerate / considerately
consistent / consistently
constant / constantly
continual / continually
cooperative / cooperatively
courteous / courteously
creative / creatively

D

decreasing / decreasingly
definite / definitely
deft / deftly
deliberate / deliberately
delicate / delicately
dependable / dependably
development / developmentally
devoted / devotedly
diligent / diligently
diplomatic / diplomatically
direct / directly
discreet / discreetly
distinct / distinctly
diverse / diversified / diversely
dramatic / dramatically
dynamic / dynamically

E

eager / eagerly
easy / easily
effective / effectively
efficient / efficiently
elaborate / elaborately
emphatic / emphatically
energetic / energetically
enterprising / enterprisingly
enthusiastic / enthusiastically
entire / entirely
equal / equally
essential / essentially
even / evenly
eventual / eventually
evident / evidently
exact / exactly

exceeding / exceedingly
excellent / excellently
exceptional / exceptionally
expedient / expediently
experienced
expert / expertly
extensive / extensively
extraordinary / extraordinarily
extreme / extremely
extrovert

F

fair / fairly
faithful / faithfully
favorable / favorably
financial / financially
fine / finely
firm / firmly
flexible / flexibly
fluent / fluently
formal / formally
frank / frankly
free / freely
frequent / frequently
fresh / freshly
full / fully

G

generous / generously
genuine / genuinely
gracious / graciously

H

harmonious / harmoniously
helpful / helpfully
high / highly
honest / honestly

I

ideal / ideally
immediate / immediately
immense / immensely
important / importantly

increasing / increasingly
independent / independently
industrious / industriously
influential / influentially
informal / informally
inherent / inherently
initial / initially
innate / innately
innovative / innovatively
insightful / insightfully
instrumental / instrumentally
integral
intellectual / intellectually
intelligent / intelligently
intense / intensely
intricate / intricately
inventive / inventively

J
joint / jointly
just / justly

K
keen / keenly
kind / kindly

L
leading
logical / logically
loyal / loyally

M
mature / maturely
meaningful / meaningfully
memorable / memorably
methodical / methodically
meticulous / meticulously
mindful / mindfully

N
natural / naturally
neat / neatly
notable / notably

O
objective / objectively
observant / observantly
occasional / occasionally
official / officially
open / openly
optimistic / optimistically
original / originally

P
particular / particularly
perceptive / perceptively
persistent / persistently
persuasive / persuasively
pioneering
pleasant / pleasantly
polite / politely
popular / popularly
positive / positively
potent / potently
powerful / powerfully
practical / practically
precise / precisely
preliminary / preliminarily
present / presently
previous / previously
principal / principally
private / privately
productive / productively
professional / professionally
proficient / proficiently
profitable / profitably
profound / profoundly
progressive / progressively
prominent / prominently
prompt / promptly
proper / properly
prudent / prudently
public / publicly
punctual / punctually

Q
quick / quickly

R

rapid / rapidly
rational / rationally
realistic / realistically
reassuring / reassuringly
recent / recently
regular / regularly
reliable / reliably
repeated / repeatedly
resilient / resiliently
resolute / resolutely
resourceful / resourcefully
respectful / respectfully
responsible / responsibly
rigorous / rigorously
robust / robustly
routine / routinely

S

safe / safely
scholarly
secure / securely
selective / selectively
sensitive / sensitively
serious / seriously
sharp / sharply
shrewd / shrewdly
significant / significantly
sincere / sincerely
singular / singularly
sizable / sizably
skillful / skillfully
slight / slightly
smart / smartly
smooth / smoothly
social / socially
solid / solidly
sophisticated
sound / soundly
special / specially
specific / specifically
spontaneous / spontaneously
steadfast / steadfastly

steady / steadily
straightforward / straightforwardly
strategic / strategically
strict / strictly
striking / strikingly
strong / strongly
substantial / substantially
subtle / subtly
successful / successfully
succinct / succinctly
sudden / suddenly
suitable / suitably
supportive / supportively
systematic / systematically

T

tactful / tactfully
tangible / tangibly
tasteful / tastefully
technical / technically
tenacious / tenaciously
thorough / thoroughly
thoughtful / thoughtfully
timely
tireless / tirelessly
traditional / traditionally
tremendous / tremendously
true / truly
typical / typically

U

ultimate / ultimately
unambiguous / unambiguously
uncommon / uncommonly
unconditional / unconditionally
undeniable / undeniably
understandable / understandably
unerring / unerringly
unexpected / unexpectedly
uniform / uniformly
usual / usually

V
variable / variably
varied
vast / vastly
verbal / verbally
virtual / virtually
visible / visibly
vital / vitally

vivid / vividly

W
weekly
well
wide / widely
willing / willingly

Websites That Have Thorough Job Descriptions

The websites listed below provide detailed job descriptions for thousands of jobs. You can use that information to help you think through all of the tasks and skills that are connected to a specific type of job.

Please do not simply copy the points in a job description and paste those points to your resume. Doing so will result in a resume that is not effective because it will not be a good reflection of your personal skills and experiences. Instead, review the points that describe a job you have done in the past; use those points to remind yourself of tasks you have performed or skills you have developed, and then rephrase the points so they are written in your own words and are a clear reflection of the specific experience and skills you can offer an employer.

The sites are American and Canadian government run sites, so the information is country-specific. Although these resources use North American information, you may still find them to be a useful starting point for researching job duties and skills if you are searching for a job in other countries.

If you are job searching outside of the United States or Canada, keep in mind that job duties, and educational and skill requirements for specific jobs can vary from country to country; however, there will be many similarities, so these resources are worth a look even if you are job searching in another country.

Also, please remember that resume expectations can vary from country to country. The resume tips in this book are based on standard expectations that most American and Canadian employers have when reviewing resumes. If you are job searching in another country, it will be important to ensure that you speak to someone in your local area who is an expert on job searching to ensure you take into account any differences in resume expectations in your country.

American sites with job descriptions

Occupational Outlook Handbook – www.bls.gov/search/ooh.htm

Simply type a job title into the search box. Review the list of results to find the one that is the best match for the job you are researching, and click on the link. You will find sections that describe the nature of the work as well as training and other requirements; both of those sections may provide information that will help you to think of items to include on your resume. Be sure to include the www prefix when you type this web address. If you omit the www prefix, you will be taken to the wrong page on the Bureau of Labor Statistics' website.

O*NET Online - onetonline.org

From the O*Net Online home page, find the search box. As of this writing, the search box is in the top right corner of the site, and it is labeled "Occupation Quick Search." Type in the name of the job title you want to research, and then review the list of results to find the one that is the best match for the job you are researching, and click on the link.

The link will take you to a summary report, which has plenty of information about skills, training and tasks connected to the job you selected. This summary report should provide enough information for most people who are using the information for resume writing help, but if you would like to access an extremely detailed report with additional skills and tasks listed, click on the tab labeled "Details" and you will be taken to a page with even more information about the job you selected.

Canadian site with job descriptions:

National Occupational Classification (NOC) -

www5.hrsdc.gc.ca/NOC/English/NOC/2011/Welcome.aspx

Scroll down to the bottom of the page, type your job title in the search box at the bottom left, and click "Go." There may be several variations of your job listed in the NOC. Scroll through the results, and click on any jobs that are a good fit for the type of work you do to review the information. Be sure to type the full address, including the www5 at the beginning. If you omit the www5 prefix, you will be sent to a different part of the Canadian government's website.

Other sources of job descriptions:

You may be able to access a database of thorough job descriptions at your local library or an employment resource center, if you have one in your area.

Some libraries and employment resource centers maintain subscriptions to excellent, but expensive, career planning software, which patrons or clients can access for free. Alternatively, you may find print-based resources with detailed job descriptions at a library or an employment resource center. Drop by your local library or employment resource center and tell the staff there that you are looking for job descriptions. They will be able to point you in the right direction.

Choosing a Career

careerchoiceguide.com/choosing-a-career.html

The link above links to all of the career planning information on my own website. It provides links to several articles about making career choices, taking career tests, setting career goals and making decisions about education.

Grammar for Resume Writing

thesaurus.com

This online thesaurus can help you come up with alternative words when you cannot quite think of the right word to express your idea. Do be careful when using a thesaurus to enhance your writing. Ensure that any word you choose from a thesaurus is a word you would realistically use in your writing. Avoid choosing words that are completely out of character with your own style of writing.

Grammar Girl - grammar.quickanddirtytips.com

The Grammar Girl site is a comprehensive guide to grammar. I love this site because the explanations are easy to understand. Simply enter a search term into the search box to find an article about your specific question about grammar.

Grammar Girl has an article specifically about resume grammar, which you can find here: grammar.quickanddirtytips.com/how-to-write-a-better-resume.aspx.

The Least You Should Know About English

The book, *The Least You Should Know About English*, by Paige Wilson and Teresa Ferster Glazier is an excellent, easy to understand overview of English grammar. If you are committed to improving your grammar, this book is a great resource.

There are plenty of English grammar books out there. I am recommending this book because I have used it to successfully teach grammar to adult students who really struggled with grammar in school. The authors avoid getting bogged down with obscure rules that are rarely used. Instead, they focus on common grammatical errors and sources of confusion that come up regularly in writing.

If you can apply all of the concepts in this book to your writing, no reasonable person would ever accuse you of having poor grammar! This book is available to download free online here: nelsonbrain.com/content/glazier01908_0176501908_02.01_chapter01.pdf

"Whatever you can do or dream you can, begin it.
Boldness has genius, power and magic in it."
Johann Wolfgang von Goethe

ABOUT THE AUTHOR

I started studying career and work counseling in 1999 because I wanted to work in a field where I could help people help themselves. Since then, I've worked with approximately 2000 clients from all kinds of backgrounds.

I'm convinced that all people need and deserve access to the knowledge and skills required to manage their own careers.

When you have good career management skills, you have a lot more freedom to direct the course of your life, and I believe everyone, no matter what strengths and challenges they bring to the table, deserves to have access to information that can help them build a rewarding career.

Over the years, my work has involved:

- Facilitating job finding club workshops
- Providing one on one career guidance
- Helping injured workers choose and retrain for new careers
- Writing about job search and career planning on my site, careerchoiceguide.com

I have worked with all kinds of clients including:

- Professionals struggling through a tough labor market
- Parents returning to work after several years out of the workforce raising young children
- New immigrants, usually well-educated and experienced professionals, struggling to land their first jobs in their new home country
- Laid off workers from manufacturing plants, and out of work administrative assistants struggling to find suitable jobs in declining industries
- Injured workers who were retraining to start new professions because their injuries prevented them from returning to their previous jobs
- Job seekers struggling to find work because they had not completed high school
- People with established careers struggling to find work because of age discrimination

All of my clients brought with them their own unique set of strengths that would help them build a rewarding career, and many brought challenges that made job searching difficult. My job was to help them find and highlight their strengths and overcome their challenges.

It has been a huge privilege to work with my clients and be a part of their lives and their career development.

Stay Connected to Current Job Search News

I publish new job search and career planning articles on my site, CareerChoiceGuide.com on a regular basis. To keep up to date with the latest information, you can subscribe to the free Career Choice Guide Newsletter at:

careerchoiceguide.com/newsletter

Or, to be informed each time I post a new article, you can also subscribe to the site's RSS feed here:

careerchoiceguide.com/career-choice-blog.html

If you have questions for me, I can be contacted via the form on this page:

careerchoiceguide.com/contact

One Last Thing...

If you enjoyed reading this book, I'd appreciate it if you would take a couple of minutes to post a short review at Amazon. Intelligent reviews help other customers make better buying choices. And because I read all my reviews personally, they will help me to write better books in the future. Thanks for your support!

All the best,

Lisa McGrimmon